I0880148

"We Believe in the Holy Spirit": Global Perspectives on Lutheran Identities

Documentation 63/2021

THE
LUTHERAN
WORLD
FEDERATION

The views expressed in this publication are those of the authors and do not necessarily reflect the official position of The Lutheran World Federation.

"We Believe in the Holy Spirit": Global Perspectives on Lutheran Identities

Edited by
Chad M. Rimmer and Cheryl M. Peterson

LWF Documentation 63

Evangelische Verlagsanstalt
Leipzig

Bibliographic information published by the German National Library

The **Deutsche Nationalbibliothek** lists this publication in the **Deutsche Nationalbibliografie;** detailed bibliographic data are available on the internet at http://dnd.dnd.de

© 2021 The Lutheran World Federation
Printed in Germany

This work, including all of its parts, is protected by copyright.
Any use beyond the strict limits of copyright law without the permission of the publishing house is strictly prohibited and punishable by law.

This book was printed on FSC-certified paper.

Cover: LWF/Albin Hillert
Editorial assistance: Kristine Greenaway and LWF Office for Communication
Design and Layout: LWF Office for Communication

Printing and Binding: Elbe Druckerei Wittenberg GmbH
ISBN 978-3-374-06949-1 / eISBN (PDF) 978-3-374-06950-7

Published by Evangelische Verlangsanstalt GmbH, Leipzig, Germany, under the auspices of
The Lutheran World Federation
Department for Theology, Mission and Justice
150, rte de Ferney, PO Box 2100
CH-1211 Geneva 2, Switzerland

Parallel editions in German and Spanish

Contents

Preface

Questions of Lutheran identity have driven joint theological reflection within The Lutheran World Federation (LWF) since its inception. What is a Lutheran understanding of the church's ministry? How do Lutherans understand the connection between justification and justice? What is the relationship between worship and culture? How do we understand ourselves as a communion of churches? What is the church's role in the public space? How do we interpret the Bible? These questions have prompted significant study processes within the communion that reveal who we are and who God calls us to be in the world.

In 2019, representatives of every region of the communion gathered in Addis Ababa to ask a new set of questions. A diverse group of teachers, diaconal ministers, pastors, youth, bishops, musicians, social workers, and more, gathered to reflect on the diverse expressions of our common Lutheran tradition.

Lutherans around the world share a tradition that is rooted in the norms of Scripture, common confessions, a catechism, and shared liturgical traditions. But the gift of Christ, present in faith, is Word that bears fruit in each one of us. While the good news of Christ is the common melody, each of us sounds individual notes that create a harmony.

This consultation rooted these questions of unity and diversity in the third article of our Trinitarian ecumenical creeds and our catechisms' teaching about the work of the Holy Spirit. The gift of faith, the life of the church, and our baptismal calling belong to the work of God's Spirit. By that Spirit, we are united in a common confession, and yet personally gifted for a life of faith and loving service to all creation.

Ours is an age when spiritual and political narratives promise easy answers to complex issues. Excluding diversity and demanding uniformity offer easy answers to complex problems. Nevertheless, they threaten the very social and ecological fabric of life and stifle the life-giving creativity of the Spirit at work in creation. Living into the unity among the diversity of our Lutheran communion is an ongoing task. It invites us to be led by the Spirit as we journey together, witnessing to the powerful message of Jesus Christ, crucified and risen. Always knowing that, ultimately, our Lutheran confession, rooted in Christian liberty, is a gift. We confess a dynamic relationship between grace and gifts that equips us to translate the good news of God's love in Christ Jesus in a variety of ways. The Spirit equips us for interdisciplinary and interfaith dialogue that responds to the multifaceted needs of a world in need of reformation and transformation.

I commend this volume of essays to member churches, theological institutions, pastors, and lay members across the communion who want to explore the Trinitarian grounding of our Lutheran tradition and our baptismal vocation to participate in God's mission.

Rev. Dr Martin Junge (Chile/Switzerland)
LWF General Secretary

"We Believe in the Holy Spirit": Global Perspectives on Lutheran Identities

Chad M. Rimmer and Cheryl M. Peterson

Lutheranism is informed by a field of biblical and confessional norms, and by theological doctrines such as law and gospel, faith and works, nature and grace, justification and sanctification, and freedom and vocation. Lutheranism is formed by our experience of the living Triune God in communities that gather around the Word, sacraments, service, and public witness. Lutheran self-understanding is shaped by ecumenical *koinonia* and interfaith dialogue and *diapraxis*. Lutherans boldly open our faith to interdisciplinary engagement including our cultural, social, political, racial, gendered, economic, and ecological contexts.

"Lutheran identities" are dynamic – never prescriptive or exclusionary: always growing new fruit of Christian liberty. Lutheranism is a living tradition that is formed and reformed by our experience of God at work in our lives and in the world. The lived experience of faith, broadly defined as spirituality, shapes our Christian identity and engagement with the world.

Spirituality is deeply personal in the sense that it relates to one's personal experience of God's Spirit. Yet, Lutherans affirm that this personal relationship is always nurtured in communities that are particularly, and universally, part of the church. Lutheran identity is formed, reformed, and transformed through the local and global reality of the one, holy, catholic, and apostolic church. Some LWF member churches call for renewal by reviving spirituality, and some churches struggle to understand the myriad expressions of spiritual gifts that call into question their experience in the Lutheran Church.

What can we say about the work of the Holy Spirit to call, gather and equip the church today? Contemporary discourse about spirituality is frequently driven by individuals who claim to receive spiritual gifts (*charismata*) via special revelations of the Holy Spirit. While the Spirit blows where it will, this type of spiritual narrative can be exclusionary. It often underwrites anthropological, social, and political narratives that are contrary to the Lutheran theological heritage. In many contexts, these narratives create anxieties about Lutheran identity and the practice of our faith, or a fundamental confusion about the gracious, reconciling, and liberating nature of the gospel. Messages and resolutions from the LWF Twelfth Assembly relate to the work of the Holy Spirit in the life of our churches. These statements use the language of church renewal, revival, or spirituality. They call the communion to provide a framework to address these fundamental questions as Lutherans.

In a 2016 report to the LWF Council, General Secretary Martin Junge asked, "How would we describe the 'being and witnessing Lutheran' today in a global perspective? What are the key features of our identity and witness, and how do they relate to the key tenets of Lutheran theology? ... How could we articulate a coherent, shared narrative that helps us recognize each other as Lutheran churches globally yet remain contextually rooted? ... It is an essential project that fosters coherence, mutual understanding and mutual accountability as we jointly continue proclaiming Jesus Christ as Lord and Savior, and witness to God's love and justice in this world."

Contemporary constellations of economic and political power, legal challenges, scientific and technological discoveries, and new psychosocial developments continuously call for new expressions of the Lutheran tradition. Emerging cosmologies and cultural realities shape the way we practice our faith and contextualize Lutheran identities. However, within these new horizons, we want to discern ways in which we creatively express our common Lutheran heritage.

With that context in mind, the LWF convened a global consultation on contemporary Lutheran identities in October 2019, starting the first phase of a study process on Lutheran identities. The consultation was held under the theme, "We Believe in the Holy Spirit: Global Perspectives on Lutheran Identities" and it was hosted by the Ethiopian Evangelical Church Mekane Yesus in Addis Ababa. LWF member church representatives, theologians, and practitioners engaged in rich theological reflection on the work of the Holy Spirit. This consultation aimed to explore how spirituality forms Lutheran identities, and shapes the life of the church around the world today. Consultation participants began the process of listening for the ways that we sound the common notes of Lutheran identity among the rich harmony of lived, contextual identities across our communion.

The essays included here follow the content and methodology of the consultation. Three days of theological reflection were divided into the following headings: "The Holy Spirit as Gift and Promise"; "The Church as Holy Communion"; and "Transformed and Freed."

Section One: The Holy Spirit as Gift and Promise

This section explores a theology of the Spirit, and spiritual theology.

Bible Study: In the first Bible study, Jun Hyun Kim explores Luther's sermons on John 14 in order to set the stage for understanding today as the "time of the Holy Spirit."

Keynote: In the day's keynote address, Kenneth Mtata sets the context for our theological reflection by centering the work and witness of the South African bishop, Manas Buthelezi. Mtata explores Buthelezi's liberation theology, by highlighting the Christological pneumatology at work in Luther's theology, in order to remind us of the rich pneumatology that is at the heart of the Lutheran tradition. Mtata examines the promise of a spiritual theology of hermeneutics, ministry, and makes the case for a renewed focus on sanctification in the Lutheran tradition, particularly in this context of the Africa region.

Papers: Mutale Mulenga-Kaunda, one of the invited ecumenical guests, represents her roots in African Pentecostalism. Exploring the nexus of African women, the Holy Spirit, and the church, Mulenga-Kaunda suggests that the subordination of the Holy Spirit is related to its feminine characterization. As a rejoinder to this subordination of the feminine, Mulenga-Kaunda applies a feminist lens to suggest how the liberty found in the work of the Holy Spirit becomes the source of liberation.

Bernd Oberdorfer roots his paper in the classical Lutheran doctrine of the Word and the emphasis on proclamation. However, Oberdorfer draws our attention to the Lutheran confessions to demonstrate that the Spirit is active in the ministry of the Word and proclamation. Therefore, Oberdorfer makes the case that the church is a creature of the Spirit, and critically assesses a Lutheran perspective on the Trinity's work in the context of "normal life."

Winston Persaud takes the Joint Declaration on the Doctrine of Justification as a starting point to underline the importance of a Trinitarian basis for Christian witness in the twenty-first century. By rooting the doctrine of justification in the work of the Holy Trinity, Persaud shows the way that Lutherans can approach open dialogue with Pentecostal and Charismatic traditions, while sustaining historic ecumenical dialogues.

Johann-Christian Põder outlines the work of the Holy Spirit in creation and sanctification, and highlights three critical questions to approach the future of pneumatology in Lutheran theology.

Chad Rimmer presents an ecotheological reading in order to define what is meant by "spirit" in our contemporary pluralistic and interfaith spiritual context. While Lutherans traditionally dwell on the relationship between faith and works, Rimmer calls for a pivot to faith and reason. He explores the Lutheran confessions and Luther's sacramental and mystical theology to demonstrate how the concept of the replete presence of God equips Lutherans to engage in interfaith and interdisciplinary dialogue about "spirits", while perceiving God's Spirit at work in the world as gift and promise.

Section Two: The Church as Holy Communion

This section probes the nexus of ecclesiology, liturgy, and pneumatology.

Bible Study: In the second Bible study, Caroline Christopher explores the calling of the priesthood of the baptized through a case study of diaconal ministry among Dalit people.

Keynote: In the keynote address for the second day, Jennifer Wasmuth returns us to Luther's *Small Catechism* in order to recover the pneumatological dimensions of our understanding of the church as communion of saints. Wasmuth reveals the "double dynamic" of the Holy Spirit's work in calling individuals, and in calling together the church as a "unique community" in the world. Wasmuth explores the connection between pneumatology and ecclesiology in order to make a strong call for Lutherans to lift up a "cross-theological pneumatology." This approach can add an element to liturgical theology, as well as understanding the church's relationship to the world. At the consultation, this paper laid the groundwork for a vibrant conversation about a "Christological-pneumatology" or a "pneumatological-Christology."

Papers: Mari-Anna Auvinen explores the concept of community through the lens of Tswana cosmology that shapes Lutheran identity in the Evangelical Lutheran Church in Botswana. The Tswana concept of personhood and intersubjective identity offers a fresh approach to conceiving the Trinity as a community, and to the Spirit's role in the way humans participate in this community.

Emmanuel Clapsis, another of the ecumenical guests, represents an Orthodox perspective on the normative theological principles that inform our understanding of how the Holy Spirit and the Word co-institute the church. By highlighting the interdependent activity of the second and third person of the Trinity, Clapsis lays the basis for the Spirit's active presence in history. Despite the ambiguities of our time, the Eucharist is the eschatological basis and criterion for the church's prophetic witness to the Spirit's presence in the world.

Nestor Paulo Friedrich also takes up the notion of the church's prophetic role in the world. From his context in the Evangelical Church of the Lutheran Confession in Brazil, Friedrich unmasks the market mentality that underwrites contemporary discourse about spirituality. Among the economic spirits of the age that would once again commodify grace, Friedrich recalls us to the "charm" of being Lutheran and to how the theological narratives that inform our Lutheran identity and spirituality help us to resist the capitalist spirits of the age.

Christopher Lee McDonald, one of the young theologians, explores the spirituality of children in order to draw attention to the corporate nature of worship. In an age when sedentary, isolated lifestyles are creating crises of embodied community, the liturgy provides the location for a spirituality that unites our bodies, minds, and souls. Through a case study of his ministry among children, McDonald makes the case for liturgical singing, movement, and communing as the location for a holistic, coordinated formation of a corporate sense of self that liberates us for community.

Another young theologian, Sebastian Madejski, continues to delve into the role of liturgy in communicating God's spirit. From his context in the Evangelical Church of the Augsburg Confession in Poland, Madejski conducted ethnographic research among new members which revealed how the liturgy played a key role in amplifying the Spirit's call to come, taste, and see God's presence.

Cheryl Peterson looks at the traditional marks of the church through the lens of pneumatology. Peterson demonstrates the fundamental role that the Holy Spirit actively plays in the apostolic, catholic, holy, and unified nature of the church's identity and mission in the world today.

Section Three: Transformed and Freed

This section turns toward more anthropological questions regarding spiritual gifts.

Bible Study: In the third Bible study, Beverly Wallace takes a womanist reading of 1 Corinthians 12. Wallace contrasts the story of Chloe and the cosmology inherited by women of African descent in order to highlight the various transformative and liberating gifts of the Spirit.

Keynote: For the third and final keynote address, Veli-Matti Kärkkäinen examines the Holy Spirit's work in gifting, transforming, freeing, and empowering all believers to live out their vocation. Kärkkäinen first reminds us of the deep and integral role that the Holy Spirit has always played in Lutheran tradition and history. Secondly, Kärkkäinen explores particular challenges that the charismatic movement seems to raise for Lutherans and Lutheran churches. Finally, Kärkkäinen lays the groundwork for a charismatic-diaconal understanding of spiritual gifts that is rooted in the notion of the priesthood (or ministry) of all believers. By drawing a golden cord between the "spheres" (or "layers") of the Spirit's activity in the cosmos, creation, society, church, and salvation, Kärkkäinen challenges the churches to broaden the concepts of spiritual gifts to include administration, teaching, service, etc., as a normal part of the Spirit's work to equip each of us for ministry.

Papers: From his context of the consultation host church, the Ethiopian Evangelical Church Mekane Yesus (EECMY), Yacob Godebo draws attention to the way in which Lutheran theological identities are formed, the contemporary significance of Lutheran theological identities, and the way in which Lutheran theological identities inform the sense of vocation and ministry in the Ethiopian context.

Sofie Halvarsson, one of the young theologians, probes the concept of the priesthood of all the baptized. Based on the doctrine of the *imago Dei*, Halvarsson interprets spiritual gifts as one way that the Spirit communicates God's story to the world, and, therefore, makes a strong claim for radical inclusion as a way to discern the diverse expressions of God's work in the world.

Another young theologian, Novriana Gloria Hutagalung, writes from the Indonesian context, offering the Batak traditional practice of mourning songs (*andung-andung*) as a means of healing. In this way, Hutagalung demonstrates the way that theological aesthetics become performative theology and serve as means of the Spirit's grace.

The fifth young theologian is Kagiso Harry Morudu from the Evangelical Lutheran Church in Southern Africa. Morudu draws attention to the spiritual gifts of young people and analyzes the need to increase youth participation and leadership to combat patriarchy and sexism, and to create inclusive spaces.

Wilfred Samuel presents a Lutheran perspective on the nexus between justification and sanctification. Samuel revisits the notion of baptismal regeneration and explores the Spirit's essential work in mission and formation.

Johannes Habib Zeiler analyzes the state of theological education and formation in the context of changing African landscapes, particularly in the Evangelical Lutheran Church in Tanzania. Zeiler explores the rich, costly, and often contested spaces where theological identities are being formed, and calls the communion of churches to renew our attention to the methods and means of theological education and faith formation.

This volume concludes with an annex that reflects on the findings from the consultation report, and points toward future questions that emerged. The findings highlight the commitment to the norms of the Lutheran tradition, as well as a need to renew our focus on core theological commitments such as the priesthood of all the baptized, the theology of the cross, and the fundamental Trinitarian perspectives of God as a community of love that forms and informs our relationship to God (*coram Deo*) and to the world (*corum mundo*).

The consultation calls us to engage more deeply in dialogue with Indigenous traditions throughout the communion, as well as other interfaith and ecumenical dialogue. It also unmasks the differences between contexts where Lutherans are among the majority or the minority, as well as the rich ways that cultural and multiple religious belonging shape our understanding of what it means to be Lutheran. While the consultation calls us to deepen a Lutheran understanding of spiritual gifts, it also calls us to affirm the need to discern gifts of the Spirit and the spirits of our age. Maintaining a focus on the link between sanctification and justification, *charis* and *charismata* helps the church to combat exploitative and exclusionary spiritual discourse and practices while doing what we can to nurture the vibrant spiritual diversity that brings wholeness and healing to the body of Christ and to our participation in the work of God's Spirit in the world.

In the end, the consultation affirms that one of the organizing principles of our tradition is Christian liberty. Lutherans are liberated by God's grace to participate in God's work in the world. While religious identity is always fluid, always porous, and always evolving, this consultation begins a rich conversation about how the Holy Spirit calls, gathers, and frees us to express God's transforming and sustaining love for the world.

We hope that this documentation encourages you and your community of faith to explore these questions. How are the biblical, liturgical, confessional, theological, and spiritual foundations of our shared Lutheran tradition translated through the beautiful mosaic of languages, cultures, and vocations where you live? It is inspiring to witness God's Spirit of grace, liberty, and love give birth to different expressions of our common tradition. When we share our stories with Lutheran friends from contexts different from ours, we deepen our own identity and sense of belonging. Their stories become part of our own story of what it means to be Lutheran.

The Holy Spirit as Gift and Promise

Bible Study

The Time of the Holy Spirit

John 14:25-27

Jun Hyun Kim

Setting the Stage

In John 13 and 14, Jesus is in the Upper Room, telling his disciples plainly that he will soon travel the path of suffering and death. The disciples, one and all, react in fear, confusion, and worry. "Where are you going? Why can we not go with you? What will we do, if you aren't with us anymore?" Jesus responds by saying that he is the way, the truth, and the life, and that if they only believe in him, they do not need to be afraid (Jn 14:6).

In John 14:15, Jesus further describes the life of faith, saying that those who believe and trust in him will also keep his commandments. That is the mark of a true disciple. Then Jesus says (Jn 14:16), "I will ask the Father, and he will give you another Advocate to be with you forever." Paul describes it this way, in Galatians 4:6, "And because you are children, God has sent the Spirit of his Son into our hearts...." So, we see God's clear promise; God will send us the Advocate, the Comforter, the Helper–the Holy Spirit–who will be with us forever.

In our text, it is plain that Jesus will soon finish his work on earth. Soon He will walk the Via Dolorosa–the way of suffering–to Golgotha. Soon he will die for all humankind and, three days later, rise to life again (though the disciples did not understand what he meant (Mk 9:10). Here, in the Upper Room, they were afraid. Jesus talked repeatedly of going away[1] referring both to his death and his ascension to heaven. This filled the disciples with fear and dread; they worried that they would have to go back to following the Old Testament system of sacrifices and rituals. They worried that they would never see Jesus again. They did not want to come back under the rule of the priests and their obligations.

So, Jesus prays to God for his fearful disciples. He speaks words of comfort and assurance, and he promises that he will send them the Comforter—the Holy Spirit—as their helper and ours too. And it is just as he promised. Disciples today are now able to "feel" Jesus and "experience" God through the ministry and presence of the Holy Spirit, which is not "in" the earth or "of" the earth, but truly is with us always.

The Time of the Holy Spirit

Today is the "Time of the Holy Spirit." If the Old Testament era can be called the "Time of God the Father" and if the incarnation, life, death, and resurrection of Jesus is the "Time of God the Son," then the time of the Church—from Pentecost to the present day—may rightly be called the "Time of the Holy Spirit."

If we believers "experience God" today, it is through the power and work of the Holy Spirit. To "grow in the grace and knowledge of our Lord and Savior Jesus Christ" (2 Pt 3:18) is to gain wisdom through the Holy Spirit, which enables us to know Jesus more, learn more, and understand him better. Even when we share the sacrament of the Lord's Table, it is the Holy Spirit which enables us to see with the eyes of faith, and recognize that in, with, and under the bread and wine we truly receive the body and blood of our Lord. Truly, in our lives of faith, nothing can be done without the Holy Spirit!

Yet, as believers, we face a challenge: people all around us ask, "What is the evidence that the Holy Spirit is with you?"

Some people would answer that speaking in tongues is the trustworthy proof of the Holy Spirit. But this claim is not fully biblical, because speaking in tongues is given as one of the gifts of God not as evidence of God. Then on what basis can we testify that the Holy Spirit is with us?

Let me ask it a different way: (1) Is the Holy Spirit inside of you or outside of you? (2) If the Holy Spirit is outside of you, is the Holy Spirit right next to you or one step away?

I think you can see for yourself that these questions are the wrong kind to be asking because the Holy Spirit is everywhere, and that is important.

In John 14:23, Jesus talks about the Father and the Son making their home with the believer. This expression certainly harkens back to his words

[1] See, for example, John 14:2, 12, 19.

at the beginning of John 14, but it also evokes the rich Old Testament imagery of the tabernacle and the temple, as YHWH's dwelling place (Ex 25:8). The idea that YHWH dwelt among YHWH'S people through the divine service of tabernacle and temple, according to his own scriptural mandate, is surely reflected in the New Testament incarnation of Jesus dwelling among us.

At the end of John 14:24, Jesus reminds his disciples that the words they hear are not his alone, but also God's, who sent him. In this way Jesus alludes to the work of the Holy Spirit of whom he will speak in the next verses.

The anticipation is fulfilled in John 14:26 where the Savior says: "the Holy Spirit, whom the Father will send in my name, will teach you everything, and will remind you of all that I have said to you." Put another way, God promises that the Holy Spirit will always help us, lead us, and be with us so that we fulfill our calling to love our neighbors as ourselves; growing in sanctification—sometimes called our "horizontal" or *coram mundo* righteousness.

Who and What Is This "Holy Spirit"?

The Holy Spirit of Scripture is not presented as merely some kind of "motion created in things"[2] an impersonal being or a mere "power." Rather, the Spirit is presented as someone called alongside to help, an advocate, defender, comforter, and counselor (παράκλητος). The Holy Spirit's "office" is to bring to our remembrance all that Jesus has spoken and done.

Martin Luther connects John 14:26 to the Confession of the Church in his 1537 sermons on the Gospel of John. He writes, "'I believe in the Holy Spirit and the Holy Christian Church', so we confess in the Creed, because the Church is the place where the Holy Spirit brings to our remembrance all that Jesus has spoken. In doing so, the Holy Spirit dwells in and continuously sanctifies the Church through Word and Sacrament."[3]

Further, he reminds us, "If you yourself were holy, then you would not need the Holy Spirit at all; but since we are sinful and unclean in ourselves, the Holy Spirit must perform his work in us...."

Reflecting on his own condition, Luther admits, "I am not holy through myself but through Christ's blood, with which I have been sprinkled, yes, washed in Baptism, and also through his Gospel, which is spoken over me daily."

---

[2] *Augsburg Confession* (hereafter, CA) I:6.

[3] Martin Luther, *Sermons on the Gospel of St. John, Chapters 14-16*, in *Luther's Works*, American ed., vol. 24, ed. Jaroslav Pelikan and Daniel E. Poellot, trans. Martin H. Bertram (Saint Louis: Concordia Publishing House, 1961). [*Luther's Works*, hereafter LW.] This and the remainder of the quotations in this section are from pages 168-71.

And he joyfully concludes, "He (the Holy Spirit) baptized me; he proclaimed the Gospel of Christ to me; and he awakened my heart to believe..."

In this way, Luther encourages the baptized to look for the Holy Spirit at the place he is found "not up above the clouds" but "down here on earth" where "the Word and the sacraments" are going on.

Let us now consider the last verse of today's reading.

Where Can I Find Peace?

In John 14:27, Jesus is preparing to end his years-long earthly sojourn with his disciples, and he leaves his peace with them as his legacy. What he gives is measured neither by silver nor by gold; it is neither social status nor worldly success, it is the incomparable gift of his peace (Rom 5:1).

The peace Jesus speaks of has nothing to do with "the absence of warfare." In fact, it is precisely in the context of the Christian's daily battle against enemies both from within (our sinful flesh) and from without (the devil and the world) that Jesus gives us peace.

But if this is so, where can we find this peace? Where in all the world can believers flee when the storms rage against us? Where is the church to find shelter and peace? Luther answers, "Nowhere else than in his baptism, in the Sacrament and in the office of the ministry."[4]

We live in the "Time of the Holy Spirit." As believers, we know God the Father, we know Jesus Christ, God's only Son, we know the Holy Spirit who proceeds from them. We have the promise of the word that through the power and working of the Holy Spirit, we will change; we will grow in the grace and knowledge of Jesus Christ and in our sanctification.

How is one to grow like this? How are we to receive the blessings the Spirit bestows? Brothers and sisters, you know as well as I do, that there is a virtually endless collection of theories, studies, seminars, and arguments about how to "get" or "grow in" the Holy Spirit. Perhaps the simplest is the best after all (even if the "wise" and "learned" of the world would mock us). Let's seek the Holy Spirit where the Spirit promised to be found—in the pure and holy word, and the blessings of the sacraments. To God alone be the glory!

[4] LW 24:180.

Martin Luther to Manas Buthelezi: Toward a Lutheran Pneumatological Identity

Kenneth Mtata

Introduction

The title of this conference is "We Believe in the Holy Spirit: Global Perspectives on Lutheran Identities." At face value, the theme may give the impression that the Holy Spirit is at the heart of Lutheran self-understanding. Luther was obviously aware of the Holy Spirit if one looks at how he treats the third person of the Triune Godhead, especially in both the *Small Catechism* and the *Large Catechism*. But Martin Luther's pneumatology was not answering contemporary questions about the Holy Spirit in relationship to Lutheran identity. In his theology, Martin Luther was answering the questions of his time and it looks like Christology rather than pneumatology provided the main tools for his response.

How Self-Understanding Happens

Martin Luther was not, however, a Lutheran. It is we contemporary Lutherans who are asking ourselves who we are and what features of the Holy Spirit inform our self-understanding. The reason we seek to understand our Christian identity in relationship to the Holy Spirit and not, for example, in relationship to the Father or to the Son, is caused by how identity happens. Human beings tend to understand themselves in terms of their differences with others. But the moment they find that an identity they thought they shared is being presented with a different emphasis, they begin to ask themselves: Are we authentic? Are we the real thing? In my view, the rise of pneumatic Christianity in the form of Pentecostalism has made Lutherans, and other Christians of a similar tradition, question their identity. In his recent paper, Hans-Peter Grosshans has actually concluded that contemporary interest in pneumatology in Western scholarship has been awakened by the presents of migrant Christians whose emphasis on the Holy Spirit has reawakened old questions.[1]

Back to the Roots

When one reaches such moments of identity crisis, one tends to trace one's roots with the aim of resetting or rebooting, to use computer language. As contemporary Lutherans seek to reboot, they must go back to the past, to their foundations. This instinct to go back to the past is not new. At the time of the Reformation when Martin Luther and his contemporary reformers felt that authentic evangelical Christianity had lost its vitality and character, they went back to the past, to the founding normative sources, namely the scriptures and the confessions of the early Christian traditions. It is also possible that it was the rigorous study of the scriptures in the first place that could have made them aware of the disjuncture between their contemporary Christianity and that exhibited in the scriptures. We can, therefore, conclude at this point that this conference is necessitated by the realization that the Holy Spirit seems not to be given an appropriate place in Lutheran identity, yet other expressions in other Christian traditions seem not to adequately represent how Lutherans could understand the Holy Spirit.

Structure of this Presentation

To contribute to this quest for a Lutheran pneumatology, I will look briefly at some of the key features of Martin Luther's pneumatology. I will then look in some detail at how Manas Buthelezi related to this Lutheran heritage in his

[1] English translation, Hans-Peter Grosshans, Vernachlässigter Geist? Zur Bedeutung der Pneumatologie in der neuesten evangelischen Dogmatik, in: *Wir glauben an den Heiligen Geist. XVII. Begegnung im bilateralen theologischen Dialog zwischen der EKD und dem Ökumenischen Patriarchat (Konstantinopel XVII)* (eds) Petra Bosse-Huber, Konstantinos Vliagkoftis and Wolfram Langpape, Beiheft zur Ökumenischen Rundschau Nr. 130, Leipzig (Evangelische Verlagsanstalt). 2021, 93-118, 100.

own pneumatology. I chose Buthelezi because (a) he was a Lutheran in his self-understanding (identity), (b) he was consciously a contextual theologian (not every theologian has this self-awareness), (c) he gave special attention to the theme of the Holy Spirit in conversation with Lutheran heritage.

After looking at some continuities and discontinuities between Buthelezi and Luther, I will conclude by suggesting how contemporary Lutheran pneumatology could speak to, and answer, some of the pressing issues, especially in my own context.

Martin Luther's Pneumatology in Retrospect: How Lutheranism Has Grown in 500 Years

When Martin Luther posted his 95 theses in Wittenberg in 1517, he would not have anticipated that 500 years later, a movement bearing his name, and its offshoots, would have spread into the whole world, and indeed in Africa. Martin Luther would never have dreamt that by 2017, the largest and the fastest growing Lutheran church would not be in Germany or Europe, but in Africa, with the Ethiopian Evangelical Church Mekane Yesus with a membership of 8.6 million in comparison to 25,000 in 1959! Indeed, Luther would not have imagined that 500 years later, there would be debates among Africans, Asians, Latin Americans, North Americans, and Europeans as to what was the most faithful way to uphold the evangelical Christianity which Luther propounded. This would have confirmed his understanding that the Holy Spirit invites people from all nations through the proclamation of the gospel of Jesus Christ.

Dynamism of New Lutheranism

Martin Luther would be impressed by how the proclamation of the gospel of salvation through faith in Jesus Christ alone has been embraced in traditionally non-Lutheran regions of the world. He would be excited to see the joy and dynamism of worship in some of these new churches in comparison to some dull and half-hearted preaching he chastised during his time. Luther would have seen his pneumatology confirmed as he witnessed the Holy Spirit illuminating scriptures and convicting hearts to faith. He would be overjoyed to see the Old and New Testaments being used to proclaim Jesus Christ as the center of preaching. He would value the revelation of the Spirit and the hermeneutical creativity in this preaching, the conviction of such preaching, and the childlike faith of appropriation of such preaching.

Growing Displacement of Christ with Spiritual Experience

Martin Luther would have been disturbed by the tendency in some Lutheran churches, and indeed in other Christian traditions, to replace faith in Christ as the basis of salvation with special experiences of the Holy Spirit. He would be equally disturbed by the replacement of the scriptures with special revelations of the new prophets claiming to have special access to God through dreams and other insights. He would recall his pneumatology that God does not speak to God's people apart from God's word illumined by the Holy Spirit.

Replacement of Solus Christus

Martin Luther would have been shocked by some Spirit-led churches claiming that by paying tithes or seed money to a prophet one could earn their salvation. He would have been angry to see the rise of religious entrepreneurs literally selling the gospel for money. He would be disgusted with excessive hierarchies emerging in the church on the basis of the spiritual gifts. Not that Luther would prefer a democratic polity, he would not be aware of it. But he would continue to rebuke political authority that is unjust and business that was charging excessive interest.

Martin Luther would probably maintain his Christological pneumatology, which is an understanding of the role of the Holy Spirit revealing God's love to the world in Christ, as he says in his commentary on the third article of the Creed in the *Large Catechism.*

Luther's Hermeneutic of the Spirit

In the Small Catechism and Large Catechism, Luther views the confessions as providing the lens through which biblically based understanding of the Holy Spirit should be pursued. He sees the creeds providing the "entire essence of God, his will, and his work exquisitely depicted in very short but rich words." While the law demands something from the believer, Luther sees in the creeds the heart of faith which are "taught by the Holy Spirit alone."[2] In other words, the character, function, and operations of the Holy Spirit must be understood within the full witness of the scriptures in conversation with the earlier theological traditions of the church. Luther does not see himself saying anything new as far as the Holy Spirit is concerned but saying the old truths in new ways. He

[2] Large Catechism, II, 63-64; Tappert, 419.

highlights the Holy Spirit as one who (a) makes holy through (b) the church, (c) forgiveness of sins, (d) resurrection of the body, and (e) life everlasting. We will come back to some of these highlights in our concluding remarks.

Manas Buthelezi and Lutheran Identity in Africa: The Forming of African Lutheranism

Christianity in Africa was not established on the basis of doctrinal differentiation but on the basis of the multiplicity of founding missionaries. This also applied to Lutherans. That Lutherans in Africa were rarely concerned with doctrinal purity can be seen in the way pastors with no Lutheran training could run a Lutheran church. There is a case of a group of Lutherans who had fled from Nigeria in 1995 and settled in Cameroon where they organized themselves into a number of parishes and invited a pastor from the Full Gospel church who had fallen out with his own church leadership and made him their pastor. For fifteen years, members of the Wisconsin Synod would come once in a while to provide in-house training for pastors there.

Double Identities

Initially, the Lutheran churches in Africa mimicked the practices of their founding European mother churches but their beliefs differed. Some African Lutheran Christians tended to be Lutherans during the day under the surveillance of their European missionary founders, but secret members of the African Indigenous or Spirit churches during the night. The reason was simple to understand; many of these Christians identified with the practices in the Spirit churches because the latter represented African spirituality better than the Lutheran and other missionary-founded churches. I remember during my days as a pastor in an urban Lutheran church when members of my congregation would disclose how they used to visit a prophet in the African Indigenous church in order to get the service that we in the Lutheran liturgical practices could not provide. In a sense, the way the Lutheran and other reformation traditions were passed on through the medium of the European missionaries did not fully meet the needs of the African person, especially the spiritual inclination.

Africans Come into Their Own

When African theologians, even those trained in the West, started theologizing from their indigenous spiritual disposition, the subject of the Spirit became an important one. As Veli-Matti Kärkkäinen has observed, the growth of contextualized understandings of the Spirit in the global South, but especially in Africa, have tended to "complement the mainly Western approach that" had dominated the Reformation theological reflection for a long time.[3] In this light let me commit some space to Manas Buthelezi, an eminent African Lutheran theologian who made a detailed study about the Holy Spirit from his African perspective.

Apartheid Context of Buthelezi

Bishop Dr Manas Buthelezi (1935–2016) is mainly known for his black theology and liberation theology work from the 1970s.[4] His work emerged from the context of apartheid and racial discrimination in South Africa. In his black theology, Buthelezi sought to develop a theological anthropology highlighting the equality of all before God, hence criticizing the apartheid program of separate development. His theological method was shaped by the black consciousness of Steve Biko and the 1960s' Civil Rights movements in the United States of America (USA). Through this theology, he sought to stimulate the agency of black people so that they could contribute to their own emancipation and development.

Buthelezi's Transition from Liberation to Pneumatic Theology

On the surface, the Buthelezi of black theology appears drastically different from the one after 2000; the latter talks about the Holy Spirit. While during his days in liberation theology, he was a political activist, after his tenure as bishop of the Central Diocese of the Evangelical Lutheran Church in Southern Africa, he became more of an evangelist and spiritual healer.

[3] Veli-Matti Kärkkäinen, *Pneumatology: The Holy Spirit in Ecumenical, International, and Contextual Perspective* (Ada, Mich.: Baker Academics, 2002), 147.

[4] Relevant works by Manas Buthelezi include the following: 1) "The Theological Meaning of True Humanity," in *The Challenge of Black Theology in South Africa*, ed. Basil Moore (Atlanta: John Knox Press, 1974); 2) "An African Theology or a Black Theology" and "The Theological Meaning of True Humanity," in *Essays on Black Theology*, Black Theology Project, ed. Mokgethi Mothlabi (Johannesburg University Christian Movement, 1973), 3–9; 70–80 ; 3) "African Theology and Black Theology: A Search for a Theological Method," in *Relevant Theology for Africa: Report on a Consultation of the Missiological Institute at Lutheran Theological College*, Maphumulo, Natal, 12–21 September 1972, ed. Hans-Jürgen Becken (Durban: Robinson & Co., 1972), 18–24.

During his days of liberation theology, his interlocutors and audience were the university students, pastors, church leaders and international organizations whom he sought to mobilize against the apartheid regime. As a teacher on the Spirit, his audience became the ordinary members of the Lutheran churches in the rural areas of KwaZulu Natal. When I asked him why such a shift, he told me that he, as a contextual theologian, always sought to answer contemporary questions in light of the scriptures and his theological tradition. For him one of the most pressing questions for the Lutheran church was that of the Holy Spirit.

Lutheran Roots of Buthelezi's Pneumatology

In his earlier work, Buthelezi had made scattered references to the Holy Spirit. But one of his most comprehensive treatments of the subject is the presentation he made in June 2002 at a Lutheran World Federation consultation on Renewal Movements in Lutheran Churches in North and South, held at Moshi, Tanzania.[5] Here he articulated the circumstances surrounding the shift of his theological focus and his theological approach. In terms of theological method, Buthelezi presented his approach as "something between a sermon, a Bible study and personal sharing."[6] He saw himself theologizing within the Lutheran tradition, hence he begins by making reference to the Lutheran reformation tradition saying, "according to our confessions..." By referring to the creeds in his treatment of the Holy Spirit, he shares the same starting point with Martin Luther. From the creeds he notes that the Holy Spirit as God is "worshiped and glorified" together with the Father and the Son.[7] It looks as if from the onset Buthelezi wants to resolve the question of the subordination of the Holy Spirit to the Father and the Son. This is indeed addressing a long-standing challenge in pneumatology.

Experience of the Holy Spirit

Buthelezi was not interested in metaphysical explanations of the nature of the Spirit but rather the operational function of the Holy Spirit and the

[5] LWF Department for Mission and Development report on the consultation on Renewal Movements in Lutheran Churches in North and South, 2002

[6] Manas Buthelezi, "The Gifts of Holy Spirit for the Healing of World," in *Consultation on Renewal Movements in the Lutheran Churches in North and South*, ed. Péri Rasolondraibe (Geneva: Lutheran World Federation, 2002), 9.

[7] Ibid.

Spirit's gifts as the "vital deposits of power for effective ministry." As a true contextual theologian, he starts with his own experience and the experience of his church. In so doing he confirms what Carter Lindberg has called the "neuralgic point for Lutheran" approach to the Holy Spirit, i.e., starting with human experience.[8]

As a true contextual theologian, Buthelezi does not focus on just any human experience, but on one which causes the human being to ask the fundamental questions of faith and life. For Buthelezi it started when one of his congregants asked him how one could be filled with the Holy Spirit. This question is not very far from the question Martin Luther asks about how the Holy Spirit sanctifies. In continuity with Luther, Buthelezi affirms that (a) the Holy Spirit is received through the preaching of the Word and the administration of the sacraments, (b) the Holy Spirit does not have her own ministry in the life of the believer but that which continues and completes the work of salvation in Jesus Christ, and (3) the Holy Spirit serves other functions as provided for in the third article of the baptismal creed. Notably, the Holy Spirit gathers the saints to hear and believe in the gospel, effect membership in the church, and maintain the unity of the church.

The Academy and the Congregation

Buthelezi goes on to say that this classical Lutheran pneumatology was not user-friendly. It was something that made sense only to theologians but did not allow for "practical application to the simple needs and activities of an ordinary congregation."[9] So how does Buthelezi think this deficiency could be addressed? For Buthelezi, the Holy Spirit should first and foremost be sought in the ministry of Jesus. One cannot understand the "Holy Spirit and open ourselves to His power, if we forget in the first place what Jesus said about the Holy Spirit."[10] Here Buthelezi is consistent with Luther's Christocentric pneumatology. For him, Jesus Christ is not only a principle and content of preaching and theology, but also an exemplar upon which ministry must be modeled. According to Buthelezi, one goal of ministry is to equip ministers to be multipliers of what Jesus did in his lifetime. Buthelezi says the gifts of the Holy Spirit allow ordained and lay ministry

[8] Carter Lindberg, *The Third Reformation: Charismatic Movements and the Lutheran Tradition* (Macon, Ga.: Mercer University Press, 1983), 234.
[9] Buthelezi, 10.
[10] Ibid., 11.

to converge around the same source of power and replicate the signs and wonders that Jesus performed in his earthly ministry.[11]

Hermeneutics in Buthelezi's Pneumatology

As a Lutheran, Buthelezi wants to show that his understanding of the Holy Spirit is biblical. So, informed by John 14, Buthelezi was confident that Jesus expected his disciples to "do greater works" (Jn 14:12) than he himself had done while he was still on earth.[12] Jesus said this in the full awareness of the limitations of human nature, which could only be addressed by the Holy Spirit, Buthelezi argues. For Buthelezi, this dispensation of the work of the Holy Spirit "includes our time, the year 2002."[13] The Holy Spirit, according to Buthelezi, "is still with us in the Lutheran Church, but we have unfortunately ignored him."[14] Buthelezi was aware that such a position could be viewed as suspicious by his fellow theologians, especially from the global North. In his defense, he would say, "The maturity of the African church is only evident when Africa is able to produce its own heretics."

Buthelezi, in continuity with Luther, saw the Holy Spirit playing a central role in the process of interpreting the scriptures. He argued that while an *exegete* was able to attain head knowledge by appropriately rearranging and reconstructing the biblical text, this remains the "letter that kills" without the Holy Spirit's illumination.[15] His conclusion on this subject of interpretation is that there is "a difference between knowing certain facts as part of head knowledge and being led by the Holy Spirit in understanding the practical application of those facts."[16] Buthelezi says it was the day the scriptures came alive through the power of the Holy Spirit after diligent study that Luther felt as if he was born again.

Justification vs Sanctification?

Buthelezi was aware that those emphasizing the ministry of the Holy Spirit in their Lutheran churches in his diocese were confronted by the injunction, "it is un-Lutheran." Buthelezi was also aware, more than his congregants,

[11] Buthelezi, 13.
[12] Ibid., 12.
[13] Ibid., 13.
[14] Ibid.
[15] Ibid., 14.
[16] Ibid.

of the debates on justification and sanctification. For him, Lutherans had made mistakes in overemphasizing one aspect of theology above the rest. He says, "If Luther were to rise from the dead he would be shocked at the strange things, which are done, under the cover of his name."[17] One such shocking thing for Buthelezi is the overemphasis of "justification at the expense of teaching and preaching the totality of the principles of sanctification."[18] For Buthelezi, this separates "Jesus from the Holy Spirit" whom Jesus taught so much about.[19]

Buthelezi sees two main functions of sanctification in this context: (a) It is not about morality but ministry since the sanctified are likely to be "more productive in their ministry and to be agents of the repetition of the apostolic tradition of performing signs and wonders, which Jesus initiated"[20]; (b) It is a means of grace, that is, it is an undeserved experience which God endows to a sinful human being and is what Paul meant when he said, "But we have this treasure in clay jars, so that it may be made clear that this extraordinary power belongs to God and does not come from us."[21] In other words, sanctification for Buthelezi provides the foretaste of the perfected life the children of God would experience in fullness at the end of times. By making the gifts of the Holy Spirit part of the means of grace, Buthelezi adds to the traditional Lutheran understanding of the word and the sacraments as the means of grace to move toward John Wesley's understanding.[22] For Buthelezi, the work of justification is not superior to that of sanctification for they are both the results of the Holy Spirit.

The Holy Spirit Today, Beyond Luther and Buthelezi: Back to the Bible

Now that we have heard Luther and his conversation with Manas Buthelezi, we must ask ourselves how we advance towards a contemporary Lutheran pneumatological identity. In the first place, just as Luther drew from the scriptures and the confessions of the past, and Buthelezi drew from Luther and from past confessions in answering contemporary questions, we should follow suit. The Holy Spirit must generate deeper insights into

[17] Buthelezi, 13.
[18] Ibid.
[19] Ibid.
[20] Ibid.
[21] Ibid., 13-14. See also 2 Cor 4:7.
[22] John Wesley, *The Means of Grace: A Sermon on Malachi 3:7* (Farmington Hills, Mich.: Gale ECCO, [1835] 2010).

self-understanding among Lutherans today in proportion to their commitment to rigorous and prayerful study of scriptures through the lens of their Lutheran heritage and the confessions of faith. God speaks anew through the ancient scriptures because they are breathed by the Holy Spirit who opens the eyes, ears, and hearts of contemporary believers to faith.

The Holy Spirit and the Creative Reordering of the World

This vitality of the word of God illuminated by the Holy Spirit is realized in proclaiming this word with faithfulness. The proclamation of the word in the power of the Spirit is meant to gather God's people across space and time and bring them into the fold of the faithful. In this fellowship of brothers and sisters, people of faith also fellowship with the Father, the Son, and the Holy Spirit, and hence participate in the life of the Divine. We see an example of this active relationship when God sent the word as spirit to brood over the waters in Genesis 1, which unleashed a creative process that ordered the universe. If this creative impulse remains available wherever the word is released in the power of the Holy Spirit, we must see possibilities of creative solutions to the chaos that bedevil the contemporary context; the theology of the Holy Spirit could be a resource to reimagine creative order in contemporary chaos.

The Holy Spirit beyond the Church

In his paper, Hans-Peter Grosshans sees a possibility of looking at the Holy Spirit in relationship with the sanctified human spirit:

> If one would like to draw a special achievement of the Holy Spirit into this very general understanding of the activity of the Spirit, then this could be (beyond the certainty of the Spirit) *love*: Christians should bring their hope in the Kingdom of God, founded by the Spirit of God in the historical process, into social relations in such a way that these are not only ordered by law and order, but also determined by the Spirit of love - also mediated by the Spirit of God.[23]

[23] Grosshans, 93–118, 100.

The Holy Spirit and Reawakening of Transformative Human Agency

In my view, a Lutheran pneumatology of our time must see the Holy Spirit not in terms of the "division of labor" between the Father as creator, the Son as the redeemer, and the Holy Spirit as sanctifier, but to recognize that the "wind blows where it chooses, and you hear the sound of it, but you do not know where it comes from or where it goes. "So it is with everyone who is born of the Spirit" (Jn 3:8). This freedom of the Spirit refuses the dogmatic boundaries of what the Holy Spirit can do through the unleashed agency of those born of the Spirit. The association of the Holy Spirit with stimulated and released, individual and collective, human agency in situations of need has not been adequately emphasized. Afraid of persecution, the church in the Acts of the Apostles would seek special agentic power of the Holy Spirit to proclaim the gospel: "When they had prayed, the place in which they were gathered together was shaken; and they were all filled with the Holy Spirit and spoke the word of God with boldness" (Acts 4:31).

Three Areas Where Transformation Is Required

This agency, caused and aided by the Holy Spirit, is not only confined to the religious sphere. The cup of those filled with the Holy Spirit runs over, to satisfy the thirst of the world outside the community of believers. In this understanding, the Holy Spirit becomes the cause and energy behind the task of "improving the quality of the conditions in a society (with Christian love) … ."[24]

In my view, this relationship of the Holy Spirit with the spirit of the times in my situation in Zimbabwe must happen at three levels, namely the level of dominant ideologies, the level of dominant structures, and the level of daily practices. As observed by Luther, that there is a Holy Spirit means also that there are forces of ideas, structures, and practices that are against what we believe in the third article of the Apostles' Creed: "We believe in the Holy Spirit, the Holy Christian Church, the Forgiveness of Sins, the Resurrection of the Body and Life everlasting." The Evil Spirit of this age should of necessity contradict the holiness of the fellowship of the saints; must accuse instead of forgiveness; must be the spirit of death and not of resurrection; and must work with a short horizon of life and not eternal life. This is what Paul says as he speaks to the Ephesians: "For our struggle is not against enemies of blood and flesh, but against the rulers,

[24] Grosshans, 93–118, 101.

against the authorities, against the cosmic forces of this present darkness, against the spiritual forces of evil in the heavenly places" (Eph 6:12).

But the reason why we must realize that this battle of the spirits is at three levels is, as Paul puts it in Corinthians:

> "Yet among the mature we do speak wisdom, though it is not a wisdom of this age or of the rulers of this age, who are doomed to perish. But we speak God's wisdom, secret and hidden, which God decreed before the ages for our glory. None of the rulers of this age understood this; for if they had, they would not have crucified the Lord of glory. But, as it is written,
>
> "What no eye has seen, nor ear heard,
> nor the human heart conceived,
> what God has prepared for those who love him"–
>
> these things God has revealed to us through the Spirit; for the Spirit searches everything, even the depths of God" (1 Cor 2: 6-10).

The Disruptive Nature of the Holy Spirit

The church of Jesus Christ, driven by the Holy Spirit, in this sense no longer serves as "stabilizer and ennobler of a bourgeois world shaped by law and order and learned culture, but as irritation of this world and its orders."[25] The Holy Spirit must embolden human agency like that of Jeremiah through which God speaks "See, today I appoint you over nations and over kingdoms, to pluck up and pull down, to destroy and overthrow, to build and to plant" (Jer 1:10). In this understanding, the Holy Spirit must function to work "new beginnings", breaking up existing orders, providing for "discontinuities in the lives of people and societies. The Holy Spirit does not bring about the ordinary, but the extraordinary."[26] The Holy Spirit in our time must be what Paul Tillich understood as the "power that causes spontaneous interruptions of human existence, followed by new adjustments of human life, including community life."[27]

[25] Grosshans, 93-118, 101.
[26] Ibid.
[27] Ibid., 93-118, 102.

Renewal of the Church for the Sake of the World

This newness of the Holy Spirit's work in our midst must happen in the context of a church, which tends to fossilize in structures and institutions. These are not bad, but without the dynamism of the Holy Spirit, the ecclesiastical structures and institutions become too predictable and too domesticated to allow fresh outpouring of the Spirit. Renewal of the church, which is always not a very comfortable process, must characterize the churches of the Reformation. Lutheran pneumatology must characteristically lead to the revitalization of the ministries of the church not for the church's sake but for the sake of the world. A church must not have the Holy Spirit but be filled with the Spirit because the church can only touch the world through its spiritual overflow. There is no renewal of the church that will allow society to maintain the status quo.

Conclusion

In this paper, I looked at some highlights of Luther's pneumatology and observed how Buthelezi, someone separated from Luther by about 500 years, developed his pneumatology from Luther and the early creeds. I then finished by proposing how a contemporary Lutheran pneumatology could look. I conclude by highlighting that it should create a holy people so that they can transform society. It must give new impetus for the proclamation of the word of forgiveness of sin in a world of guilt and accusation. It must speak life in situations of death. It must also speak of abundance of life, everlasting life, in place of short-lived lives.

I cannot not finish this without referring to my own contemporary situation. Since our transition in November 2017, lives of Zimbabweans have become dire; doctors have been on strike for more than eight weeks; prices of commodities have been going up every week. There is no fuel. About eight million Zimbabweans, half the population, are in desperate need of food. There is no clean water in urban areas; we are praying that we do not have a cholera outbreak. Politically motivated violence, characterized by abductions and torture, is back. In times like these, we pray as John 14 states that Jesus send us the Advocate, the Holy Spirit, whom the Father will send in his name, to teach us all things and remind us of all the things Jesus promised us, especially that, "I will never leave you or forsake you" (Heb 13:5). The Holy Spirit emboldens us in this situation to speak the truth without fear. The Holy Spirit also gives us wisdom and protection. A Lutheran pneumatology is therefore relevant for my personal life as it is for the broader Lutheran community.

"Transformed and Freed?" African Pentecostalism, Women's Identity and the Subordinated Spirit

Mutale Mulenga-Kaunda

It is for freedom that Christ sets us free—the freedom of others—those on the margins who are different from us to whom much is given. This requires of us to love even more.

Introduction

I am delighted to have been accorded this opportunity to speak at this consultation on the theme, "We Believe in the Holy Spirit: Global Perspectives on Lutheran Identities." It is important that the theme depicts the plurality in which we find ourselves as scholarship has informed us that there is no one way of expressing an identity or even Christianity. Even within the same denomination, the multiplicity of identities is evident. Nevertheless, the specific focus of my presentation is to interrogate the theme from a Pentecostal African woman's perspective.

Allow me to begin with my life as it is this journey that embodies my ecumenical experiences. Having been raised in the United Church of Zambia, the single largest church next to the Roman Catholic Church, as a teenager I explored my faith and settled in the Pentecostal church and later married a Pentecostal pastor. Having realized that my vocation is not limited to the Pentecostal church, I went on a quest to enrich my Christianity, which led me to often preaching in the Baptist and Presbyterian churches in South Africa. However, having been in other denominations has not negated my Pentecostal roots which continue to define my religious experiences. However, it has broadened the way I experience and conceive of the Holy Spirit. I believe that when you are transformed by the Holy Spirit you become conscious of the real challenges that the world is facing today, the challenges of injustice, challenges of HIV, challenges of racism and xenophobia, challenges of gender inequalities–the list is endless. In other words, you become an embodiment of the life that the world is seeking in all these struggles.

It is because of this that I approach my talk from an African feminist pneumatological perspective. In this frame, women's experiences are the chief cornerstone of African women's theologizing. At the core of this pneumatology is an emphasis on the interplay of African cultures, women's experiences, and the Holy Spirit. African scholars have demonstrated that all conceptions of God, including the notions of the Holy Spirit, are culturally situated and, as such, are to be "treated with suspicion because of their potential to perpetuate a patriarchal ideology, which is the root cause of women's oppression."[1] Thus, African feminist pneumatology stresses women's experiences of the Holy Spirit and how such experiences disempower or empower them for resistance against relations of power, sexism, heterosexism, exploitation and oppression in the church and society.[2]

This means that African women's thinking about the Holy Spirit takes personal experiences seriously in any theological conversation. That is why storytelling has always been at the core of African women theologians' thinking as a way of engaging with African women's realities. A story:

> At the age of 17, my mother who was a single parent after divorcing my father, died. I became the head of the family, caring for my two sisters. After a funeral in Zambia, we have what we call *isambo lyamfwa,* (an indigenous postmortem)[3] where families gather to discuss how the sickness was handled, the cause of death, and how the children will be taken care of in cases where one parent or both parents have died. After my mother's burial, we held *isambo lyamfwa* and it was clear that my sisters and I would be on our own. Usually, families would decide to take a child or two in order for them to feel they still belong to a family and have a sense of security. This did not happen with my sisters and me. Then

[1] See Chammah J. Kaunda and Isabel A. Phiri, "African Instituted Churches Pneumatology and Gender Justice in the Work of GC Oosthuizen: An African Feminist Pneumatological Perspective," *Scriptura* 115, no. 1 (2016): 1–12.

[2] Kaunda, and Phiri, "African Instituted Churches Pneumatology,"

[3] After a funeral in Zambia, family among the Bemba people gather to inquire what caused the death, what is the way forward, how the rest of the family can be of assistance, and everything in between.

> the pastor of my church pledged that the church would assist us financially each month or with groceries. It was settled. We would be in a child-headed household and, with help from the church and a little that I was getting from my untrained preschool and kindergarten teaching, we would be alright. We were never alright. The church kept their word only for the first month, every other month I had to go and ask for assistance from the church and it felt like I was begging. I decided that the church was my last resort. Only if the worst came to the worst, would I go and seek financial assistance from the church. Whenever I went to the church treasurer to seek assistance, he referred me to the pastor, and then the pastor would send me back to the treasurer with approval that they release the finances to me. This was not my problem though. The problem was that the church had no office, so I had to move between two houses that were very far from each other and, most often, I had not eaten for several days. They could have made an arrangement for approval to be in place, especially as the pastor had made that promise to my extended family and me. I slowly stopped asking for this help. At the time, I was a youth leader, I was a Sunday school teacher, and I was a worship leader in this church. My two sisters were in the church choir as well.

I had joined the Pentecostal church as a teenager when my mother's health was deteriorating. I was hopeful that the church would be of help to my mother and to us as a family. My mother had lost her nursing career on medical grounds and it was difficult to make ends meet. The Pentecostal church was a safe space that would assist in my daily struggles against poverty, marginalization, and injustice. Recalling this story brings a realization that I could have been abused by the leadership of the church. I was vulnerable and needed assistance often; the possibility of being taken advantage of and violated in such instances is high. Statistics show that a girl child in need of financial assistance is a recipe for abuse. Often when a girl is in such a vulnerable state, leaders of institutions where she should get a livelihood abuse their power and, in the process, violate her. News of how pastors are "preying" on young girls is all over the media. The case in October 2018 of Cheryl Zondi in South Africa is one example. Her pastor repeatedly raped her when she was just 14 years old. I never experienced any abuse of that nature from the pastor nor the church treasurer, I only wished they could have made the handing over of financial assistance easier because, by the time I would go to seek this assistance, I would not have had food for days.

How else should the church show care to struggling orphaned teenagers? Being each other's keeper goes beyond the call to greet one another. It includes reaching a place where we are able to find out how things really are and how we can serve others better. I came to learn the significance of the church intricately linking the relationship between spiritual gifts and social praxis, because the church is not only the locus, but the embodiment, of the Spirit's missional activities of justice, empowerment, inclusion and solidarity.

African Women, Holy Spirit, and the Church

African women and girls negotiate through life at every turn and level. For African women, whether it is at work, home, church or even in how they experience the Holy Spirit, there is a journey of negotiations. Women's experiences of the Holy Spirit's workings are not neutral because the experiences and working of the Holy Spirit are socially and culturally constructed. Patriarchal apparatus has been deployed to define how a woman should experience and express the Holy Spirit.

While the Pentecostal church has been applauded for being gender-inclusive in its engagements, women are simultaneously excluded, marginalized, and exploited on various levels. For example, Pentecostal churches in Zambia encourage women to take up leadership roles in public spheres, but it appears the churches are doing this to be politically correct. Thus, it seems women's empowerment and the cry for justice are just good ideas to discuss, even in ecclesiastical spaces. In Pentecostal churches, as in various other patriarchal spaces and institutions, the idea of a strong woman is liked until a woman actually stands up, projects her voice, and begins to offer the same status of empowerment for other women. Then she becomes too much. She has forgotten her place and all sorts of accusations are thrown her way. Such women should just be an idea, a fantasy something the church should keep talking about, but it should not become a reality. A real breathing, strong, competent, living woman who embodies all this is perceived as a risk and a threat. That is why it is "absolutely essential that the oppressed [women] participate in the revolutionary process with an increasingly critical awareness of their role as subjects of their transformation" as Paulo Freire maintains.[4] By this I mean that a woman who goes against the master narrative of experiencing the Holy Spirit is often perceived as rebellious and her commitment to the faith is questioned. Women are under pressure to experience the Holy Spirit in an already defined direction so that their experiences of the Holy Spirit do not destabilize the status quo. In some churches, a woman who is a prophet cannot stand at the pulpit and preach when she has her monthly periods. Driving in Pietermaritzburg in South Africa one Saturday afternoon, I noticed a gathering of an African Initiated Church under a tree and one woman was

[4] Paulo Freire, *Pedagogy of the Oppressed* (London: Bloomsbury, 2018), chapter 4.

kneeling outside the circle of stones; everyone else was inside that circle. Curiosity got the better of me and, when I enquired why, I was told that she was having her menstrual period and she had to worship outside the circle[5]. Does this mean that when a woman is menstruating, she cannot have access to the Holy Spirit? I often wonder why women still go to worship when their bodies and sexualities are policed and regulated by male-defined and male-engineered barriers to accessing the Divine. Looking at this from an African feminist pneumatology perspective, it appears the Holy Spirit is repulsed by women's menstrual blood. How do we even begin to discuss freedom and transformation when women in faith communities are still policed and regulated about how to approach God on certain days?

Shouldn't we begin by transcending these barriers and definitions that have been placed on what it means to be a woman, especially in ecclesiastical spaces? The constant policing and regulating of women's dress, sexuality, behavior, and being points to ways the Holy Spirit has been historically and socially defined in patriarchal terms. Radical shifts in order to experience the freedom that the Holy Spirit gives is imperative. This means being freed in our attitudes, conceptions, and perception of one another, and of women. Perhaps the paraphrase of the famous South African Archbishop Desmond Tutu, "your humanity is bound up with mine," would express this better. Overcoming those limitations–understandings of the working of the Holy Spirit that are shaped and defined by patriarchy–means a struggle for freedom and transformation. Those policing and regulating attitudes that come from men and some women (because they have been nurtured into this system) need to be rejected. We have constructed and boxed the workings of the Holy Spirit; that is the challenge we face. For me, when we talk about transformation from the Holy Spirit, it is about reading the signs of times. The United Nations has developed Sustainable Development Goals (SDGs) which recognize that women's empowerment is critical and a global priority. Therefore, young women and girls should be viewed and empowered as agents of their own transformation and change, not as beneficiaries of change. Their inclusion in the implementation of the SDGs is crucial. The SDGs assume that, through gender equality, genuine transformative change can be achieved. The transformation and freedom that the Holy Spirit bestows should also be accessed by women. As a church we cannot leave anyone behind in our progress. This means that there is a need for church leadership that is competent, committed, compassionate and consistent in their following of Jesus who welcomes all and "leaves no one behind." [The phrase is used to promote the SDGs–Ed.] While African

[5] The desire to worship God even on days that a woman is on her menses and knows she won't be allowed in the circle, yet she goes to worship still.

women do not take patriarchy lying down, as Nigerian scholar Nnaemeka Obiomma has demonstrated, women and men should work as partners of equals, working together to achieve gender equality in ecclesiastical spaces.

"Freed and Transformed": What Does it Mean for African Women?

At the beginning of this year, the reverend Vukile Mehana, a senior minister in the Methodist Church of Southern Africa, South Africa's ruling party's chaplain general, and a highly networked private and business sector leader, was recorded on a WhatsApp conversation expressing his sentiments about a female clergy person, the reverend Nompithizelo Sibhidla who was robbing the men's guild. His vile sentiments were, "What kind of a woman is this who fiddles with men's chests? What do the wives of these men think when there is this woman with big breasts fondling the chests of (their) men? From where does Nompithizelo get this tendency?" Sarojini Nadar and Tinyiko Maluleke raise pertinent questions: "If Sibhidla cannot robe the men, can she touch their foreheads when she blesses them? Can she serve them communion? And when she does, how far must she stand from the untouchable chests of men? Can she bury the dead, and minister to the sick, in spite of her 'big breasts'?"[6]

An African theology of liberation must care about patriarchy and gender insensitivity in order to be relevant.

As already argued, stories such as Sibhidla's confirm that men define the way the Holy Spirit works. The spirit of God has been "patriarchalized" and domesticated, like women; the Holy Spirit shares a subordinate relationship to men who have seen themselves as situated on top of human hierarchy in God's plan. Patriarchal ideology keeps in check the way in which the Holy Spirit is defined and works in the lives of African women. The unconscious feminization of the Holy Spirit has meant the Holy Spirit is at the service of male humanity and women experience the transformation of the Holy Spirit through their male counterparts. Scholars argue that the Spirit is relegated to effective subordination despite the rhetoric of full equality with the two other persons in the Trinity. This has some important implications for the status of women in church. What is seen as arbitrary for women in church turns out to be a gendered ballast for church life, especially for women. Can we reclaim the Spirit of God as a liberating Spirit? I challenge us to go beyond just reclaiming the Spirit

[6] "No Holy Cows in Hate Cases," *Mail & Guardian*, 10 January 2010, https://mg.co.za/article/2019-01-10-00-no-holy-cows-in-hate-cases/.

of God as Sophia, the wise feminine Spirit. We have to reclaim the Holy Spirit as liberating agency for the suffering and marginalized, especially women. The Holy Spirit liberates humans only as partners–women and men able to live with and affirm each other as equals before God and ourselves. This means we must move from individualistic understanding of the transformation and empowerment of the Holy Spirit to a more communal and partnership orientation between women and men. If we claim to be freed and transformed by the Holy Spirit, the manner in which we define relationships through our perception of those who are on the margins, those who are different from us and those with whom we do not agree, shows whether the Holy Spirit is indeed at work in our lives and whether we are liberated, formed and transformed. There is no better way of proving that the Holy Spirit is at work except through sound and just relationships. As Paul argued, "where the Spirit is, there is liberty."

Women face all sorts of social challenges and the Spirit of God gives them freedom because they are human in their own right, without societal norms and definitions. I always looked to God and prayed earnestly as a teenager. I believed in my heart that God would use the church to alleviate my suffering. I was committed to God, to the Pentecostal church and to hard work because I knew that as a Bemba proverb says, "*Lesa afwa abayafwa*" (God helps those who help themselves). So, while I was hopeful that the church would empower me, I was also working to empower myself. The definition of the Holy Spirit is central in the process of transformation and freedom for women. The Holy Spirit is a power that speaks, defines, directs, and frees individuals and faith communities, and often speaks and works through human beings. Luke narrates in Acts 2:1–4:

> "When the day of Pentecost had come, they were all together in one place. And suddenly from heaven there came a sound like the rush of a violent wind, and it filled the entire house where they were sitting. Divided tongues, as of fire, appeared among them, and a tongue rested on each of them. All of them were filled with the Holy Spirit and began to speak in other languages, as the Spirit gave them ability."

"They were all together": What defined them was not gender, not their sexual orientation, rather their humanity, their waiting for God, their connectedness to one another. "All of them were filled with the Holy Spirit": There was no discrimination on account of gender or sexuality. The Holy Spirit empowered them all equally. They were all destitute and marginalized in their societies. It was the Holy Spirit who transformed and freed them as human beings created with dignity. So, what does it mean to be "freed and transformed" for African women?

First, it is a call to walk with those who have been at the receiving end of marginalization, oppression and exclusion, especially African women and others who are minorities. It is when the church has recognized, stood in critical solidarity, and walked with, the vulnerable, and listened to their stories, that transformation can be seen. The church is not a neutral space it is political and must be engaged critically to attain gender equality for women's experiences of the church, the Holy Spirit and life in general. "There has been a consistent call in missiological circles to understand mission as not just [spiritual] conversion but indeed as spreading the good news of justice and love, a move which of necessity requires transforming injustice in the world."

Second, we need radical connection between church talk with the prophetic actions to help the marginalized, especially women, through the power of the Holy Spirit to freely name their reality. As can be seen in Acts chapter 2, the Holy Spirit came on the marginalized people to empower them to find their own voice in order to name their situations of oppression and exploitation. Paulo Freire warns, through oppression, the marginalized lose their identity and too often tend to name the "oppressor's reality as their own, and therefore contribute to their own oppression." The church must incarnate in the marginalized and through them begin to name realities of injustice in order to transform them. There is a need for "a deliberate and a conscious process of developing awareness of the contradictions of the sociocultural, political and economic reality" shaping the marginalized and rethink the work of the Holy Spirit in the process of transforming oppressive and exploitative realities.[7]

Finally, without a shadow of doubt, the church, through the power of the Holy Spirit, has potential for fostering liberation and transforming the church itself and nations. We need to create spaces that can bring about just transformation and authentic freedom in women's lives. There is a need to begin recognizing the hard work by African women within the church and society, which for too long has gone completely unrecognized and their ideas which are often not only unappreciated, but not taken seriously even though they make up the majority of church membership. The late Nelson Mandela once said this: "For to be free is not merely to cast off one's chains, but to live in a way that respects and enhances the freedom of others." How do we live that out? By inclusion of women in decision-making policies in institutions. In short, all human experiences have their source and final goal in the Divine. Thus, the question of right contemplation of God, right

[7] Chammah J. Kaunda, "'A Voice Shouting in the Wilderness': Desmond Mpilo Tutu's Contribution to African Theology of Public Prophetic Preaching for Social Justice and Wholeness," *International Journal of Public Theology* 9, no. 1 (2015), 44.

speech about God, and experiencing of the Holy Spirit all hang together. Let me end with a poem I wrote recently:

> Before I am a woman, I am human
> I am also black
> But not just black, but I am an African
> I bear the marks of colonialism on my back
> I can hide scars of patriarchy on my breast
> I am oppressed within
> I am exploited without
> Because I am a woman, I am an African
> Where is the Holy Spirit?
> God has sided with my oppressors
> Justice I call, justice I long for
> Take everything, but give me the Holy Spirit
> That's all I ask, that's all I want

Embodied Spirit: Outlines of Lutheran Pneumatology

Bernd Oberdorfer

At first sight, it does not seem to be a wise idea to focus a conference about Lutheran identity on pneumatology. Lutherans, to say the least, have not been widely known for advocating the Holy Spirit. On the contrary, did they not themselves practice a strict cautiousness with reference to the Holy Spirit, condemning everyone who directly referred to the Spirit instead of meditating God's revelation in the words of the Holy Scripture (*sola Scriptura*) as being "Spiritualist" or "Schwärmer"? And has their Christocentric approach to theology (*solus Christus*) not prevented them from developing elaborated ideas on pneumatology? Moreover, in the Reformers' internal conflict about the Holy Communion, was it not the Swiss Reformers who explicitly linked the sacramental commemoration (Zwingli) or representation (Calvin) of Christ to the Holy Spirit whereas the Lutherans in their rigid emphasis on the real and substantial presence of the whole Christ did not give the Spirit a special attention? Thus, it actually makes sense to characterize Zwingli's or Calvin's theology essentially as a "Theology of the Holy Spirit," but it would be an ambitious, if not vain, endeavor to do so for the work of Luther or Melanchthon.

In the specter between –as has been said in a German word play–*Geistvergessenheit* und *Geistversessenheit*[1] (oblivion of, and addiction to, the Spirit), the Lutherans seem to come quite close to the extreme of oblivion (and particularly orthodox theologians regularly accuse them of being

[1] See Christian Danz and Michael Murrmann-Kahl, eds., *Zwischen Geistvergessenheit und Geistversessenheit: Perspektiven der Pneumatologie im 21. Jahrhundert* (Tübingen: Mohr Siebeck, 2014).

oblivious of the Spirit) and definitely are not in danger to become addicted. If Lutherans speak of the Spirit (and of course, they do), it seems to be a well-tempered, domesticated Spirit which, as it were, works in the shadow of Christ and hides as a captive behind the bars of the Holy Scripture.

But (even apart from the fact that the shadow sometimes is not the worst place to be and, at times, it is preferable to meet domesticated rather than wild animals) this first sight deserves a second glance. Indeed, the Lutherans were not silent when it came to the Spirit. It is true that they distrusted any claims of a freewheeling wafting of the Spirit. But they did so because they wanted to secure the authenticity, sufficiency, completeness and perfection of God's revelation in Christ to which we have access in an open book –the Holy Scripture. They wanted to prevent Christians from the temptation of searching for a second "spiritual" truth besides, or in addition to, or above, the truth which is revealed in the scriptures. They fought against the idea that there might be "higher" truths available by intercession of the Holy Spirit, truths that might be necessary to achieve full Christian perfection. Thus, they insisted that the Spirit's work be found within, not beyond the one, concrete revelation in which God makes Godself present in the world. This implies, however, the conviction that the Spirit itself is really, and substantially, present in the revelation and, moreover, that the revelation cannot be understood without reference to the Holy Spirit. The fact that the Spirit, according to Lutheran theology, is an "embodied" Spirit does not make the Spirit superfluous or reduce the Spirit to a subordinated tool. It rather implies that whenever we speak of God and God's revelation we have to speak about God's Spirit as well. In the following, therefore, I would like to elaborate outlines of Lutheran pneumatology focusing on the idea of the Spirit's embodiment.

The Spirit's Embodiment in the Word

Locus classicus of Lutheran pneumatology is article 5 of the Augsburg Confession. There we read:

> So that we might receive this faith, the ministry of teaching the gospel and administering the sacraments is established [sc. by God]. For through the Word and sacraments, as through tools, the Holy Spirit is given who effects faith, whenever and wherever it pleases God, in those who hear the gospel.[2]

[2] Latin version, my translation.

According to the systematic arrangement of the Confession, this article explains how the faith is achieved, which article 4 declared to be the cause and form of the justification of the sinner. Article 5 repeats the core message of the gospel, "not because of our own merits, but for Christ's sake, God justifies those who believe that they are received into grace because of Christ." Unambiguously, article 5 identifies the Holy Spirit as the source and effective cause of our faith. The Confession, on the one hand, by binding the Spirit's work to the human practice of preaching the gospel and administering the sacraments as the Spirit's "tools" (*instrumenta*), as it were, "earths" or "grounds" the Spirit's presence; the Spirit commits itself to use these instruments to create faith. On the other hand, the Confession underlines that the Spirit does not work, so to speak, automatically; the Spirit "effects faith, whenever and wherever it pleases God." However, this does not qualify the unique relevance of the gospel; the Spirit, whenever and wherever it works, effects faith "in those who hear the gospel."

The text of article 5 is very dense and complex; the translation therefore has to be very concise (which, by the way, is not always the case in the English translations to which I had access). The complexity even increases if we compare the Latin with the German version because the comparison displays significant differences with reference to the question who "acts" in the process of faith-based justification:

In the Latin text, the Holy Spirit is given through the instruments of Word and sacraments and effects the faith. In the German text, the Holy Spirit itself uses the instruments of Word and sacraments in order to effect faith. In the German version, thus, Word and sacraments are instruments of the *work* of the Spirit. In the Latin version, however, these are instruments of the *gift* of the Spirit. In other words, in German, the Spirit *works* through Word and sacraments; in Latin the Spirit *comes* through Word and sacraments. It seems that the German text binds the Spirit even more strongly to Word and sacraments than the Latin does.

The German version gives a more elaborate expression of the Spirit's work saying that the Spirit "comforts the hearts and gives faith." Thus, it emphasizes the dimension of the heart and makes clear that faith is more than knowledge. I will come back to this later.

In the German text, it is the Spirit who works "whenever and wherever it wants to," whereas in Latin, it is God who gives the Spirit "whenever and wherever it pleases God." As in the first bullet point, the German version seems to ascribe the Spirit a more active role. We could take from this that the German version more explicitly reflects the Spirit's status as a trinitarian person (although, of course, the Latin version is far from denying that).

In the Latin version, the "ministry of preaching (*docendi*) the gospel and administering the sacrament" is established (by God), whereas in German, God established "the ministry of preaching, gospel and sacraments." This subtle difference could be read in a way that the Latin focusses more strictly on the *ordained* ministry whilst the German, in a more general sense, ascribes the ministry of preaching, gospel and sacraments to the whole church. In any case, the discussion on whether article 5 speaks of ordained ministry in particular (some would even say, exclusively), or of the ministry of the church in general, runs through the whole history of Lutheran theology and has not yet been resolved unanimously. Of course, this is of great relevance for ecclesiology, but in the context of pneumatology I will not go deeper into that question.

Clearly these differences do not mark substantial contradictions, but rather indicate a variety of possible interpretations. However, with respect to pneumatology, both versions have in common that they describe gospel and sacraments as means and media of the Holy Spirit's saving and sanctifying advent and presence in the world. The Spirit's presence displays itself by causing people to believe in the truth of what is being proclaimed in the gospel. The Spirit does so, we must add, by revealing the real meaning of the Holy Scripture's words, in other words by making people *understand*. And with reference to Luther's basic concept of biblical hermeneutics – "was Christum treibet" (what moves to Christ, or more precisely, to believing in Christ) – this means to understand the words of the Bible as testifying Christ as Savior. The Spirit, therefore, does not actually testify for itself. Instead, the Spirit's presence reveals itself indirectly when it testifies for Christ. In this dialectical sense, we could apply the biblical words "Blessed are those who have not seen and yet have come to believe" (Jn 20:29) to the Spirit as well, so that we understand it as "Blessed are those who have not seen the Spirit and yet have come to believe." In other words, the Spirit is visible when it makes Christ visible as Savior. It is visible in the mirror of Christ, the open book of the Holy Scripture.

This becomes even clearer in the anathema that concludes article 5. The reformers confirm they "damn the Anabaptists and others who think [German version: teach] that the Holy Spirit comes to people without the external word [German: without the bodily–*leiblich* –word of the gospel] through their own preparations and works." It has been rightly remarked that this damnation does not really strike the "Anabaptists" who declined the baptism of infants with explicit reference to the Holy Scripture, but rather the "Spiritualists" who stressed a saving presence of the Holy Spirit which is neither bound to the media of Scripture and sacraments nor to the saving work of Christ. This way of understanding the Spirit's presence, then, does not "move to Christ." This explains why the Confession states that neglecting the media of Word and sacraments leads to the conviction that we have to prepare ourselves for the Spirit's advent. This is because, without the Word, we would not know that, due to what Christ already has done for us, we need no longer prepare ourselves for the coming of God. In other words, if we search for the Spirit beside and beyond, Christ (and Holy Scripture as Christ's medium), we will never find the Spirit. The Spirit is only present when and where the presence of Christ is affirmed or, even more precisely, when and where the Spirit affirms the presence of Christ.

This strong emphasis on the presence of Christ might explain why the Lutherans did not elaborate the role of the Spirit in their understanding of the Holy Supper. They wanted to prevent any suspicion that an explicit reference to the Holy Spirit might qualify the reality of Christ's presence which is indicated and induced by the powerfully promising word of consecration. This does not mean that they underestimated (or even contested) the presence of the Spirit in the Eucharist. But this presence, once again, is mediated through the Word—and only through the Word.

Spirit and Understanding: The Spirit Is Not a Sceptic

The phrase "powerfully promising word" might be used as a short formula for the Lutheran emphasis on the *sola Scriptura*. The Holy Scripture entails everything we have to know about our salvation: it is "sufficient." And it not only entails its salvific content, it also reveals it. It is *sui ipsius interpret*, its own interpreter. There is nothing to add to the scriptures to make them understandable, neither an external authority nor a tradition—not even the Holy Spirit. The latter might be surprising because it seems to suggest that we do not need the Holy Spirit to understand the Holy Scripture. Yet, the contrary is true. However, the Holy Spirit is not something to be added to the scriptures to make them understandable. Rather it already is within the scriptures and reveals its salvific content. We do not need to first achieve the Spirit in order to turn toward the scriptures and understand them. Rather, the Spirit is within the scriptures and opens up our understanding.

This is the reason why Luther, in his famous controversy with Erasmus of Rotterdam, pointedly says, "The Holy Spirit is not a sceptic." *(Spiritus Sanctus non est skepticus).*[3] In this controversy, which has become crucial to Lutheran hermeneutics, Erasmus argued that the Bible is a book with very diverse content, including cryptic passages and ostensive contradictions. Therefore, it does not offer a clear understanding of itself but rather requires an external authority which is capable and entitled to give an

[3] Martin Luther, *The Bondage of the Will*, trans. J.I. Packer and O. R. Johnston (Grand Rapids, Mich.: Baker Academic), 70.

authentic interpretation. Moreover, Erasmus stressed the relevance of longtime church traditions; if a specific interpretation of a biblical phrase is supported by a significant number of 'Church Fathers, Synods, Popes' and respected theologians, this "cloud of witnesses" makes it more probable that this interpretation is true—more probably at least than if only a single theologian advocates it. Ironically, he asked Luther why he on the one hand so frankly doubted the decisions of Synods, Popes, and Church Fathers, and on the other hand was so sure to be right. It is more than evident that he accused Luther of subjectivism. For Luther, however, to accept that the Holy Scripture is not clear in itself would have meant to qualify the revelation itself. But God does not reveal Godself in vague adumbrations and ambiguous announcements because this would destroy the reliability of God's word and make it uncertain to trust in it. According to Luther, the certainty of faith depends on the clarity and accessibility of the word of God. If the Holy Spirit were a sceptic, God would leave us alone in doubts and presumptions. Therefore, the Holy Spirit, being no sceptic, represents the reliability of God's salvific presence. As to subjectivism however, Luther was convinced that the way the scriptures had spoken to him revealed their meaning. It was not just his subjectivist imagination but rather, as it were, an objective truth coming from outside (*extra nos*), and thus could be plausible to others as well. And he did not proclaim his interpretation of the scriptures as a mystic experience which cannot be further explained but only humbly accepted; he always argued exegetically. In his famous speech at the Diet of Worms in 1521, he announced that he was willing to retract when he was disproved "by Scripture and reason." But undoubtedly, within the reformers' movement, a plurality of interpretations of the Bible has arisen, all of them trusting in the revealing power of the Spirit, and questions of Bible hermeneutics, therefore, have always remained a crucial challenge for Lutheran theology. Thus, it does not seem exaggerated to say that the pathos and ethos of reading and understanding the Bible—and the struggles resulting from that—form an essential part of Lutheran identity.

The Work(s) of the Spirit

Let us go back to the Augsburg Confession. Article 5, as we have seen, focuses the Spirit's work on the creation of faith. By strictly linking this work of the Spirit to the preaching of the gospel, the Lutheran tradition also implies a concentration on understanding this gospel; the Spirit reveals the Christological and soteriological meaning of the scriptures. This might raise the assumption that Lutheran pneumatology is restricted to cognitivism and subjectivism. Only the German version of article 5 indicates something that goes beyond the dimension of understanding when it says that the Spirit "comforts the soul." And implicitly, moreover, there is also a nod to ecclesiology in that preaching the gospel is an act of the church. This excludes a subjectivist misunderstanding of the Spirit's work.

In article 3, we find a more elaborate description of the Spirit's dynamics in Christian life. Article 3 summarizes the classical Christology with reference to the Apostles' Creed. Coming to explain the way Christ rules "seated at the right hand of the Father," the article, in its German version, states that Christ "through the Holy Spirit sanctifies, purifies, strengthens, comforts all who believe in him, also gives them life and all kind of gifts and goods und protects and guards them against the devil and the sin." Interestingly enough, in the Latin version, Christ "sanctifies those who believe in him by sending the Holy Spirit into their hearts," and it is the Holy Spirit then who "reigns, comforts and vivifies them and defends them against the devil and the power of sin." Here the Spirit plays a more active role. Both versions, however, have in common that they give a broader picture of Christian life which is formed by Christ and inspired by the Spirit. We could even say that the ruling of the ascended Christ is realized in this Christian life of the believers. Christ and Holy Spirit are almost synonymous; Christ is present through the Spirit and its work.

Lutheran theology, thus, roots Christian life in the work of the Spirit. This becomes even more evident in Luther's interpretation of the third article of the Apostles' Creed in his *Small Catechism*. Here we read, "The Holy Spirit has called me through the gospel, illuminated me with his gifts, sanctified and preserved me in the right faith, as well as (the Holy Spirit) calls, collects, illuminates, sanctifies the whole Christianity on earth in the one unanimous right faith." And it continues, "In this Christianity (the Holy Spirit) daily forgives me and all believers all sins and will resurrect me and all dead people on the day of judgement and give me eternal life together with all those who believe in Christ." Here the Spirit explicitly is the subject and driving force of the whole of Christian life. Here, moreover, the Christian life is clearly embedded in the church. Conversely, this means that the presence of the Spirit always has an ecclesial dimension.

The Church as Creatura Spiritus

It has often been remarked that the third article of the Apostles' Creed, after naming the Holy Spirit, immediately switches to the church. Different from the Nicene Creed, it says nothing about the Spirit itself. This could mean that the Spirit's presence in the world is realized in the church and its work of communicating the faith. The church, then, could be called the (visible) face of the (invisible) Spirit. Although this does not give a full picture of the Spirit and its work (which is not limited to the church) and although the church should not be too self-reliant and forget that the church's face always also shows traces and scars of sin, it nevertheless is true that the Spirit reveals itself (by, as it were, hiding itself) in the church as the "congregation of the believers among which the gospel is preached purely and the holy sacraments are administered in accordance with the gospel" as article 7 of the Augsburg Confession in its German version puts it.[4]

In some ecumenical documents, therefore, the church has been called a "creature of the Word and of the Spirit." This fits perfectly with a Lutheran understanding of the church as "Creature of the Word (*creatura Verbi*)" as long as the "and" (sc. of the Spirit) does not imply an addition but rather an explanation, "creature of the Word, which means of the Spirit." Lutherans always were convinced that through baptism we are integrated into the one spiritual "body of Christ" and become a living part of it. Luther emphasized that because all members are baptized, they all enjoy the same status and dignity. There is no internal religious hierarchy in Christianity although, of course, there are different gifts, tasks, and responsibilities. Reformation historians say that this concept of the "common priesthood of all believers (or of all baptized)" was the core element of the Reformation's dynamics and thus forms an identity marker of all types or "wings" of the Reformation. Above all, this concept implies a critique of any qualitative differentiation with respect to the presence of the Spirit and contradicts any monopolistic presumptions about the spiritual competences of the clergy. "Whoever has crawled out of baptism," Luther said provocatively, "has already been ordained as priest, bishop or pope."[5]

The concept of the "common priesthood of all believers" has at least a two-fold scope. On the one hand, it ascribes to all believers a competence to do what a priest does, namely, to be a mediator (*Mittler*) between God and humans by interceding for others in prayer to God, and by presenting God's word to others. This includes the competence to read and interpret the word of God in the Holy Scripture, which is no longer an exclusive right of the clergy. On the other hand, it stresses that each and every task in the church has a spiritual dimension or, in other words, is a *charisma*, a gift of the Spirit. There are no higher or lower forms of *charisma*, there are no more perfect or less perfect forms of being Christian. This anti-elitist focus had the consequence that the Reformers prioritized the, as it were, "normal" and "natural" gifts of the Spirit and distrusted the interest in "supernatural"

[4] The Latin version is slightly different: "congregation of the saints in which (sc. congregation), etc."

[5] *Weimarer Ausgabe* (hereafter, WA) 6:408, 11-21.

or extraordinary spiritual gifts like celibacy or miracles. The emphasis to avoid a first-and-second-class Christianity is a most significant heritage of the Reformation because it resulted in a new perception of the dignity of "normal life" as being the full form of Christian life and witness.[6] But it had the price of discrediting any forms of special vocations which are not open to everybody. It took centuries, e.g., until Lutheran churches rediscovered that monasticism does not necessarily result in religious elitism but rather can be an inspiring form of Christian witness. In the following paragraph, I would like to comment on both the dignity of "normal life" and the challenge of "paranormal" Christian lifestyles.

THE SPIRIT'S EMBODIMENT IN "NORMAL LIFE"

It was a great discovery of the Reformation that clergy and monasticism are neither the only nor the highest forms of Christian vocation. The Reformers taught instead that every profession, every way of living, has a special vocation and is a form of Christian witness. The German word for "profession," *Beruf*, mirrors the idea that a profession is not simply a job but a vocation, *Berufung*. Not only a monk is "called" by God but also a mother or father who nourishes their children, a farmer who produces food, a politician who cares for the good order of a city or a state, etc. They all, by fulfilling their duties, practice love of the neighbor and thus witness to their Christian faith. Luther could even say that "normal life" always entails a dimension of asceticism which is at least as significant as the asceticism of a monk: parents who sit by the beds of their ill children; couples who care for one another in good as well as in bad days; farmers who harvest, if necessary, in rain and storm; politicians who assume responsibility, notwithstanding the circumstances–they all abstain from following their own interests by subordinating those interests to the needs of others. In his treatise "On Christian Liberty," Luther pointed out that justification through faith makes one free from the necessity of caring for oneself and thus frees one to be "a willing servant" of anyone who needs help. Because Christ has given me everything I need for worldly and eternal life, I can "selflessly" use my capacities in favor of others. We can add that this selflessness also has a pneumatological dimension because it images the Spirit's "selfless" witness for Christ.

[6] See Bernd Oberdorfer, "Aus der Klausur ins 'normale Leben': Reformatorische Leitbildtrans-formationen," in Bernd Oberdorfer and Eva Matthes, eds., *Reformation Heute, vol. 5: Menschenbilder und Lebenswirklichkeiten* (Leipzig: Evangelische Verlagsanstalt, 2019), 32–44.

This idea of "vocation" has resulted in a Lutheran ethos of "complying with duties" (*Pflichterfüllung*) which had a strong impact on the cultural, political, and even economic history of countries with significant Lutheran populations. The positive effects are so evident that they hardly can be overrated. One problem, however, cannot be denied. Lutherans had the tendency to read this ethos of complying with duties as implying an unconditional obligation to political obedience. If complying with duties is implicit in Christian freedom, then, quite paradoxically, political obedience becomes a requirement of Christian freedom, and, conversely, political disobedience appears as a selfish act of individuals who are not willing to subordinate their own interests to the common good. Political protest, in this regard, displays a lack of Christian freedom. As an act of the *homo incurvatus in seipsum* (human being crooked in him- or herself), it is an expression of sin. Not surprisingly, therefore, Lutherans have not belonged to the avant-garde of the concept of human rights. Instead, they had to learn belatedly that Christian freedom can also be expressed by defending the rights of individuals against the pressure of totalitarian states or powerful communities.[7]

It seems that this tendency to prefer loyalty to the state or community over individual freedom has the same anti-elitist focus as the Lutheran cautiousness with regard to "extraordinary" gifts of the Spirit. The philosopher Charles Taylor, in his comprehensive study on "The Secular Age"[8], has argued that the Reformation played a significant role in the process of reducing the richness of religious expressions (by eliminating relics, saints, periods of fasting, most religious holidays, etc.) which in the long run resulted in a secular culture where religious practice has almost become invisible. Taylor concentrates on Calvinism (and does not seem to know much about Lutheran Reformation), and he does not ignore the positive effects of this process of reduction and purification (e.g., a decrease of superstition or an emphasis on equality and social justice). But although he definitely underestimates the inspiring potential of the Reformation to create new forms of religious expression (particularly in music and hymns),

---

[7] See Oberdorfer, "'Freiheit von ...' Kleine theologische Apologie des Individualismus—im Horizont von Luthers Freiheitsschrift," in *Kontroverse Freiheit. Die Impulse der Ökumene*, eds. Thomas Söding and Bernd Oberdorfer (Freiburg im Breisgau: Herder, 2017), 219–236; Oberdorfer, "Reformation und politisch-gesellschaftliche Emanzipation," *Evangelische Theologie* 74 (2014): 118–126.

[8] Charles Taylor, *A Secular Age* (Cambridge, Mass: Harvard University Press, 2007). Cf. Oberdorfer, "Exkarnation und geahnte Fülle: Zu Charles Taylors Diagnose des Glaubens im 'säkularen Zeitalter,'" in *Mission zwischen Proselytismus und Selbstabschaffung*, eds. Jutta Koslowski and Andreas Krebs (Leipzig: Evangelische Verlagsanstalt, 2017), 11–22.

he points to an important issue. Did the wonderful Lutheran emphasis on anti-elitism and "normal life" and the dimming out of the "extraordinary" gifts of the Spirit, not create –as an unintended side effect–the risk of losing the dimension of "overcoming the world," of expressing a distance to the world, of eschatology? The challenge then would be to regain this dimension without breaking the anti-elitist framework.

The Spirit as Lord: Trinitarian Perspectives

I cannot end without some, albeit very sketchy, remarks on the Trinitarian dimension of pneumatology.[9] The Reformers defended the dogma of the Triune God (cf. CA 1). However, they were very hesitant to continue the medieval speculations about the immanent life of God. Two famous phrases of Melanchthon mark a general consensus of the Reformers' Trinitarian hermeneutics. He recommended the "secrets of God better be adored than explored," and he stated that "to know Christ means to know his benefactions." The knowledge of Christ–as the godly-human person of the dogma–is strictly rooted in the knowledge of Christ's work of reconciliation and justification; there is no need for speculations that go beyond. This goes as well for the Trinity as a whole. To speak in modern terms, the Reformers maintained a strict correspondence between "immanent" and "economic" Trinity. There is no difference between the "immanent," intrinsic being of the Triune God and God's reality towards, and within, God's creation. This also refers to the mutual relations among the Trinitarian "persons." The Reformers underlined that, on the one hand, the Holy Spirit is –in the full sense – God and fully participates in all actions of God *ad extra*. Therefore, Luther could praise the vivifying presence of the Spirit as creator, *Spiritus creator*, in nature. Yet, on the other hand, they insisted on a very strong Trinitarian link between the Son and the Spirit. If, in the history of salvation, the Spirit is Christ's Spirit and is sent by Christ and witnesses for Christ, this mirrors their eternal, intrinsic relations–the Spirit receives its eternal being not only from the Father but also from the Son. The Reformers, therefore, saw no problems to maintain the Western tradition of the "Filioque" although they did not use it polemically against the Orthodox tradition. In the ecumenical dialogues of the twentieth century, however, it became evident that in the history of salvation, the relations between Christ and the Spirit are mutual. It is the Spirit which, after Christ's baptism in the river Jordan, empowers Christ to preach the gospel. If the

[9] See Oberdorfer, *Filioque: Geschichte und Theologie eines ökumenischen Problems* (Göttingen: Vandenhoeck & Ruprecht, 2001), 267-275.

correspondence between "economic" and "immanent" Trinity is essential for Lutheran theology, this mutuality must be made visible in the conception of the eternal relations between Son and Spirit; the "Filioque" proves to be not false but one-sided and insufficient. This opens the door to a new and fruitful dialogue with the Orthodox Churches.

Challenges of Lutheran Pneumatology

I hope that my paper shows that Lutheran theology was not at all tacit about the Holy Spirit but rather developed rich ideas on pneumatology. Nevertheless, I would like to end with three challenges which result from the specific concentration of Lutheran pneumatology and need further reflection:

- First, its focus on embodying the Spirit in the Holy Scripture and its understanding evokes the question of what we can, and have to, say about "extraordinary" ways of the Spirit's witness of God's salvific presence.

- Second, its focus on faith evokes the question of what we can, and have to, say about the presence of the Spirit in creation.

- Third, its focus on Christian faith evokes the question of what we can, and have to, say about the presence of the Spirit outside the church, in other religions, in the secular world, etc.

It is clear that these questions are not supposed to qualify the soteriological focus of Lutheran pneumatology. But it is clear as well that they formulate essential challenges for Lutheran self-understanding and Lutheran identity within the context of our time and age.

A Theological Reflection on the Person and Work of the Holy Spirit in the Face of Contemporary Challenges to Christian Witness in the Twenty-First Century

Winston D. Persaud

Introduction

Given the focus of this theological consultation, in this paper I have chosen to point to primary theological facets of Lutheran identity in relation to the question of "the person and work of the Holy Spirit," calling attention to insights from Martin Luther, the *Joint Declaration on the Doctrine of Justification*, and common statements of the Lutheran-Roman Catholic Dialogue, USA. Given the decisive and definitive role of the doctrine of justification in Luther's and Lutheran theological articulation and confession of the Christian faith, the focus on the doctrine of justification should not come as a surprise. At the same time, it may be surprising, given a common assumption that the Reformation's accent on justification by grace alone (*sola gratia*), through faith alone (*sola fide*), in Christ alone (*solus Christus*) means that the overriding focus was on the second article of the Creed. Consequently, in that vein, focus on the third and first articles of the Creed are subordinate. In this paper, the essential, dynamic interrelatedness between Christ and the Spirit is both assumed and explicitly noted. Indeed, the theological argument in this essay rests on the conviction that what the church confesses about the person and work of the Holy Spirit, the person and work of Jesus Christ, and the person and work of God the Father is essentially, and inextricably, Trinitarian.

Further, the approach is grounded in the theology of the cross whereby we make the confession that it is through the Spirit that, in faith in Jesus Christ, the crucified and risen Savior and Lord, we are able to discern God's gracious, saving and liberating presence where God appears to be absent. In his "Heidelberg Disputation" (1518), theses 19-22, Martin Luther declares:

> 19. That person does not deserve to be called a theologian who looks upon the invisible things of God as though they were clearly perceptible in those things which have actually happened (Rom 1:20).
>
> 20. One deserves to be called a theologian, however, who comprehends the visible and manifest things of God seen through suffering and the cross.
>
> 21. A theologian of glory calls evil good and good evil. A theologian of the cross calls the thing what it actually is.
>
> 22. That wisdom which sees the invisible things of God in works as perceived by humans is completely puffed up, blinded, and hardened.[1]

In a cursory reading of the foregoing theses, it is easy to overlook the assumed, essential presence and work of the Holy Spirit, who is not mentioned. Yet, we confess that in the death of Jesus in which the theologian of the cross "comprehends the visible and manifest things of God seen through suffering and the cross"[2], God, who raised Jesus from the dead through the power of the Spirit, is most present. In the power of the Spirit the eternal word became incarnate in Jesus. In the power of the Spirit, who descends on Jesus at his baptism, Jesus enacts the kingdom of God and, consequently, suffers death on the cross. Thus, in the framework of the theology of the cross, we have to consider the paradoxical and ambiguous character of power. The theology of the cross exposes and judges us in our denial of the truth about God and consequently the truth about ourselves. The theology of the cross cuts through ideologies of glory and triumph. For example, in 1 Corinthians 1:18-31, the Apostle Paul speaks about the paradoxical power of God in the cross of Christ. In raising Jesus from the dead, God identifies with Jesus in his death. Indeed, it is through the Spirit

[1] *Martin Luther's Basic Theological Writings*, 3rd edition, eds. Timothy F. Lull and William R. Russell (Minneapolis: Fortress Press, 2012), 15.

[2] *Luther's Basic Writings*, Thesis 20.

that God raised Jesus from the dead (Rom 1:4). Later in his letter to the Romans, the Apostle Paul writes, "If the Spirit of him who raised Jesus from the dead dwells in you, he who raised Christ from the dead will give life to your mortal bodies also through his Spirit that dwells in you" (Rom 8:11). The very Spirit through whom God the Father sends the Son and raises him from the dead will empower and guide the life and witness of the believer in Jesus Christ.[3]

Jesus Christ and the Spirit: Trinitarian Confession

It is central to the Christian confession that, in dealing with Jesus of Nazareth, we are dealing with God. Communion with God is through Jesus Christ in the power of the Holy Spirit.

Through the calling of the Holy Spirit, through whom God raised Jesus Christ from the dead, human beings are justified in Christ in this world, the world in which we live. In this world, we live with the foretaste of the promised new creation in Christ (2 Cor 5:17). In this experience of the new creation through God's justifying grace in Jesus Christ, God does not make us useless in the world. In the power of the Spirit, who is present and active in the world, the sinner who is justified through faith in Jesus Christ is consequently sent into this world for the sake of the well-being of the world. In the power of the Spirit, Christians are called to live the truth and reality of who they are through faith in Jesus Christ. If, through the power of the Holy Spirit, Jesus gets into the messiness of life, then believers who are called to follow him, precisely in that messy world, will be changed. Admittedly, we do not readily embrace the call to change.

The essential relationship between Jesus Christ and the Spirit cannot be overemphasized. Indeed, it is essential to speak in Trinitarian terms about the person and work of the Holy Spirit. Characteristically, in theological reflection and articulation, description of the dynamic relationship between the Spirit and Jesus Christ points both to the reality that the Spirit makes Jesus Christ present–the word mediated through created means–and engenders in sinners, faith in Jesus. Here, I offer an illustration:

> The story of Peter and Cornelius's encounter (Acts 10) places the challenge of discerning the inclusive significance of Jesus within cultures and religions right at the center. The Spirit had prepared them for their encounter with each other. Cornelius, we are told, was "a centurion of the Italian Cohort....He was a devout

[3] See, for example, John 16:13–14; Acts 1:8.

> man who feared God with all his household; he gave alms generously to the people and prayed constantly to God" (Acts 10:1–2). Cornelius, a Roman officer, occupied a place of power in the structures of the Roman Empire. For his part, Peter was an emerging pillar of the newly emerging community and he was a Jew. Cornelius's household shared in his "fear" of God. Peter, also, was awed by God's inclusiveness: "I truly understand that God shows no partiality, but in every nation anyone who fears [God] and does what is right is acceptable to [God]. You know the message he sent to the people of Israel, preaching peace by Jesus Christ. He is Lord of all." (vv. 34–36) Peter's confession leads the reader to ask who the converted ones are in this text. Was it a one-way street or did Peter have to learn something about the magnanimity of God's love? Peter's mind was changed even as Cornelius's, and that of his household, were. Through the Spirit, Peter and Cornelius met, and at the center of the encounter was the naming of Jesus Christ, who is Lord of all. In the baptism of Cornelius and his household, we have a timely reminder that the Christian message is transcultural, trans-political, and intergenerational. The work of the Spirit is centered in the message concerning Jesus Christ.[4]

One of the places where Martin Luther perspicuously writes about the essential unity of the work of the Spirit and the work of Jesus Christ is in Luther's explanation to the third article of the Apostles' Creed. There, Luther provides some of the essential elements which constitute a description of Lutheran theological identity. Luther writes:

> I believe that by my own understanding and strength I cannot believe in Jesus Christ my Lord or come to him, but instead the Holy Spirit *has called* me through the gospel, *enlightened* me with his gifts, *made me holy and kept me* in the true faith, just as he *calls, gathers, enlightens, and makes holy* the whole Christian church on earth and *keeps it* with Jesus Christ in the one common, true faith. Daily in this Christian church the Holy Spirit *abundantly forgives all sins*—mine and those of all believers. On the Last Day the Holy Spirit *will raise me and all the dead and will give to me and all believers in the Christ* eternal life. This is most certainly true.[5]

In this explanation (English translation) which has twelve verbs that describe the unique work of the Spirit, we notice the overriding dominance of the action of the Holy Spirit. Further, the work of the Spirit is explicitly Christologically and pneumatologically focused.

---

[4] Winston D. Persaud, "Believing in Jesus Christ in This Postmodern World," *Word & World* 27, no. 3 (July 2007): 268.

[5] Robert Kolb and Timothy J. Wengert, eds., *The Book of Concord: The Confessions of the Evangelical Lutheran Church*, trans. Charles Arand (Minneapolis: Fortress Press, 2000), 355f. Emphasis added.

Grammar, Language, Prepositions, and Verbs

In speaking about the presence and decisive work of the Holy Spirit, it is illuminating to note in the text the use of prepositions and verbs to describe the dynamic work of the Spirit. In so doing, we see in the work of the Spirit intimations of who the Spirit is. This phenomenon reflects the thesis, *we come to know who the Spirit is through what the Spirit does.*

Joint Declaration on the Doctrine of Justification

In the Joint Declaration on the Doctrine of Justification (JDDJ), it is made clear that the joint agreement between the LWF and the Roman Catholic Church has come about through the prompting and guidance of the Holy Spirit. Indeed, it is a decisive breakthrough which has emerged in this concrete expression on account of the Spirit's work of giving new insights, etc. Thus, as the member churches of the LWF and the Roman Catholic Church look forward to the vital, necessary work ahead, in consequence of the JDDJ, the Spirit is named. In the closing paragraph (44) of the text, we read: "We give thanks to the Lord for this decisive step forward on the way to overcoming the division of the church. We ask the Holy Spirit to lead us further toward that visible unity which is Christ's will."[6]

In paragraph 11 of JDDJ, which presents a summary of the meaning of justification that is present in the New Testament, we note the reception of the Holy Spirit by the believer in Christ, on account of God's grace alone. Together, Lutherans and Romans Catholics declare:

> 11. Justification is the forgiveness of sins (cf. Rom 3:23–25; Acts 13:39; Lk 18:14), liberation from the dominating power of sin and death (Rom 5:12–21) and from the curse of the law (Gal 3:10–14). It is acceptance into communion with God: already now, but then fully in God's coming kingdom (Rom 5:1f). It unites with Christ and with his death and resurrection (Rom 6:5). It occurs in the reception of the Holy Spirit in baptism and incorporation into the one body (Rom 8:1f, 9f; 1 Cor 12:12f). All this is from God alone, for Christ's sake, by grace, through faith in "the gospel of God's Son" (Rom 1:1–3).[7]

Further, in paragraph 15, Lutherans and Roman Catholics again point to the reception of the Holy Spirit—specifically, "receive the Holy Spirit"—when

---

[6] *Joint Declaration on the Doctrine of Justification* (Grand Rapids, Mich.: Wm. B. Eerdmans Publishing Co., 2000), 27.

[7] *Ibid.*, 11.

they describe the decisive, dynamic presence and work of the Holy Spirit in justification, which is effected by grace alone, through faith alone, in Christ alone. Note the use of "through the Holy Spirit" and "the Holy Spirit, who renews our hearts while equipping and calling us to good works," the "common" language Lutherans and Roman Catholics use in JDDJ to speak of the Reformation's definitive declaration on justification:

> 15. In faith we together hold the conviction that justification is the work of the triune God. The Father sent his Son into the world to save sinners. The foundation and presupposition of justification is the incarnation, death, and resurrection of Christ. Justification thus means that Christ himself is our righteousness, in which we share through the Holy Spirit in accord with the will of the Father. *Together we confess: By grace alone, in faith in Christ's saving work and not because of any merit on our part, we are accepted by God and receive the Holy Spirit, who renews our hearts while equipping and calling us to good works.*[8]

In the common language in JDDJ, Lutherans and Roman Catholics emphasize that faith in Christ is a gift of the Spirit who effects the transformation of the sinner that begins in this life and is completed in the life that is eternal. This is totally God's work. Paragraph 18 states, "Faith is itself God's gift through the Holy Spirit who works through word and sacrament in the community of believers and who, at the same time, leads believers into that renewal of life which God will bring to completion in eternal life."[9] God's gracious self-giving in Christ to the believer is through the Spirit. Thus, in paragraph 18, JDDJ states, "Lutherans and Catholics share the goal of confessing Christ in all things, who alone is to be trusted above all things as the one Mediator (1 Tim 2:5f) through whom God in the Holy Spirit gives himself and pours out his renewing gifts."[10]

The Holy Spirit and the Church: Lutheran and Roman Catholic Dialogue in the United States of America

The church is called to address the question of how we structure our lives-in-community, for the way the life of the community is structured is integral to the mission of the church. The church receives power from the Spirit, it lives by the power of the Holy Spirit, and it is by the Holy

[8] *Joint Declaration*, 15. Emphasis added.
[9] Ibid., 16.
[10] Ibid.

Spirit that it bears witness to the new life God gives in Jesus Christ, the crucified and risen Lord.

The church was not only called into being by the Holy Spirit on the day of Pentecost, but it is through the Holy Spirit that the mission of the church has continued through the centuries in the complex, diverse world in which we live. Thus, Lutherans and Roman Catholics declare together:

> 10. The witnesses who set forth this gospel shared in the authority of Jesus Christ. During his earthly ministry Jesus had sent forth disciples to carry on his mission by proclaiming the message about the kingdom of God (Mark 3:15; 6:7; Matt: 4:23; 9:35). After Easter the risen Lord commissioned followers with his authority to go forth into all the world, to the close of the age (Matt. 28:19-20) and promised them his presence in their corporate mission as his Church (Matt 18:20). When they proclaimed his word, they shared in the authority of Jesus himself. Jesus said, "He who hears you hears me" (Luke 10:16); cf. Matt. 10-:14, 40; John 17:18; 20-21). The witnesses to Jesus are enumerated in such groupings as apostles, prophets, teachers, evangelists, pastors; etc., and in lists of names such as those of "the twelve." Although those who exercised this apostolic ministry are often anonymous and little is known about them, their boldness, confidence, and assurance are striking. They did not hesitate at times to assert that the Holy Spirit guided the decisions they had made, "It had seemed good to Holy Spirit and to us." (Acts 15:28); they invoked anathemas on those who preached a false gospel (Gal 1:6-9). Their statements reflect confidence that the truth of their message is ultimately anchored in God (paras. 16-18).[11]

It is instructive to note that, to date, throughout the Lutheran and Roman Catholic dialogue in the USA there has not been a focus on "the person and work of the Holy Spirit" since that is not an area of doctrinal dispute. Indeed, at the outset of the dialogue, the first three rounds were devoted to topics which were areas not in dispute. In the common statements that emerged from the eleven rounds of the dialogue which have been concluded, there are repeated references to the Holy Spirit; specifically, the references are to the work of the Holy Spirit, with the implied assumptions about the full divinity of the Holy Spirit.

Further, it is illuminating to note how faith is defined in *Teaching Authority & Infallibility in the Church*, which emerged from Round VI of the Lutheran and Roman Catholic dialogue in the USA, which had taken place more than two decades before the JDDJ in 1999. We read:

---

[11] Paul C. Empie, T. Austin Murphy, and Joseph A. Burgess, eds., *Teaching Authority and Infallibility in the Church*. Lutherans and Catholics in Dialogue VI (Minneapolis: Augsburg Publishing House, 1978), 17–18. Emphasis added.

Faith as trust and obedience is the proper response to the Lord Jesus Christ (Rom. 1:5; 10:8-10; Phil 2:12; 3:21). No one can confess him to be the Lord without the Holy Spirit (1 Cor. 12:3). In the perspective of faith all creation is subject to him (Phil. 2:10): he has a role in creation (1 Cor. 8:6; John 1:3) and in the preservation of the world (Heb1:3); he will sit upon God's judgment seat (2 Cor. 5:10; cf. Rom 14:10) as the one designated by God to judge the living and the dead (Acts 10:42). Past, present, and future are under the authority of Christ, in whom all God's promises are affirmed (2 Cor. 1:20).[12]

The use of "and obedience" in conjunction with "trust" in defining faith gives us reason to pause. "In the perspective of faith" indicates that faith is here *fide quae*. Through the power of the Holy Spirit, it is possible to know, preserve with integrity, and keep returning to the content of faith that is believed and is to be believed.

Thus, it is through the inspiration of the Holy Spirit that the vital, necessary, unavoidable work of making possible faithful, evangelical interpretation of Scripture in new, diverse, and challenging contexts comes into being. Here, we call attention to the "Summary Statement" of Round I, "The Status of the Nicene Creed as Dogma of the Church," of the Lutheran and Roman Catholic dialogue in the USA, which affirmed that the "Nicene Faith" was necessarily a contextual answer to the "Arian question," as "the Church was obliged to state her faith in the Son in non-biblical terms."[13] The clear implication is that the philosophic, religious, and linguistic world of the fourth century not only provided the question(s) concerning Jesus' identity in relation to the Father, but it provided the linguistic framework for the answer (s). This use of non-biblical categories must be viewed as emerging out of the Spirit's inspiration to make a defense of the faith. In so doing, the church was, and is, believed to have faithfully presented the authentic biblical witness which may serve as normative for future confession of the gospel. "The church" as the authoritative interpreter of Scripture, and Scripture as the authoritative norm, formed an intrinsic unity and wholeness.

In their deliberation on the relationship between "doctrine and the cultural context," Lutherans and Roman Catholics make this common statement:

[12] Empie et al., *Teaching Authority*, 16.

[13] Joseph A. Burgess and Brother Jeffrey Gros, FSC, eds., *Building Unity: Ecumenical Dialogues with Roman Catholic Participation in the United States*, Ecumenical Documents IV (Mahwah, N.J.: Paulist Press, 1989), 88.

> 24. Lutherans and Catholics share the confidence that the Spirit is present and guides Christian teaching not only in the first periods of Church history but also in later developments.... Further, Lutherans have their confessional writings, and Catholics, various later dogmas. The churches have traditionally attached a high degree of authority to such formulations of their teaching, so that to deny the faith confessed in these documents has been seen as amounting to a rejection of the gospel.
>
> 25. By Christ's own commission, the gospel had to be preached in diverse civilizations and cultures, and to be transmitted from generation to generation to the close of the age. This communication of the gospel has implied that the Church has the obligation and the authority to formulate its faith in such a way that this faith can be recognized and believed. Such an authority is spiritual, for it is fundamentally the authority of the Spirit guiding the faithful. It is evangelical, for it is the authority of the gospel (the evangel) itself, knowledge of which is transmitted through the church's preaching and teaching. It is apostolic, for it is rooted in the early apostolic commission and community. It is centered upon Christ, the word of God Incarnate who is the one mediator (1 Tim. 2:5-7) of God's self-revelation to humankind. It derives from God's gracious gift and not from any human work or merit. It is not a product of human culture or philosophy.[14]

The confession that Scripture is the word of God is grounded in the conviction that the Holy Spirit is the author and decisive "interpreter" of Scripture whereby it is read and heard as God's word. It is instructive to read and ponder the following from *Scripture and Tradition* from the Lutheran and Roman Catholic dialogue in the USA:

> The basic aim of such interpretive activity for Lutherans, however, is not to supplement a supposed insufficiency of Scripture or to clarify its alleged obscurities. Rather it is the attempt to allow the light of Scripture to illumine our darkness, to have the subjectivism of our spirits overcome by the Spirit who speaks through Scripture. Everything in the church's practice, preaching, and teaching is to be subordinate to the Word of Scripture. Both the structure of transmission and the content of what is transmitted must be judged according to the norm of Scripture.[15]

Given the confusion that has arisen, and continues to exist, among Christians when we speak of the Bible (Scripture) as the word of God which norms all doctrine of the faith and is itself not subject to another norm (*norma*

[14] Empie et al., 23–24.

[15] Harold C. Skillrud, J. Francis Stafford, and Daniel F. Martensen, eds., *Scripture and Tradition*, Lutherans and Catholics in Dialogue IX (Minneapolis: Augsburg Publishing House, 1995), 30.

normans), it is crucial to note the three-fold meaning of "word of God," as presented in *Scripture and Tradition*:

> 5. Among Lutherans and Catholics as among other Christians who confess faith in the Triune God, the Word of God is often identified in three ways. The Word of God is, above all, the eternal Son of God who became incarnate as Jesus Christ by the power of the Holy Spirit. As the incarnate Son of God, crucified and risen, Jesus Christ reconciles the fallen world with God, revealing the salvation of humankind and the advent of a new creation.
>
> 6. The Word of God is also God's message to humankind, proclaimed as judgment and mercy. Beginning with the Word in creation and continuing in the calling of Israel, the Word of God culminates in the person and work of Jesus Christ, attested through the ages by the power of the Holy Spirit
>
> 7. Furthermore, the Word of God, witnessed through the ages by power of the Holy Spirit, is a written word, the Holy Scripture. The written word of God is inspired by God's Spirit, who communicates through its authors God's revelation centered in all its fullness in Christ.

It is evident in the foregoing that the conviction that Scripture is the word of God which is the norming norm that is not normed (*norma normans*) is grounded in the decisive work of the Holy Spirit. This conviction is accented further in *Scripture and Tradition*:

> The church in every age and in every part of the world continues to preach and receive the Word of God in faith and to respond actively in word and deed. Through its proclamation and response, the church echoes the Word of God communicated through Scripture and earlier tradition, and makes it possible for believers everywhere to have access to the Word of God, no matter how far removed they may be in time, place, and culture from the original events of revelation. Through the power of the Holy Spirit the Word of God lives on in the memory of the church and is differently interpreted in different contexts.[16]

One of the crucial areas of the Christian life in which the Spirit calls and moves the believer to listen to the word of God as promise and invitation is in relation to the ongoing, vital question of prayer for others. Here, we note that for the Lutheran and Roman Catholic dialogue in the USA:

[16] Skillrud et al., 41.

> Prayer for others in their life of faith, their "growth in grace" and witness to the gospel, are (sic) to be part of the Christian life in the knowledge that God has promised to hear such prayers and that they are done in the Spirit who makes faith in Christ possible. Thus, we read: 'By the work of the Holy Spirit the ministry of word and sacraments "mediates" the present Christ to whom the faithful respond with worship, with good works, and with other fruits of the Holy Spirit. Growth in grace, knowledge, love, and hope are the unfailing consequence of justifying faith. The interim between Christ's first coming in Israel and his final return at the end of time is filled with the advance of the gospel and, through the power of the Holy Spirit, response to it. All of Christian life is nurtured and sustained by the Christ who is "mediated" through the gospel and the Holy Spirit. Thus, Lutherans speak of God's solidarity (oneness) with creatures, of God "for us" (*pro nobis*) in Christ and of unmerited salvation "outside us" (*extra nos*).[17]

Openess to, and Welcome of, Pentecostal and Charismatic Experiences Grounded in Fidelity to the Doctrine of Justification

Faith in Christ, which becomes active in love for the neighbor, occurs in, and through, the Holy Spirit. The unity of faith in Christ and love of neighbor calls us to be grounded in an unequivocal commitment to the doctrine of justification.[18] Here, it is instructive to ponder the following questions raised by Anthony C. Thiselton:

> (2) In spite of claims to the contrary, does Pentecostal zeal for renewal and purity risk that which invited Luther's complaint about the radical Reformers? Is there more than a hint of receiving the Holy Spirit when faith, obedience, and prayer

[17] Winston D. Persaud, "A Lutheran Reflection on The One Mediator, The Saints, and Mary in Relation to the Question: How Do Lutherans Understand Prayer for Other People?", in *Dialog*, vol. 52, Number 1, Spring (March) 2013, 62. Citation is from *The One Mediator, The Saints, and Mary*, eds. H. George Anderson, J. Francis Stafford and Joseph A. Burgess, *Lutherans and Catholics in Dialogue VIII* (Minneapolis: Augsburg Publishing House, 1992), 41.

[18] In his treatise, "The Freedom of a Christian," Luther makes the connection about how the righteous is to live "in the liberty of the Spirit" in serving others, including political or governing authorities. Luther writes, "The counsel and advice of St. Paul in Romans 13:1-7 and Titus 3:1 also apply to this topic. He admonishes Christians to be subject to the ruling powers and be ready to do good works—not in order to be justified, for they are already righteous through faith—but that in the liberty of the Spirit they might serve the authorities and all, obeying them freely out of love." See *Martin Luther's Basic Theological Writings*, 421f.

> are first offered? Or does the Spirit himself originate and cause faith, obedience, and prayer? Was Luther right in claiming that the "radical" Reformers unintentionally undermined Paul's doctrine of justification by pure grace through faith?[19]

A positive way forward in responding to Thiselton's questions might be forged through honest theological pondering on how we might respond to the following question: Does the historical, characteristic confessional way in which Lutherans, among others, assume, and speak about the presence and work of the Holy Spirit in creation, and in speaking about the identity and work of Jesus Christ—even as there is more explicit recognition of the presence and work of Holy Spirit in and through the church—provide a significant basis to explain why Lutherans miss and ignore, and are even skeptical about, facets of what the Spirit is doing in Christian communities which are clearly Pentecostal and charismatic? We need to find a way to integrate Lutheran confessionalism and pietism with a keen awareness of religious and cultural diversity,[20] in order to speak positively about experiences which have been customarily deemed outside the Lutheran confessional and liturgical norm because those experiences are Pentecostal and Charismatic and (therefore) continue to be regarded as undercutting the doctrine of justification.[21] Is the Holy Spirit, who bears witness to the new creation in Christ in whom we are justified by faith in him, to the glory of God, calling us to find within the Lutheran tradition the theological impetus to openness and welcome?

[19] Thiselton, *The Holy Spirit*, 62.

[20] See Wonsuk Ma, "Lord and Giver of Life: The Holy Spirit among the Spirits in Asia," in *Asian Christian Theology: Evangelical Perspectives*, Timoteo D. Gener and Stephen T. Pardue, eds. (Carlisle, Cumbria, UK: Langham Global Library, 2019), 119–138.

[21] Anthony C. Thiselton calls attention to the difference within the Pentecostal and Charismatic Movement, when he writes, "Again, we encounter differences within the Pentecostal and Charismatic Movement. Max Turner and Frank Macchia, for example, are more concerned than Robert Menzies and I. R. Williams to find "middle ground" or openness." Ibid.

The Work of the Holy Spirit in Creation and Sanctification: On the Future of Lutheran Pneumatology

Johann-Christian Pöder

In the following reflections, I will focus on the work of the Holy Spirit in creation and sanctification. When discussing the Holy Spirit, we are often perplexed and confronted with basic questions:

- Who or what is the Holy Spirit?
- How and where do we experience the Holy Spirit?
- How should we speak of the Spirit?
- How does our Lutheran tradition shape our apprehension of and dealing with the Spirit?

The American writer Walter Lippmann once said, "For the most part we do not first see, and then define, we define first and then see." This can be true also in case of the Holy Spirit. It is hard to attempt to "see" (experience) the Spirit and not to take refuge in traditional or new definitions. This does not mean that we do not need definitions. However, we should try to track back different definitions to the very roots of their experiential content and situation.

With such questions in mind, I will proceed in three steps. After some introductory remarks, I will first recall the lament about the oblivion of the Spirit which emerged in the second half of the twentieth century. Second, I will refer to some recent counter-positions to this lament. And third, I will discuss the connection between the work of the Spirit in creation and in sanctification. This final step also includes some basic reflections on the doctrine of Trinity.

Introduction

In 2002, the Danish theologian Niels Henrik Gregersen wrote the following in his "Ten Theses on the Future of Lutheran Theology":

> A Trinitarian theology of the Holy Spirit has not been adequately articulated within classical Lutheran tradition. Usually, the work of the Spirit divides up the work of the Spirit as life-giving Creator and as sanctifying Redeemer. What is needed, however, is a theology of the Holy Spirit that is able to articulate that the vivifying and transforming work of the Spirit is always coordinated for the one and wholehearted purpose of sanctification.[1]

In this observation, Gregersen was concerned about other religions and the world outside of Christianity in their relation to the redemptive will and work of God. In my view, this is indeed a vital question to reflect in a theology of the Spirit. I will, however, turn to this subject a bit later and consider first what Gregersen mentions to be the usual way of thinking of the Spirit in the Lutheran tradition—the division of the Spirit's work as life-giving and life-sustaining Creator, and as sanctifying Redeemer. As we shall see, even an articulation of this double action is not as uncontroversial and usual as one may assume.

The Oblivion and Renaissance of the Spirit: Exploring the Spiritus Creator

In the *Oxford Handbook of Martin Luther's Theology*, Jeffrey G. Silcock points out that for Luther, the Spirit's activity cannot be limited to matters of faith and church, even if Luther's focus mainly lies on the third article. He adds that the Spirit's ongoing work in creation and preservation needs to be further developed in the twenty-first century. Silcock's brief remark about the need for a broader and more balanced apprehension of the Spirit reflects a sense of dissatisfaction characteristic for many theologians in the last decades.[2]

---

[1] Niels Henrik Gregersen, "Ten Theses on the Future of Lutheran Theology: Charisms, Contexts, and Challenges," *Dialog* 41, no. 4 (December 2002): 270.

[2] Jeff Silcock, "Luther on the Holy Spirit and His Use of God's Word," in *The Oxford Handbook of Martin Luther's Theology*, eds. Robert Kolb, Irene Dingel, and Lubomire Batka (Oxford: Oxford University Press, 2014), 308. Cf. Veli-Matti Kärkkäinen, *Pneumatology: The Holy Spirit in Ecumenical, International, and Contextual Perspective*, 2nd ed. (Ada, Mich.: Baker Academic Publishing, 2018).

Indeed, since the second half of the twentieth century, there has been wide criticism of a Lutheran tendency in pneumatology to focus on matters of the third article. This has been considered too reductive and narrow or even as a "forgetfulness of the Spirit." More precisely, this oblivion has been associated with an intimate link between the Spirit and Jesus Christ in Western theology, as well as with the traditional Lutheran emphasis that the Spirit is bound to the "external word" of God in the Bible and proclamation.

This focus on salvation and the redemptive work of the Spirit–on the Spirit as a channel of salvation–was seen as too narrow and unhelpful in responding to new and urgent issues of society. Ecological problems, questions of peace and social justice, and a new, intensified awareness of other religions led theology's interest to the realm of creation and the wider society–to the Holy Spirit as *Spiritus Creator.*

This change was further facilitated by a new, postmodern openness to, and sensitivity for, the spiritual dimension of life and all reality. Furthermore, for Lutheran theology, new and intensified encounters with Eastern Orthodoxy as well as with the rapidly growing Pentecostal movements triggered an interest in a broader, renewed understanding of the Spirit. Not surprisingly, all these trends also motivated biblical scholarship to focus on the diversity of biblical references to the Spirit, which in turn shaped novel approaches in pneumatology.

The Spirit Reminds Us of Christ: Back to a Narrow, Soteriological Pneumatology?

The renaissance of the Spirit which aimed to extend the activity of the Spirit to creation and other religions has, however, also provoked protest. The critics point to a specific systematic interest of universal or "holistic" pneumatologies. The function of such universal concepts of the Spirit was to show that an experience of God is also possible *extra Christum*, before and beside God's revelation in Christ. A theology of the Spirit aimed at offering a universal interpretation of reality–of culture, society, nature and ecosystem, etc. It aimed to discover God's presence in social liberation, ecological processes, charismatic movements, and other religions. All this mirrored a deep concern about the declining relevance of Christianity in a rapidly changing modern world.

However, one could argue that such a cosmic widening of the scope threatens to make the notion of the Holy Spirit vague and blurry, to empty it of any clear content. According to this criticism, the lament about an oblivion of the Spirit has led –paradoxically enough–to a new *disappearance* of the Spirit. If the Spirit is–in confusingly different ways–everything and everywhere, the Spirit is in fact nothing and nowhere. For example, this observation led the German theologian Christian Danz to ask critically what exactly the Spirit *is*, if every experience of "liberation," "wholeness" or "criticism of modernity" can be ascribed to the Spirit's activity? Is the universal reality of the Holy Spirit, often seen as divine energy or power, not lacking any distinctive contours? How can the Spirit still be distinguished from the spirits of the world?[3]

A diagnosis of this kind was for some theologians a reason to go back to what they see as the classical Protestant, clearly soteriologically oriented understanding of the Spirit. Thus, they argue again for linking the Spirit to Jesus Christ and to the verbally or bodily mediated personal appropriation of salvation. According to this view, the Holy Spirit is the Spirit of Christ, and the central work of the Spirit is to mediate Christ's presence to the people—to remind us of Christ. The Holy Spirit signals our dependence on such a reminder and is always bound to embodied mediation of Christian religious communication.[4] This last aspect is also sharply stressed by the German theologian, Philipp Stoellger, who elaborates the insight that the Spirit has a body—the external, written, and oral word or sign. Without a body, the Spirit would be a free-floating, terrifying ghost. Pneumatology can thus be seen, pointedly, as a media theory of Christianity.[5]

Three Critical Questions

There is not much doubt that for Luther and the Protestant tradition, the work of the Holy Spirit focuses intensely on the matters of the Third Article. The Holy Spirit is the spirit of Christ, the mediator of salvation to the people. However, since Regin Prenter's famous book *Spiritus Creator*, we are also aware of Luther's universal, creation-based view of the Spirit. Yes, Prenter admits that it is possible to put such thoughts aside as something unessential to be found only occasionally in Luther's exegetical studies of the creation story. Still, he points out that a cosmic view of the Spirit is of genuine importance for Luther's theology. The Spirit in sanctification is the

---

[3] Christian Danz, Gottes Geist: Eine Pneumatologie (Tübingen: Mohr Siebeck, 2019), 94. Cf. Christian Henning, Die Evangelischer Lehre vom Heiligen Geist und Seiner Person: Studien zur Architektur protestantischer Pneumatologie im 20. Jahrhundert (Gütersloh: Gütersloher Verlagshaus, 2000).

[4] Danz, *Gottes Geist.*

[5] Stoellger, Philipp, "Die Medialität des Geistes oder: Pneumatologie als Medientheorie des Christentums," in *Risiko und Vertrauen: Festschrift für Michael Welker zum 70*, eds. Heike Springhart and Günter Thomas (Leipzig: Evangelische Verlagsanstalt, 2017), 139–174.

very same creative Spirit who is at work in all creation—"the Holy Spirit is given the work of the sanctifying love of God to preserve and sustain his whole creation."[6] In Luther's Trinitarian view, the Spirit is not limited to the religious communication of Christ's presence.

In accepting this view, we find ourselves confronted with three complex questions. First, what is the critical lesson of the above-mentioned rejection of the cosmic Spirit? Is it not the insight that we need a better account of the Spirit's cosmic work? Second, how should we see the relationship between the Spirit's work in creation and in redemption? And third, how do we understand our Trinitarian faith—both in general and in thinking about the Spirit?

In the following, I will mostly reflect on the second question and address, above all, the concern about the universality of God's redemptive will or, in the words of Niels Henrik Gregersen, "that the vivifying and transforming work of the Spirit is always coordinated for the one and wholehearted purpose of sanctification" (see above).

The Spirit's Work in Creation and in Sanctification: Tension and Unity

Indeed, traditional Lutheran pneumatology has not much reflected on the unifying intention or the identity of the Spirit's creative and redemptive work. The Holy Spirit seems to perform quite different tasks in creation and sanctification, and accordingly, members of other religions and the world outside of Christianity seem to be excluded from salvation—they may be part of the Spirit's life-creating and life-sustaining work, but they have not heard the redemptive gospel of Christ.

To bring just one example: Regin Prenter points out that the Spirit's works in creation and redemption are only "two stages" of the one act of God. They are part of the very same all-encompassing divine activity. However, despite this unifying perspective, he also observes a tension between these two works of the Spirit in Luther's theology. This "hiatus" is the problem of predestination—the tension between all who exist and those redeemed and elected. Luther's Trinitarian view does not rationalize or harmonize this tension—the only way out is to hold on to the living word of the gospel. The unity of the Spirit's creative and redemptive work is a testimony marked by a tension, not a theological insight about which we can elaborate rationally. This pneumatological "mind the gap" reminds us of the worldly situation of faith (2 Cor 5:7).

[6] Regin Prenter, *Spiritus Creator* (Philadelphia: Muhlenberg Press, [1946] 1953), 192.

This gap can also provoke, however, a search for other and more satisfying ways of thinking about the unity of the Spirit's work. I will refer here *pars pro toto* to Niels Henrik Gregersen who has called for a generous modification of Lutheran theology. According to him, we should take leave of Luther's Augustinian notion of double predestination and be inspired, for example, by Gregory of Nyssa and his idea of universal salvation. Indeed, Schleiermacher and in his footsteps, Karl Barth – both important figures for today's Lutheran theology—were greatly attracted by the idea of an *apokatastasis panton* of universal salvation. It is easy to understand why, since this doctrine powerfully mirrors the very heart of Reformation theology—the radical, all-embracing grace of God. For pneumatology, this generous reorientation will mean a much clearer unity of the Spirit's work in creation and in sanctification. How can such an understanding of the Spirit be envisioned?

A Trinitarian Theology of the Holy Spirit: A Lutheran Deficit?

Gregersen recommends we develop a more adequate Trinitarian understanding of the Spirit. For Luther, it was usual to appropriate different divine works to different persons of the Trinity. A revised pneumatology should, however, stress that the works of the Father, Son, and Holy Spirit always take place in a "mutual agreement" or integration—that the Spirit's work of sanctification always integrates the divine works of creation and redemption. "The works of the Spirit are always attuned to both the mind of the Father, from which the Spirit was sent (*ex patre*), and to the Wisdom of the Son through whom the Spirit is flowing (*per filium*)."[7] This view allows us to see the work of the Spirit as always being coordinated by the "redemptive will of the eternal Word of God," by the unifying purpose of universal salvation. Yet, importantly, the Spirit is not bound to the external word of God or to the reality of the church. Thus, the sanctifying presence of the Spirit can also be found outside of Christianity—a perspective which notably widens the traditional lens of Lutheran theology (ibid.).

In the wake of the influential renaissance of Trinitarian theology in the twentieth century, this— or a similar kind of Trinitarian approach—will surely find resonance. However, a universalization of the Spirit's redemptive work is possible also for a Lutheran theology which is critical of classical Trinitarian thinking. For this significant direction of Lutheran theology, the classical doctrine of Trinity is marked by unresolvable *aporias* and

[7] Gregersen, 270.

problems. This approach often rejects the notion of the immanent Trinity and the "persons," and stresses the oneness of God. Mostly, it adopts a kind of modalist view of the Triune God—different persons of the Trinity are, in fact, different experiences or "modes of encounter" of God. In this view, the Holy Spirit can be understood as quite identical with God himself; the Spirit can be seen, for example, as a metaphorical expression for God as the all-present ground of being.[8] Thanks to its revelation in the human Jesus, we can understand God's all-embracing spiritual presence as a universal redeeming, loving presence. For the Christian faith, the salvation of all people was God's loving intention from the beginning of the world. This can be articulated, for example, through a pneumatological interpretation of the old doctrine of *logos spermatikos*—through the loving presence of the divine Spirit, people outside of Christianity can also participate

On the Future of Lutheran Pneumatology

I will finish with the following questions concerning a future Lutheran pneumatology:

- Will it be clearly oriented on the idea of universal salvation or will it still need to mirror the Lutheran-Augustinian doctrine of predestination?

- Will it work out a wholehearted unity of the Spirit's vivifying and sanctifying work or will it look at such theological endeavors with cautious reservations?

In a way, this is also a question about Lutheran identity as both these approaches claim to represent something that is deeply rooted in the Lutheran Reformation. The idea of *apokatastasis* reflects, in a powerful way, the genuine Lutheran insight into radically generous, universal grace. At the same time, this motif seems to overlook the insight that the worldly situation of faith is always marked by an indelible eschatological tension—an experience and idea clearly reflected both by Luther and later Lutheran theology (cf. Luther's idea of *Deus absconditus*).

Besides this question, a future Lutheran pneumatology has to respond to different challenges. The lively turn to the cosmic Spirit in the last century, with its continuously changing accounts, has also brought confusion about the Spirit's work. The question of how to speak of God's creative and life-sustaining work in a precise, experience-related manner has to be further

[8] Dietz Lange, *Glaubenslehre*, Bands I and II (Tübingen: Mohr Siebeck, 2001).

developed. Also, the Spirit's sanctifying presence in the church calls for further reflection, for example, on Luther's emphasis on the external word of God. As Simeon Zahl has pointed out, the scholarship emerging from the Pentecostal and charismatic tradition rightly challenges us to examine the affective, unmediated side of the Spirit's work.[9]

In these and similar questions, pneumatological reflection can still greatly profit from the impulses of liberation theology–from the insight that soteriological concerns always are linked to concerns of earthly liberation. Without identifying worldly well-being and eternal salvation, one might well say that concern for eschatological salvation "spills over into the world now."[10] Also, at this point, further reflection is needed–especially in a Lutheran context, which has traditionally been more reserved about the emancipatory power of the Spirit. The future of Lutheran pneumatology is in the making.

[9] Simeon Zahl, *Pneumatology and Theology of the Cross in the Preaching of Christoph Friedrich Blumhardt: The Holy Spirit between Wittenberg and Azusa Street* (London: T&T Clark, 2010).
[10] Samuel Shearn, correspondence with author, 2019.

After Justification: An Ecotheological Look at the Holy Spirit as Gift and Promise

Chad M. Rimmer

The 500th anniversary of the Reformation inspired a great deal of critical reflection about the legacy of Lutheran theology as well as a shift in perspective toward the future of Lutheran theology for the next five hundred years.

The Lutheran tradition is a living tradition. Faith calls and equips us to face the questions and crises of our day with the gospel of divine love and grace. But the questions we face today are not the same polemics and powers of the sixteenth century.

Interdisciplinary dialogue with the social and natural sciences, the arts, and interfaith, Indigenous and other wisdom traditions help us to broaden our perception of God's work. Multilinguistic, interdisciplinary conversations invite Lutherans to consider our Christology in light of diverse sources of knowledge. They include the experiential wisdom from mystical modes of being in the world (*sapientia experimentalis*), and liberation, feminist, womanist and ecotheological methods of reflecting on this experience of God's presence in the world.

In an age of ecumenical consensus about faith and works, Lutheran theology can shift its weight to the axis of faith and reason in order to engage these epistemological realities.

Niels Henrik Gregersen anticipated this pivot in an article entitled "Ten Theses on the Future of Lutheran Theology: Charisms, Contexts and Challenges". Thesis number 6 points to the importance of engaging in Trinitarian theology to interpret Luther and the Lutheran tradition:

> Luther's rediscovery of the external word of law and gospel presupposes an ontology of divine reality prior to, simultaneous with, and after the proclamation of the Word. Today it is particularly important to recover a notion of God's presence in the world at large. Luther's doctrine of the hidden God is a necessary placeholder for an awareness of God's majestic being, but the identification of the reality of God can only be offered via the doctrine of the Trinity.[1]

Engaging in these dialogues will help Lutherans reflect on our tradition and correct where necessary. But Lutherans can also make this pivot by re-entering our tradition with new eyes, in order to recover and build on aspects of our tradition such as a rich theology of the Spirit and spiritual theology. In this essay, I will show how Luther's sacramental theology and our confessions provide us with rich entry points, and yet maintain a crucial "placeholder" to guard against abuses in today's spiritual marketplace. With a radically expansive Trinitarian framework for perceiving the Holy Spirit as gift and promise, Lutherans today can confidently ask new questions about God's work in the world at large.

Liberty of the Spirit

Among the scriptural, confessional, theological, and liturgical diversity of the Lutheran tradition, perhaps the organizing principle of Lutheran theology is Christian liberty. Liberty drove the reform of sixteenth century political, social, and educational systems, and contributed to the flourishing of modern science and philosophies that would shape modern discourse about international law and human rights. Luther's concept of liberty was the logical extension of his confession about God's freedom to form, reform and transform the world. The experience of Luther's Reformation began with a renewed focus on justification by grace through faith as proclaimed in the Word. But that breakthrough was triggered by Luther's frustration with ecclesiastical practices that usurped God's revelatory freedom.

Priests acted as gatekeepers with shamanic powers to conjure God through sacramental rites and the power of the keys. By claiming unique spiritual capacity, the ordained priesthood was understood as *the* holy vocation. God's holiness was accessible via priests. But if priests had the power to dispense the Spirit, then God was not free. God's work in the world (or at least our perception of that work) was captive to the church.

[1] Niels Henrik Gregersen, "Ten Theses on the Future of Lutheran Theology: Charisms, Contexts, and Challenges," *Dialog* 41, no. 4 (December 2002): 264–272.

After visiting the parishes of Saxony, Luther wrote the small catechism to reinforce the people's understanding that the Christian life was rooted in the third article of the ecumenical creeds. The ministry of the Church, our faith, the shape of the Christian life and the renewal of creation are sustained by the ongoing work of the Holy Spirit. But in our interfaith contexts, we cannot simply say "Spirit" and think that we have consensus.

Defining "Spirit"

Across our communion, there is no lack of discourse about "spirit". The challenge lies in the fact that there is an abundance of ideas about spirit, which lead to a spiritual marketplace of competing ideas about spirituality.[2]

Luther critiqued popular philosophical understanding of the Spirit in his time, particularly those inherited from Aristotle. Luther criticized Aristotle for suggesting that we have the spiritual capacity to perfect good works through habit or repetition, as an artist perfects her trade. Pekka Kärkkäinen recently demonstrated that Luther's critique is not quite accurate, because they were talking about two different concepts of "spirit".[3] Aristotle used the word "spirit" to describe a force that physically moves us. Today we might call it metabolism or our nervous system. For Aristotle "spirit" describes animation, as opposed to what we might call "soul" or our spiritual nature. Keep in mind that Luther was reading Aristotle through Aquinas' theological interpretation of Aristotle. So, Luther's misunderstanding says more about the contemporary scholastic usage of the term.

In a reference to this Aristotelian logic, the first article of the Augsburg Confession condemns the teaching that "'the Holy Spirit' is a created motion (movement) in all creatures."[4] When Lutheran confessional documents make such references, they are not referring to a spiritual aspect of human being or the concept of the soul. Luther is clear that humans do not possess the personal capacity to be more or less divine than any other creature. As far as salvation is concerned, we are all equally saint and sinner (*simul justus et peccator*), equally capable of virtue and vice, and

[2] This experience of the spiritual marketplace led to the LWF Asian Church Leaders Conference in Manila (23–27 November 2017) focusing on this question of spiritual or renewal movements. lutheranworld.org/news/churches-crossroads-asia-goes-through-rapid-change

[3] Pekka Kärkkäinen, "Luther's Theological Psychology and the Spirit," in *Lutherjahrbuch 2018, 85* (Göttingen: Vandenhoeck & Ruprecht Verlage, 2018): 154–171.

[4] CA, I.

most significantly, equally incapable of claiming a particular capacity to conjure God's Spirit.

While Luther's goal was to prevent claims of special spiritual revelation, this generally pessimistic theological perspective on the spiritual status of human beings contributed to the disenchantment of bodies and the earth that led towards the scientific revolution of the seventeenth century, the western philosophical Enlightenment of the eighteenth century, and materialist political and economic theories that continue to this day.

Disenchantment underwrites all manner of colonial, racial, gender-based, and ecological violence. Many churches struggle to address oppressive or exclusionary cultural, political or religious systems precisely because the discourse is strongly rooted in narratives that lack attentiveness to Spirit or spirituality. But Luther never disavowed the metaphysics of the human spirit or soul. He simply acknowledged that when we talk about the Spirit, we refer to the presence of God's Spirit in, with, and under creation, including you, me, and the church.

While disenchantment of the Earth and creatures is a fundamental problem in parts of the world where churches seek spiritual revival, discourse about Spirit and spiritual gifts in other contexts are rooted in the wisdom of Indigenous religion or animism. I served as pastor and teaching theologian with the Lutheran Church in Senegal. In this Muslim context Lutheranism is a minority denomination within a minority religion. Senegalese often say they are 94 percent Muslim, four percent Christian and 100 percent animist. Among Lutherans there are Christians who wear talismans (called "gris-gris"), participate in various purity rites, and do not leave a baby unaccompanied in a room for fear that a malevolent spirit may change the "spirit" of the baby. Among certain groups within the social caste system, certain shamanic rites are still part of daily practice of Marabouts and others. The presence of spirits is assumed. The only question is, are the spirits fundamentally good or bad, and how does that influence our church members' understanding of the work of the Holy Spirit.

When exploring contemporary Lutheran identities, we need to take localized contextual approaches to this question with an eye to sub-regional hermeneutical questions. It is not enough to think in terms of East or West, global North or global South, or between racial or gendered groups. There are diverse beliefs and practices between local cultures, people groups, villages, and within parishes of the same diocese.

We must listen to the most localized culture and try to identify the ways diverse religious or traditional beliefs and practices about the Spirit influence our parishioners.

For instance, in Hinduism and Buddhism the concept of Spirit is Atman. Spirit is eternal, imperishable, and beyond time. This metaphysical spirit, commonly referred to as Brahman, permeates the body, mind, or consciousness, but is opposed to them. Dalit, Adivasis and feminist theologians critique the denigration of bodies that is often associated with this Brahmanic concept of the spirit. Nirmal, Devasahayam, Gnanadason, and Prabhakar are theologians who find their liberating voice against spiritual injustice and exclusion through Christian theologies of creation, incarnation, and the holiness of the poor, marginalized, and all the Earth's creatures.

On the contrary, Daoism and Confucianism suggest a fusion of spirit and body, which leads to a near denial of metaphysics. There is almost no need to talk about spirit. Life is ordered by ethics of responsibility or shame as experienced in increasing circles of belonging to family, nation, and cosmos. In this way, Confucian and Daoist perspectives have a certain resonance with Aristotelean concepts in their approach to spirit. They see spirit as that which motivates the body and its senses, and informs moral discernment about what is good or brings honor. This complementarity is the yin and yang of body and spirit. But it is not a Holy Spirit as such. Confucian and Daoist ways of thought strongly influence the way Asian Christians interpret being members of the Church and what role grace plays in liberating the individual (salvation and sanctification).

Recent Sino-Christian and Indigenous scholarship about Spirit and spirituality[5] are clear that contemporary concepts of spirit and holiness have many influences. While this is a broad sketch, it demonstrates how multiple religious belonging can inform Christian concepts of spirituality, and impact Lutheran self-understanding.

This point was evident in the internal report of the 2014 Conference on Asian Lutheranism, "Towards and Asian Lutheran Identity and Self Understanding". Among several issues related to culture and church polity, power, social roles, and the shape of ministry, papers focused on the Holy Spirit's constitutive role in the church, as well as the renewal, revival, reformation, or transformation of the Christian. The report suggests it is natural for someone from the Asian context to interpret the Spirit as dynamism. Eastern concepts of Spirit as *dynamus* resonate with concepts of theosis and holiness that we see at work in our churches today.

Merely synergizing doctrines or practices runs the risk of misappropriating faith claims and traditional or Indigenous wisdom. But I will now describe how Luther's writings and the Confessions reveal a deep faith in the freedom of God's Spirit that free us to perceive it.

[5] Such as Alexander Chow, *Theosis, Sino-Christian Theology and the Second Chinese Enlightenment: Heaven and Humanity in Unity* (London: Palgrave Macmillan, 2013).

Confessions about the Holy Spirit

The first article of the Augsburg Confession restates a Nicene, creedal understanding of the Trinity. This notion of Divine simplicity is more than a claim about the substance of God. It is the foundation of God's work in the world. God's being and act are simple. The community (unity) of Divine love (*perichoresis*) is the source of life, its reconciliation, and renewal. At the most basic level when Lutherans speak of the Holy Spirit, we refer simply to the Spirit of God. Not spirits, benevolent or otherwise, but the Spirit of the Triune God.

Creating is God's proper work. But by extending our understanding of the "Word" to include the Logos, as holy wisdom of God described in Proverbs 8, we see how the work of the Holy Three of the Trinity are united in one economy. The breath, or wind, was the dynamism of *creatio originalis* that gave the Earth its creative agency.

While the Lutheran Confessions regarding the second person of the Trinity are unremarkably ecumenical, Lutherans have interpreted the implications of the incarnation in particular ways. During controversies with Zwingli and Calvinists over whether Jesus was really present in the bread and wine of Communion, the incarnation precluded the idea of any radical opposition between body and Spirit (such as exists in some forms of the Hindu and Buddhist concept of Atman). Luther claimed that if our bodies, or the elements of creation such as bread, wine and water, are not beloved enough to participate with God's Spirit (*finitum capax infinitii*), then the incarnation is not possible. This logic underwrites feminist and eco-theological concepts of deep incarnation. Christ's birth, baptism, suffering, death, and resurrection demonstrate that all creation participates in the cosmic reconciliation. Calls of justice for black, brown, female and trafficked bodies, and for creatures and the Earth resound with this confession of the immanence of the Holy Spirit in creation.

Psalm 104 testifies that the life-giving Spirit is present in and among every creature and creation itself as the renewing, transformative energy of *creatio continua*. Renewal, sanctification, or revival is part of the same economy of the Trinity. There are deep synergies between our confession of the renewal or revival of creation and modern theories of evolution.[6]

But even before modern scientific or psycho-social theories, Luther made this confession against the "radical" wing of the reformers, who suggested a radical dis-enchantment of the sacrament. In his treatise *The*

[6] See Elizabeth Johnson, *Ask the Beasts, Darwin and the God of Love* (Bloomsbury Continuum, 2015); Michael Northcott and R. J. Berry, eds., *Theology After Darwin* (UK: Paternoster Press, 2009).

Sacrament of the Body and Blood of Christ Against the Fanatics, Luther confesses Christ is present where the Word is proclaimed, and the sacraments administered. In CA VII they constitute the Church precisely because the Spirit is present. Firm in the logic of that confession, Luther affirms that the Holy Spirit is imminently present behind the "Masks of God" (*larvae Dei*), which include all of creation. Luther writes "God is present in all creatures, and I might find God in stone, in fire, in water, or even in a rope, for God is there."[7] Luther would not disagree with Indigenous traditions that speak of the immanence of God's Spirit in nature. To disagree would be to deny the possibility of Christ's presence in the sacraments.

God Is Everywhere but God Is Hidden

In Luther's 1528 *Confession Concerning Christ's Supper*, Luther describes three ways in which Christ is present.[8] The first is circumscribed, which means in a particular form, such as Jesus's body. The second is definitive, meaning taking up space, but not circumscribed. For instance, the post-resurrection Christ who can pass through doors is obviously present but is not delimited by physical boundaries. The third, replete presence, describes the ubiquitous presence of God. Here Luther resonates with Nicolas of Cusa who describes God as the center and circumference of the universe.

Notice that the replete presence of the Spirit in and behind creation is not an attempt to describe the substance of God's presence in all creatures. Rather it describes the subsistence of all creation in God. After basing this confession of God's replete presence in his confession about the Eucharist, Luther extends the logic by saying "God may have and knows still other modes whereby Christ's body can be in a given place."[9]

This panentheistic perspective is a significant entry point for deep dialogue with Indigenous and other wisdom traditions. Serious dialogue with Indigenous or traditional religions reveals that many shamans or healers do not actually claim access to special revelations. They simply perfect their capacity to perceive that which the natural world communicates. This is less magic and more the practice of deep attentiveness to our intersubjective relationships to other-than-human creatures and the land.[10] If one claims that each creature and the energy that binds us all subsist in God,

---

[7] WA 19, 492, 5; LW 36: 342.

[8] LW 37: 214–218.

[9] LW 37: 223.

[10] For a thorough consideration of this topic, as well the phenomenology of Husserl and Merleau-Ponty that serves as an interpretive framework, see David Abram,

then is there a qualitative difference between the presence of God that we perceive in silent communion with more-than-human creatures in a forest, and the presence of God that we perceive when we pray with one another in a church? I believe that Luther would not see a qualitative difference as far as God's presence is concerned. But he would caution that we must be clear about whose presence are we invoke, whose initiative we proclaim, and what end we seek by participating in this particular communion.

Luther was a mystical theologian. He embraced mysticism in the tradition of the Teutonic Mystics. Luther's experience of God (*sapientia experimentalis*) was indebted to Eckhart's work as probably received through Tauler.[11] But Luther undeniably had mystical experiences of God, which led him to promote a spirituality of daily life, including a method of prayer (*oratio/meditatio/tentatio*) that recognized holiness in the vocation of all the baptized and the capacity to engage in moral reasoning to discern how they were freed to acts of love and justice.

This faithful mode of being-in-the-world is a mark of what it means to "be Lutheran" or "do" theology as a Lutheran. By praying, meditating with scripture or writings, and testing what we experience in daily life (more on this later), we discern our experience of God in daily life.

This mode of spiritual theology is one reason that I join Vitor Westhelle and Walter Altmann in considering Luther to be a proto-liberation theologian.[12] Luther's contextual, pastoral method of "doing" theology (*tentatio*) resounds in the theological methods of feminist, womanist and eco-theologians like me. These methods hold doctrine and experience in one theological ecology of wisdom. The question is what qualifies as theological data? When salvation is not in question, Luther draws the circle wide.

Without contradicting confessions about God's revelation in Christ Jesus, we can expect to perceive God's Spirit at work in the natural world because the world subsists in God. At this point, Luther echoes the apostle Paul in the book of Acts. Standing in the Areopagus, Paul says he sees that they[13]

The Spell of the Sensuous: Perception and Language in a More-Than-Human World (New York: Vintage Books, 1997).

[11] See Bengt R. Hoffman's foundational work on Luther's mysticism and relationship to German theology, including *Luther and the Mystics*, and *Theology of the Heart: The Role of Mysticism in the Theology of Martin Luther*, trans. Pearl Willemssen Hoffman (Minneapolis: Lutheran University Press, 2003), as well as Luther's own introduction to *The Theologia Germanica* (1516).

[12] See Vitor Westhelle, *Transfiguring Luther: The Planetary Promise of Luther's Theology* (Cambridge: James Clarke & Co., 2017); *The Scandalous God: Use and Abuse of the Cross* (Minneapolis: Fortress Press, 2006); Walter Altmann, *Luther and Liberation: A Latin American Perspective*, 2nd ed. (Minneapolis: Fortress Press, 2016).

[13] Acts 17:22–23.

are extremely religious. Paul does not fault them for their perceptive spirituality. He acknowledges the hiddenness of God and affirms their human drive to know this God. Because the question is about human perception of God's presence, and our moral reasoning to respond, there is little risk of heterodoxy with respect to revelation (justification). And there is much to gain from interdisciplinary and interfaith perspectives on perception. As Gregersen suggests, this dialogue can help Lutherans correct and expand our understanding of "an ontology of divine reality prior to, simultaneous with, and after the proclamation of the Word". Creation can be, as Joseph Sittler wrote, "evocations of grace".[14]

In turn, Lutherans have much to contribute to the conversation about the hiddenness of God with respect to the distinction between law and gospel. Luther knows that struggling with this hidden God can be terrifying.[15] This is why Luther maintains a healthy distinction between faith and reason. In the 1520 Heidelberg Disputation, Luther wrote on the theology of the cross. The simple claim is that we cannot reasonably discern our way to knowledge of salvation. God reveals God's self in Christ crucified. Scripture, and proclamation in preaching and the sacraments, are means of this grace (*charis*).

Here lies the foundation for a perceived conflict between faith and reason that persists in the dialogue between theology and the natural sciences. But Luther and Melanchthon were robust supporters of reason and the natural sciences. Luther demonstrates the essential role of reason to order daily life and moral discernment in pastoral letters such as *Whether one may flee from a deadly plague*. In Luther and the Lutheran tradition, there is no conflict between theology and the natural sciences. Reason is critical to maintaining good order, as evidenced in the positive use of civil law *(usus civilis)*. Discerning our ethical responsibility and the freedom to act lovingly toward our neighbor depends on a complex engagement of faith and reason. Luther equates this liberty *coram mundo* to good works and sanctification.

As mentioned above, faithful *tentatio* necessarily includes our experience of God's Spirit at work in the world. Luther also knew that reason could correct many pastoral abuses of bad theology. One of his main concerns is the *Schwärmers*, or "enthusiasts", who claim to have received special revelations of grace (*charis*) and, therefore, gifts (*charismata*).

---

[14] Joseph Sittler, *Evocations of Grace: The Writings of Joseph Sittler on Ecology, Theology, and Ethics* (Grand Rapids, Mich.: Wm. B. Eerdmans, 2000).
[15] Stephen D. Paulson, "Luther on the Hidden God," *Word & World* 19, no. 4 (October 1999): 363–371.

Returning to the question of other religions, there are priests, such as those who practice Vodou religions, who claim the power to manipulate spirits for better or worse. Here we are in sensitive territory that requires a highly sophisticated understanding of revelation versus manipulation in these traditions. Notwithstanding these notable exceptions, the epistemological claims of most Indigenous traditions are consistent with Christian spiritualities of perceiving God's presence in the world. At the same time, there are Christians who claim to have received special revelations or spiritual dispensations that border on the magical, and exploitative practices of other religions.

Here it is helpful to return to Gregersen's thesis at the beginning of this essay. He cautions that with respect to discerning God's work in the world at large, the concept of "the hiddenness of God is a necessary placeholder." This "placeholder" is not meant to preclude attempts to discern experiences of God through our relationship to creation, or the experience of daily life. Rather, it is necessary to safeguard against modern day enthusiasts who would claim individual capacities to divine God's will or manipulate God's Spirit. This distinction is crucial in discerning spiritual claims and preventing spiritual abuse.

As we maintain theological rigor regarding the domains of revelation and reason it is worth noting that Luther affirms reason even in relation to revelation. In the *Confession Concerning the Lord's Supper*, he writes, in affirming Christ's real presence, "we must use our reason or else give way to the fanatics."[16]

Naming the Spirit

Like the apostle Paul, Luther affirms that one way to safeguard confusion or exploitation is to name this hidden God. Luther joyfully acknowledges that the Holy Spirit is everywhere – in a stone, fire, water, and a rope. However, so that you do not stumble on the rope, burn yourself in the fire, drown in the water, or hang yourself with the rope blindly groping to find God, the Spirit of God reveals itself where Christ promised, where the Word is proclaimed, and the sacraments administered rightly.

Luther affirms the primacy of revelation in this way because he knows the terror of having to discern God all on your own. Otherwise, I am left to the whims of any self-proclaimed prophet. In my confusion, what do I attribute to God, and what do I attribute to luck, deceit, or psychology? This becomes acutely important when spiritual healers or prophets claim

[16] LW 37: 224.

to have special access to revelations of the Spirit. If not properly discerned, these claims lead to spiritual abuse, manipulation and commodification, or the terror at thinking that there is a class of people who can conjure the Spirit while others cannot. So, let us remember the last phrase of Jesus's words about the Holy Spirit in the Gospel of John, "the Holy Spirit...will teach you all things and will remind you of everything I have said to you...I do not give to you as the world gives. Do not let your hearts be troubled and do not be afraid."

Luther and the confessional writings are clear at this point. So that you will not be afraid, groping for a revelation of the Spirit, Christ promised to be revealed in Word and sacrament. God's Spirit comes as promise, freely given. Luther writes in the *Large Catechism* that this is God's proper work. The proper function of the Church is as the place where the Spirit of God promises to meet us. In that communion, the Spirit calls, gathers, enlightens, and sanctifies the church so that we can go out into the world and discern God's gracious, loving, and life-giving presence behind the other masks of God, without fear.

In the interfaith context of dialogue with traditional, or Indigenous beliefs, how do Lutherans balance this promise with our mystical capacity to perceive God revealed in nature or through cultural practices? Synergies await, for those of us who are patient and open to this dialogue.

Spirit as Promise

To refer to the Spirit as promise is not to not to say that the presence of the Holy Spirit is never sublime, awesome, or overwhelming. Otto has rightfully referred us to the fact that the revelation of God's presence is part *mysterium tremendum*.[17] Just as Moses can only look upon the backside of God[18], mystical experiences of God's Spirit can be sublime and paralyzing as much as they are inspiring. I am thinking of the mystics, Julian of Norwich, Teresa of Avila, Lutheran mystic Jacob Boehme, and many of us who could share religious experiences of God's in-breaking that occurs at times outside of the proclamation of the Word and sharing in the sacraments.

I have perceived God's sublime and comforting presence many times at the face of a cliff, on a rushing river, or in silent communion with my more-than human co-creatures while fasting on a solitary retreat on a

---

[17] Rudolf Otto, *The Idea of the Holy: An inquiry Into the Non-Rational Factor in the Idea of the Divine and Its Relation to the Rational*, trans. John W. Harvey (New York: Oxford University Press, 1936).

[18] Exodus 33:19–23.

mountaintop. I have also perceived God in the sterility of a hospital room, keeping watch with my wife suffering through chemotherapy, radiation, and post-surgical recovery.

But Luther's point is that while we may meet God hidden behind these masks, we can be sure to meet God's Spirit where Christ promises to be revealed, namely, Word and sacrament. In Luther's *Sermon on the Sum of the Christian Life* he writes that where the Word is rightly proclaimed it will be a gracious word that imparts love as the sum of the Law at Christ's commandment. Love is the sum of the entire Christian life (our identity). Luther says we are given appointed times to gather and hear that promise proclaimed as part of our formation.

Note that this demands those who are called to preach actually proclaim the gospel. He laments that:

> There have always been many, as there still are, who talk a lot about faith and pretend to be masters not only of the law, but also the Gospel, and say, as we also say: Faith is what does it, but then they go on and say but yet the law and good works must be added to it otherwise faith does not avail. Thus they mingle together our life and works and Christ. This is not to teach faith purely and sincerely, but is rather faith so coloured, feigned, and falsified that it is not faith at all, but a false semblance and shred of faith, because the confidence of the heart does not rest purely upon Christ as the only mercy seat, but is placed rather in our own holiness, as if this could stand before the judgement seat.[19]

Here we see the importance that Luther places on proclamation. The call to preach is an instrument of the Holy Spirit. In CA VII, the gospel proclaimed in its purity (*doctrina evangelii*) is interpreted as preaching the gospel (justification by grace through faith) as opposed to the law (ethical implications of that liberty, or good works). Preaching the law sends people to look for God revealed in all manner of things, including spiritual gifts and good works. Gifts and good works are fruits of faith. However, discernment can be like groping for God in nature. Hopefully we will find God if discernment seeks God's wisdom. But the Holy Spirit finds us where we proclaim the gospel.

True preaching is found where the non-violent, non-coercive Word of promise is graciously proclaimed. Even if we feel condemned by the truth that is proclaimed, that sublime revelation of the Holy Spirit is compelling, never coercive or exploitative. When Luther writes "the heart is made pure and the conscience good and secure before God, not out of regard for my own purity or life before the world, but for that lovely treasure which my

[19] LW 51: 280.

heart takes hold of,"[20] he points to God's presence as a gift. This Trinitarian economy of grace stands in sharp contrast to the commodification of self-appointed spiritual healers or prophets who claim God's Spirit comes at some cost, investment, or through special revelation. For Lutherans, the concept of gift and promise serves as a hermeneutic of suspicion to discern when we ought to be cautious about whether someone's gifts come from God's Spirit.

Spirit as Gift

Luther suggests that the two most important words in the whole of the liturgy are "for you". The body and blood of Christ, given "for you". That phrase points to the Spirit's presence in the sacraments. The Gift of Christ present in faith.

Luther often wrote about the gift of Christ present in faith, most poignantly in *Two Kinds of Righteousness*. The righteousness of Christ that fulfils the law, is the work of Christ in us. This love is the sum of the Christian life. Christ is the gift, present in faith. As Luther stated in his explanation of the third article of the creed, "I cannot by my own reason or strength believe in Jesus Christ my Lord or come to him." The sheer fact of my belief is because the Holy Spirit gifts me with the presence of Christ. Where I believe, love, and am sanctified, it is Christ's righteousness at work in me. Christ's self-giving in Word and sacraments is the work of the Holy Spirit. This is the Christological pneumatology, or the pneumatological Christology that Jennifer Wasmuth calls for in this volume.

Article IX in the Apology of the *CA* affirms "God gives the Holy Ghost to those thus baptized [to many who have been baptized in childhood]. For if this baptism would be in vain, the Holy Ghost would be given to none, none would be saved, and finally there would be no Church. [For there have been many holy men in the Church who have not been baptized otherwise.]" The gift of God's initiative is made more profound by the fact of children's spirituality. "It is very certain that the promise of salvation pertains also to little children [that the divine promises of grace and of the Holy Ghost belong not alone to the old, but also to children]."[21]

In baptism, the community gathers to speak the promise to the baptized. The Spirit bears Christ, on that promise, as the gift of faith. Every day we should remember the promise spoken. It reminds us of Christ's presence and renews and regenerates us with that gift. Regeneration[22] is the onto-

[20] LW 51: 280.

[21] CA, *Apology*, IX.

[22] Ibid.

logical aspect of justification. In the *Large Catechism* Luther writes, "every Christian has enough in Baptism to learn and to practise all his life; for he has always enough to do to believe firmly what it promises and brings: victory over death and the devil, forgiveness of sin, the grace of God, the entire Christ, and the Holy Spirit with His gifts."

The daily return to this baptismal reality through the study of Scripture, the means of grace, prayer, fellowship, work, and any practice that points to this gift of Christ present in faith is, in a Lutheran understanding, spirituality. The meaning that we derive from that experience can be properly understood as spiritual theology.

But this gracious narrative of Spirit as gift stands in contrast to many cultural initiation rites, or healing rites related to possession that exact a kind of religious, social, or even economic, debt for healing or blessing. A coercive rite can never be properly understood as Christian spirituality. Spiritual gifts are freely given within the Trinitarian economy. Such is the proper work of the Spirit.

The Spirit as Sanctifier and a Quick Rejoinder on Discerning the Spirit

Psalm 104 exults that the Spirit renews the face of the Earth liberally. The Holy Spirit democratizes its work, in the sense that all creation participates in sanctification. No one has more access to God. Psalm 36 sings that God's Spirit preserves humans and animals alike. The priesthood of the baptized is more than a reform of church power. It is a confession of the Holy Spirit's replete presence and the call for everyone to participate in the Spirit's work (as a little Christ to one another). Each vocation has the same potential for holiness.

The Spirit renews, revives, and sanctifies as gift and promise. But the Church's proclamation is not only an instrument of the means of grace and baptismal vocation. The community is a community of discernment about our vocation and spiritual gifts, or charismata.

Notice the Greek relationship between grace (*charis*), and spiritual gifts (*charismata*). Even this linguistic connection emphasizes that spiritual giftedness is part of the Trinitarian economy. In 1 Corinthians 12:1-14 Paul writes, "concerning spiritual gifts, brothers and sisters, I do not want you to be uninformed...For in the one Spirit we were all baptized into one body." Charismata should always build up the body. This is a critical threshold of discernment that we must uphold in contemporary discourse about spiritual gifts.

Paul is clear about the democratization of spiritual gifts. All gifts serve the body. Therefore, there is no hierarchy among gifts of administration, teaching, preaching, serving, or healing. The gifts that are often elevated in today's spiritual marketplace (such as speaking in tongues) are counted as the least because they can be unintelligible. Paul is clear that if spiritual gifts come from the Spirit of God, who is love, the outcome must be discernible as loving. This is why the subsequent chapter (13) speaks of love as the greatest of the theological virtues. Love is the mark of the Spirit's presence because the abiding presence of God is love.

Lutherans hold fast to this Biblical hermeneutic and the ethical imperative to love. Therefore, *charismata* are never proof of God's presence. The doctrine of justification by grace through faith insists that spiritual gifts are not incidences of a special revelation. They are part of sanctification that the communion of saints affirmed in our baptism. That same community of Word and sacrament is the location for moral discernment about the veracity and goodness of our spiritual gifts, and the spirits of the age. As Gregersen suggests, the hiddenness of God, and specifically Luther's theology of the cross, are necessary and helpful tools for Lutherans to maintain and exercise in the course of our individual and corporate prayer and moral discernment.

Conclusion: After Justification

In a 2017 collection of essays on the future of Lutheran theology, Hans-Peter Grosshans and Frederike Nuessel encourage Lutherans to make the link between justification and sanctification.[23] In Lutheran theology–as in Luther's theology–creation, redemption, and renewal are parts of the same Trinitarian economy. In contemporary discourse about spirituality and Christian identity, Lutherans can claim this aspect of our theology of the Spirit and our spiritual theology. In today's spiritual marketplace, a Lutheran narrative of the Spirit continues to resist any practice that commodifies or any discourse that separates the Spirit from an economy of grace.

And, twenty years after the Joint Declaration on the Doctrine of Justification, our Lutheran tradition equips us to speak in different theological and epistemological modes about God's work in the world at large and our participation in the Trinity's creative, reconciling, and sanctifying work in God's garden.

---

[23] Frederike Nüssel and Hans-Peter Grosshans, *Lutherische Theologie in aussereuropäischen Kontexten: Eine Zusammenschau aus Anlass des 500. Reformationsjubiläums* (Leipzig: Evangelische Verlagsanstalt, 2017).

The Church as Holy Communion

Bible Study

Formed and Freed

Galatians 5:1; 22-25

Caroline Christopher

At the time of creation, everything on the earth was formed with a purpose, particularly human beings who were formed in the image of God and expected "to till and to keep the earth safe." Human beings failed in this responsibility, yielding to their own desire. They were guilty and ashamed of their behavior, but God freed them from their guilt and gave them a new life. Therefore, the forming and freeing act of God began at the time of creation and is still continuing in God's creation; this redeeming act reflects the grace and the love of God toward creation. However, the development of human society brought many social changes in terms of class, caste, and creed which divide the people and become a threat to society and even to the church.

The word "formed" has various meanings, such as "bring together parts" or "combine" or "create" or "make (or be made) into a specific shape or form." The early church brought together people from different faiths, nations, and classes, and formed them into one faith in Christ. Even now—though there are different traditions and denominations, even different doctrines—we are all bound together by the Holy Spirit as Christians with one belief in the one triune God. We see the work of the Spirit of God in the lives of God's chosen people all through the Bible.

In the Old Testament, there are references to the Spirit empowering, equipping, and strengthening individuals who were chosen for special tasks by God. The Spirit of God came upon the chosen people whom God raised up to deliver Israel from the oppressors. God also empowered the kings who reigned over the nation of Israel. Their stories are found in Numbers 27:18 (Joshua); 1 Samuel 16:12-13 (David); 1 Samuel 10:10 (Saul); and the book of Judges. The Spirit of God came upon these people for specific tasks, irrespective of their spiritual condition. Once the task was completed, the Spirit presumably departed from that person. But in the New Testament, the Holy Spirit was promised to all believers who have faith in God and Jesus Christ. We cannot deny that the early church was formed and strengthened by the Holy Spirit and was vibrant among the believers. Whenever the early church struggled with its own contextual differences in religious, cultural, and traditional practices, the apostles reminded them about their salvation in Christ that formed them in faith and liberated them for a life of freedom. The text for the Bible study, Galatians 5:1; 22-25, is an important example of guidance for standing firm in the freedom in Christ and practicing the fruit of the Spirit in order to fulfill the liberating mission of God.

The purpose of the epistle is two-fold. Firstly, to refute the Judaizers who taught that gentile believers must obey the Jewish law in order to be saved, and secondly, to call people to faith and freedom in Christ. This controversy divided the Galatian church; having laid the foundation, Paul builds his case for Christian liberty. In this profound letter, Paul proclaims the reality of our liberty in Christ; freedom from the law and the power of sin, and freedom to live a new life in genuine freedom of mind and spirit, through the power of God. We are saved by faith, not by keeping the law (5:1-12); our freedom means that we are free to love and serve one another, not to do wrong (5:13-26). Because of this powerful truth, the letter to the Galatians was the cornerstone of the Protestant Reformation.

Freedom or Liberty from the Yoke of Slavery

The Galatian Christians attain their freedom (liberty) through the death of Christ on the cross. This liberty frees them from the law and forms them with the power of Holy Spirit in order to exercise the teachings of Jesus as taught by the apostles. This liberty strengthens them to stand firm in their faith. Therefore, Paul exhorts them to remain firm in that freedom from law and calls them to live a Spirit-filled life that will protect them from the yoke of slavery. The image of the yoke is not difficult to understand. It usually represents slavery, service, and control by someone else over our life; it may also represent willing service and submission to someone else.

In the Indian context, the early church was influenced by the caste system which divides and segregates people, both in church and society. It was also challenged by multifaith religious rituals and practices. The early missionaries faced many challenges in teaching the grace and love of God that is promised to all. According to the Indian caste system, the *Sudras* (lower caste) and Dalits are meant to be slaves for the so-called upper caste people. The early Lutheran church started its mission among the Dalits who are considered outcast and are deprived of health and education. They are even refused entry into places of worship. For the early Indian church, freeing people from the yoke of slavery of the evil caste system included a focus on health and education for all people, particularly the poor and needy.

We are also formed as Christians through the grace of God and freed from our sinful nature through our baptism in the name of the triune God. But we often neglect this greater gift of God who called us to act. We are called to be free to serve one another in love (Gal 5:13ff). All through the Bible, we see that people who are formed and freed by the Spirit of God do not keep this experience within themselves, but act to fulfill the purpose of God. For this, one needs to stand firm in the promise of God that enables us to follow the guidance of the Holy Spirit, which protects us from sinful desires, and leads us to yield the fruit of the Spirit for the betterment of the people.

Yielding the Fruit of the Spirit

The Spirit of God, which is promised to all the baptized, leads believers in the way of life; it nurtures our faith and is a channel of love and peace. Christian living is about path and product—choosing the Spirit's route and yielding the Spirit's fruit. We are called to live by the Spirit and promised to be guided by the Spirit. With this confidence, if we live by the Spirit, we will yield the fruit of the Spirit in every aspect of our daily life. The apostle Paul describes the temptations of the flesh in Galatians 5:19. However, in the Gospel according to John, we read about the fruit of the Spirit that is made possible by the living relationship between human beings and God (Jn 15:1-15) and extended to all creation.

Paul presents the significance of Christian duty toward our fellow human being: the results of the life of the Spirit are to extend beyond us and influence our whole conduct. We are not to live only for the spiritual enjoyment of fellowship with God; the true field of religion lies in moving among people; the true basis of all service to others is the love and fellowship of God. The fruits of the Spirit, which are the direct results of the indwelling Spirit and will never be produced without the Spirit's presence, nonetheless are truly dependent upon our manner of receiving that Spirit and on our faithfulness, and diligence, in the use of the Spirit's gifts.

Transformed by the Spirit

The Holy Spirit brings together different kinds of people from many nations through their faith in Jesus Christ (Acts 2:1-12) to be made into what God desires—that they proclaim the gospel to all creation. The Holy Spirit also frees us from all kinds of bondage and removes the restrictions that hinder us from attaining the fullness of life. Attaining the fullness of life is not our own achievement but comes by the grace of God through faith. When we experience the fullness of life with freedom, we are also called and formed to be liberators in our church and society. For this, God promises the Holy Spirit to all believers of Christ; the Holy Spirit teaches us, guides us, empowers us, and leads us in all truth. The truth leads us into freedom: Martin Luther lifted up this truth from the Gospels in order to free the church from the clutches of false doctrines and restore the church's spiritual heart and freedom; Martin Luther King Jr. used this truth to free people from oppressive social structures in the USA.

This kind of liberating mission is much needed in our church and society. For this liberating mission, we need to develop spiritual qualities in order to equip ourselves. We become Christians through the work of Holy Spirit who brings new life; even our faith to believe is a gift from the Spirit. The Holy Spirit ends our bondage to evil desires and creates in us love, joy, peace, and many other wonderful changes. We are free in Christ and yet freedom is a privilege. We are not free to disobey Christ and practice immorality, but we are free to serve the risen Christ. By believing, we can have the Holy Spirit within us, helping us to live for Christ.

"The Holy Spirit Has Called Me through the Gospel …": The Third Article of Luther's Small Catechism as a Basic Text of Lutheran Ecclesiology

Jennifer Wasmuth

Introduction

Allow me to begin this paper with two personal remarks. When I studied in Heidelberg in Germany at the beginning of the nineties, Friedrich Heyer was still teaching there. Probably, Heyer is a name known only to a few, if any, people here. In fact, however, he was a pioneer in exploring the history of Ethiopia. He traveled extensively throughout the country and wrote about the church of Ethiopia that is even today considered as a standard work.[1] He also founded the so-called "Tabor Society," an aid organization that still exists and has made the promotion of church schools its mission.[2] In his lectures, Heyer told with great passion of this country and its people, of its unique history and culture. That's why I'm so deeply touched and grateful to be here today–in a country about which I've heard so many interesting and fascinating things.

[1] Friedrich Heyer, *Die Kirche Äthiopiens: Eine Bestandsaufnahme*, Theologische Bibliothek Töpelmann, Volume 22 (Berlin: De Gruyter, 1971).

[2] Tabor Society home page, accessed 14 April 2020, tabor-society.org.

On the other hand, I felt a little like Jeremiah when I was asked to give a presentation on the Holy Spirit. As is well known, Jeremiah responded when he was called by God, "Ah, Lord God! Truly I do not know how to speak, for I am only a boy" (Jer 1:6). This feeling did not occur to me because of my age, of course, but because of the choice of topic. For I myself grew up in a traditional Lutheran parsonage and at the beginning of my studies I was influenced by a theological direction that is often called "neo-orthodoxy" in the English-speaking world, even though its representatives have always rejected this term. For a long time, therefore, I regarded the Holy Spirit only as part of the Christological event of salvation, which alone was considered central.[3]

Then, however, I had certain experiences that awakened my interest in a better understanding of the Holy Spirit and his work. First, there was my encounter with the Orthodox churches. For the Orthodox churches, the Holy Spirit has a much greater significance, both dogmatically and practically, than was familiar to me from my tradition. Conversely, the Orthodox side strongly criticized "Western" theology, and thus also the Lutheran church, for having domesticated the work of the Holy Spirit by binding it unilaterally to the confession of Christ. The introduction of the "filioque" into the Nicene Creed, which, as was argued, subsumes the Holy Spirit under the Son, was used frequently as an example for this narrowing. And so, in dealing with Orthodox theology—here in particular with the discussion about the "filioque"—as in the encounter with Orthodox piety, I was repeatedly confronted with the question of what the Holy Spirit means.[4]

Second, I have been very impressed by the Pentecostal churches and the charismatic renewal movement. This does not only concern the astonishing numbers—that there are currently 610 million Christians (and

[3] The Reformed theologian Karl Barth (1886–1968), who can certainly be regarded as the most important representative of the "neo-orthodox" direction, expressed self-critically shortly before his death that if he could start again he would not start with Christology but with Pneumatology, whereby he presumably contributed decisively to the "boom on the Spirit" in Protestant theology, which soon followed. See Wolfgang A. Bienert, "Die Reformation als dogmengeschichtliches Ereignis: Ein Beitrag zur Geschichte des pneumatologischen Dogmas," in *Der Heilige Geist: Ökumenische und reformatorische Untersuchungen*, Veröffentlichungen der Luther-Akademie Ratzeburg 25 (Erlangen: Marin-Luther-Verlag, 1996), 35–56.

[4] Thorough studies offer historical and systematic perspective. See Peter Gemeinhardt, *Die Filioque-Kontroverse zwischen Ost-und Westkirche im Frühmittelalter*, Arbeiten zur Kirchengeschichte 82 (Berlin: DeGruyter, 2002). Also, Bernd Oberdorfer, *Filioque: Geschichte und Theologie eines ökumenischen Problems*, Forschungen zur systematischen und ökumenischen Theologie 96 (Göttingen: Vandenhoeck & Ruprecht, 2001).

will be presumably 800 million by 2025) who understand themselves as Pentecostals or charismatics. It is rather the dynamism of these communities and their full confidence in the present activity of the Holy Spirit which have led me to my own roots and thus to what I want to talk about now—the meaning of the Holy Spirit for Martin Luther.[5]

The Small Catechism

Luther left us an extensive body of writings, among which, remarkably, there is not a single treatise on the Holy Spirit. This could lead to the fallacy—and has done so many times in the past—that the Holy Spirit plays only a marginal role for Luther. The opposite, however, is true. A closer look reveals that there is no dogmatic teaching of Luther without the Holy Spirit.[6]

One could show this by means of different writings.[7] For today, however, I have chosen Luther's *Small Catechism* because I assumed that we are all most familiar with this among Luther's writings. As you may know, the Constitution of the Lutheran World Federation even mentions the *Small Catechism* as its "doctrinal basis" alongside the Augsburg Confession.[8] In addition, it was in this writing that Luther wanted to express his teaching as comprehensively as possible. After the devastating experience of visiting congregations in the early days of the Reformation, the catechism aimed to impart the elementary knowledge of the Christian faith in an

[5] As an introduction to the history and present phenomenology of Pentecostal Churches worth reading, see Allan Heaton Anderson, *An Introduction to Pentecostalism: Global Charismatic Christianity* (Cambridge: Cambridge University Press, 2014).
[6] Bernhard Lohse, *Luthers Theologie in ihrer historischen Entwicklung und in ihrem systematischen Zusammenhang* (Göttingen: Vandenhoeck & Ruprecht, 1995), 252.
[7] See, for example, Cheryl M. Peterson, "Rediscovering Pneumatology in the 'Age of the Spirit': A North American Lutheran Contribution," *Dialog* 58, no. 2 (June 2019), 102-108. On the treatment of Luther's pneumatology in the field of Luther studies, see Michael Plathow, "Der Geist hilft unserer Schwachheit: Ein aktualisierender Forschungsbericht zu M. Luthers Rede vom heiligen Geist," *Kerygma und Dogma* 40 (1994), 143-169; see also Martin Timóteo Dietz, *De Libertate et Servitute Spiritus: Pneumatologie in Luthers Freiheitstraktat*, Forschungen zur systematischen und ökumenischen Theologie 146 (Göttingen: Vandenhoeck & Ruprecht, 2015), 11-23.
[8] There it says in section 2: "The Lutheran World Federation confesses the Holy Scriptures of the Old and New Testaments to be the only source and norm of its doctrine, life and service. It sees in the three Ecumenical Creeds and in the Confessions of the Lutheran Church, especially in the unaltered Augsburg Confession and the Small Catechism of Martin Luther, a pure exposition of the Word of God" (accessed 14 April 2020, lutheranworld.org/sites/default/files/2018/documents/lwf_constitution_en.pdf).

easily accessible form. "What is this?" Luther asks again and again in his catechism, and he gives short and concise answers.

Luther's catechism is characterized by certain peculiarities. This begins with the order of the catechetical pieces. Unlike medieval catechisms, the catechism starts with an exposition of the Ten Commandments and then goes on to the Apostles' Creed and the Lord's Prayer. Thus, the order expresses Luther's insistence "on moving from law (Ten Commandments) to gospel (creed and Lord's prayer)."[9] The catechism also contains other pieces different from the usual, including explanations of the Holy Baptism and the Lord's Supper, and prayers for mealtimes, morning, and bedtime. Most importantly for our context, however, is that Luther divides the Creed into three articles, dealing with creation, redemption, and sanctification, while traditionally it had been divided into twelve articles (assigning one to each of the twelve Apostles). Thus, Luther opts for a Trinitarian structure that completely ascribes the third article to the Holy Spirit.[10] Correspondingly, the heading above the third article reads: "On Being made holy."

If one takes a closer look at Luther's interpretation of the third article—the verses that read "I believe in the Holy Spirit, one holy Christian Church, the community of saints, forgiveness of sins, resurrection of the flesh, and eternal life" —you can see that the entire paragraph is divided into two parts. Each part begins with words about the calling of the Holy Spirit: "The Holy Spirit has called..." and then "The Holy Spirit calls..."[11]

I would now like to dwell a little on this article and ask what the sentences of those two parts say about the Holy Spirit and the Spirit's work.

---

[9] *The Book of Concord: The Confessions of the Evangelical Lutheran Church*, eds. Robert Kolb and Timothy J. Wengert (Minneapolis: Fortress Press, 2000), 346.

[10] In his "Large Catechism," Luther states: "Hence the Creed could be briefly condensed to these few words: 'I believe in God the Father, who created me; I believe in God the Son, who has redeemed me; I believe in the Holy Spirit, who makes me holy.'" *Book of Concord* (hereafter referred to as BC), 432 [7]. Albrecht Peters, writes aptly: The Holy Spirit "alone is the majestic subject of the entire article." *Commentary on Luther's Catechisms: Creed*, trans. Thomas H. Trapp (Saint Louis: Concordia Publishing, 2011), 222.

[11] Peters also distinguishes two main parts, but with a different content. According to him, it is first about "The foundational event for the faith" (I) and then about "The eschatological unfolding of the faith event" (II), *Commentary on Luther's Catechisms*, 219–220.

The Holy Spirit Has Called Me …

Let me quote the first part. It is very short; in fact, it is only a half-sentence and it reads:

> I believe that by my own understanding or strength I cannot believe in Jesus Christ my LORD or come to him, but instead the Holy Spirit has called me through the gospel, enlightened me with his gifts, made me holy and kept me in the true faith.[12]

We see that this sentence is about the foundational event of faith for the individual person. It was always important for Luther to emphasize that this was precisely the reason he turned away from the traditional, objectifying view of salvation: The Holy Spirit has called me, salvation has happened "pro me," that is, "for me." Luther, therefore, underlines in a Christmas sermon of 1519, "If I hear the story of Christ and do not believe that everything refers to me, namely that Christ was born, suffered and died for me, then the sermon or the knowledge of history is of no use."[13] And in his Church Postils of 1522 he accordingly describes the true faith in contrast to the "fides historica," that is, historical faith, in such a way that "you firmly believe that Christ was born to you, and that his birth was yours, and that it was for your own good. For the gospel teaches that Christ was born for our sake, and that he did and suffered all things for our sake."[14]

But how does this faith come about? How does the abstract knowledge of a past historical event give rise to the firm confidence that my own salvation is founded in this event?

The third article gives an answer to exactly this question–a double answer–in that Luther first makes it clear that it is not in one's own efforts; one can try as one pleases, one can be of incredible strength, both intellectual and emotional, yet one cannot bring about this faith. For this faith owes itself alone–this is the second part of the answer–to the work of the Holy Spirit.

Since there are papers in this volume speaking at length about the work of the Holy Spirit in this regard, I would like to comment on it today only briefly and to emphasize what is important to Luther in the context of his catechism.

[12] BC, 355 [6].
[13] WA 9, 440, 22-24.
[14] WA 10/I/1, 71, 3-10.

Luther describes a dynamic process that takes place in the form of a change of location:[15] Since we ourselves cannot come to Jesus our Lord, we depend on the Holy Spirit to call us. Without the Holy Spirit, we remain in the thicket of our own imperfection, and only the Holy Spirit can show us the way out. In his *Small Catechism* Luther does not elaborate further on this, but he does in the *Large Catechism*, on the basis of which the *Small Catechism* arose, writing:

> Neither you nor I could ever know anything about Christ, or believe in him or receive him as Lord, unless these were offered to us and bestowed on our hearts through the preaching of the gospel by the Holy Spirit. The work is finished and completed; Christ has acquired and won the treasure for us by his sufferings, death, and resurrection, etc. But if the work remained hidden so that no one knew of it, it would have been all in vain, all lost. In order that this treasure might not remain buried but be put to use and enjoyed, God has caused the Word to be published and proclaimed, in which he has given the Holy Spirit to offer and apply to us this treasure, this redemption. Therefore being made holy is nothing else than bringing us to the Lord Christ to receive this blessing, to which we could not have come by ourselves.[16]

The essential work of the Holy Spirit, therefore, is to bring the truth of the gospel out of hiding. This, however, does not only mean that the Holy Spirit brings us to acknowledge Christ as the redeemer, but also the Father as the creator. As Luther continues in his *Large Catechism*:

> For, [...] we could never come to recognize the Father's favor and grace were it not for the LORD Christ, who is a mirror of the Father's heart. Apart from him we see nothing but an angry and terrible judge. But neither could we know anything of Christ, had it not been revealed by the Holy Spirit.[17]

The work of the Holy Spirit is therefore decisive for our salvation. For without the Holy Spirit, the true meaning of the first two articles of the Creed would remain concealed. Everything would have been for our benefit, creation, and redemption, but we would know nothing about it and would be lost. Hence, Luther criticizes the papacy of his time in the *Large Catechism*, because under the papacy, following Luther, "no one believed that Christ is our Lord in the sense that he won such a treasure without

[15] For this, see Eilert Herms, *Luthers Auslegung des Dritten Artikels* (Tübingen: J.C.B. Mohr, 1987), 39–44.
[16] BC, 436 [38].
[17] BC, 439–440 [65].

our works and merits and made us acceptable to the Father. What was lacking there? There was no Holy Spirit present to reveal this truth and have preached."[18] Because the work of the Holy Spirit is of such importance, some scholars see in the third—not in the second—article of the Creed the central article for Luther. In fact, it is this article that occupies the largest space in Luther's interpretation of the Creed in the *Large Catechism*. It is the third article to which everything points.

Luther speaks in the *Small Catechism* about the Holy Spirit who "enlightened me with his gifts, made me holy and kept me in the true faith." Luther does not explain this further here but, as the German scholar Albrecht Peters writes, based "on the formulations that he [Luther] uses most regularly, something like the following could have been articulated in the Small Catechism: The Spirit enlightened and inflamed my heart in the true faith."[19] This is very revealing, since the term "heart," which is mentioned here, had a central meaning for Luther. For him the heart was the "'chief organ for the emotional-spiritual life,'" and thereby "'the place within the human being where God reveals Himself,' as well as that 'place where decisions about the entirety of one's standing *coram Deo* (in the presence of God) are made.'"[20] That means that through the Holy Spirit we are not only brought to Christ and through Christ to the heart of the Father, becoming aware of his abundant mercy, but that the insight in the heart of the Father is also given into our heart, and thus it affects—unlike what Thomas Aquinas taught—our entire existence. The "bringing to Christ" is, therefore, nothing else than the Triune God coming to the human being, "By means of His sanctifying work, the Spirit prepares us to be the dwelling place for the Son and the Father. We are to become a house of the living God, both in body and soul."[21] This, of course, cannot remain without effects. The "new heart" will give our life new direction, as Luther writes in his Pentecost sermon of 1523:

> The Spirit composes "a fiery flame in our heart and makes it lively, so that it splits up into fiery tongues and an energetic hand; a new person comes forth who detects that he now has a completely different discernment, disposition, and sense than

[18] BC, 436 [43/44].

[19] Peters, *Commentary*, 242.

[20] Peters, 243. On the significance of the heart for Luther, see also Birgit Stolt, *Martin Luthers Rhetorik des Herzens* (Tübingen: Mohr Siebeck, 2000).

[21] Peters, 256. How in detail the relationship of the Holy Spirit, faith, and love might be understood in Luther in contrast to scholasticism, see Theodor Dieter, "Du mußt den Geist haben!" Anthropologie und Pneumatologie bei Luther," in *Der Heilige Geist: Ökumenische und reformatorische Untersuchungen*, Veröffentlichungen der Luther-Akademie Ratzeburg 25 (Erlangen: Marin-Luther-Verlag, 1996), 65–88.

> he had beforehand. Everything is now enlivened, there is lively discernment, light, courage, and heart, which burn now and desires to do everything that pleases God."[22]

The Holy Spirit Calls ... The Whole Christian Church

Luther's interpretation of the third article is not limited to the half sentence I have already quoted. Rather, Luther continues:

> The Holy Spirit has called me [...], just as he calls, gathers, enlightens, and makes holy the whole Christian church on earth and keeps it with Jesus Christ in the one common, true faith. Daily in this Christian church the Holy Spirit abundantly forgives all sins - mine and those of all believers. On the Last Day the Holy Spirit will raise me and all the dead and will give to me and all believers in Christ eternal life. This is most certainly true.[23]

The most interesting, and at the same time most controversial expression of this passage, is the expression "just as he calls." Is Luther here only concerned with paralleling the work of the Holy Spirit on the individual with that on the church? Or is there a deeper connection?

There seem to be good reasons to assume that Luther not only wanted to place two statements next to each other, but that the "just as" has a similar function to the "just as" in the interpretation of the second article, which grounds the new Christian life in Christ's resurrection and reign.[24] And that is because in the following sentence it says that it is the Christian church, in which "the Holy Spirit abundantly forgives all sins–mine and those of all believers." And even more clearly, the *Large Catechism* states that the Holy Spirit "first leads us into his holy community, placing us in the church's lap, where he preaches to us and brings us to Christ."[25] The church is described here in other words as "the protective space and the divinely designated location for the work of salvation as it is given to the

---

[22] WA 12, 570, 12, see Peters, 244. It seems remarkable that Luther mentions among the different gifts of the Holy Spirit expressively only faith. This has to do with the fact that only faith and the selfless love that springs forth from that faith is saving in eschatological terms, all other gifts belong for him "under the temporal rule of God" (Peters, 246-248).

[23] BC, 355-356 [6].

[24] BC, 355 [4].

[25] BC, 435-436 [37].

individual, the means and organ 'through' which the Spirit carries out His office as the one who sanctifies."[26]

Thus, the church plays a decisive role for Luther. If the third article can be regarded as the article toward which everything is converging, then in the third article itself the church can be regarded as the one toward which everything is converging, in which the work of the Holy Spirit culminates. It seems important to note this, because Protestants, and thus also Lutherans, are often accused of being interested in individual salvation only. Luther's interpretation of the third article, however, proves the opposite. For him there is no salvation of individuals unless they are at the same time being placed in the holy community.

For a better understanding of the third article, one would expect, as often happens in medieval catechism interpretations, that the four attributes of the church, confessed with the Nicene Creed, are then the object of Luther's explanatory note which says that the church is the one, holy, catholic and apostolic church.[27] The Nicene Creed was the creed spoken in worship during the Reformation period. Luther himself respected it highly, and he dealt intensively with the attributes of the church elsewhere, too. Nevertheless, in his interpretation in the *Small Catechism*, as you can see from the quotation above, he refers neither to the Nicene Creed nor to the attributes, at least not directly. In the German original version, he even does not use the term "church," but rather prefers to speak of "Christian people." How can that be explained? What's in the background here?

What Luther writes in the *Large Catechism* is again very revealing. For he explains here why he has difficulties with the German term "Kirche," that is "church." He writes,

> The word *ecclesia* properly means nothing more than an assembly in German. But we are accustomed to using the word *Kirche*, which the common people understand not as an assembled group of people, but as a consecrated house or building. But the house would not be called a church if it were not for a single reason that the group

[26] Peters, 289.

[27] Very often unity, holiness, catholicity, and apostolicity are referred to as the "marks of the church" (*notae ecclesiae*). This is nevertheless a problematic terminology since it is difficult to identify the church by its unity, holiness, catholicity and apostolicity. Hence, for Luther they are not marks but essential qualities ("Wesenseigenschaften") or theological attributes of the hidden ("verborgene") church. The marks in the proper sense, which Luther also calls *tesserae, symbola, igna*, and *characters* are according to him the preaching of the gospel and the sacraments of baptism and the Lord's supper. For more information, see lutheranworld.org/sites/default/files/2018/documents/online_course_-_module_6_-_ecclesiology._church_and_churches_-_jennifer_wasmuth.pdf.

> of people come together in it. [...] Therefore, [...] it ought to be called 'a Christian community or assembly,' or best and most clearly of all, 'a holy Christian people.'"[28]

Luther, therefore, rejects the term "Kirche" because for him it is connected with a misleading understanding of the church as merely a house or building. But for him the church is rather:

> ... on earth a holy little flock and community of pure saints under one head, Christ. It is called together by the Holy Spirit in one faith, mind, and understanding. [....] The Holy Spirit will remain with the holy community or Christian people until the Last Day. Through it he gathers us, using it to teach and preach the Word. By it he creates and increases holiness, causing it daily to grow and become strong in the faith and in its fruits, which the Spirit produces.[29]

It is clear from that description that Luther has no difficulty with the attribute of holiness, quite the contrary. The holiness of the church is certain to him. However, this is only true if the church is a community called by the Holy Spirit and guided by the Holy Spirit. The holiness of the church therefore has its sole reason for existence in the fact that the Holy Spirit takes it into his service, proclaims the word of God, and pronounces the forgiveness of sins in the church. Holiness, therefore, is not something that belongs to the church in itself but depends on the work of the Holy Spirit in the church alone.[30]

If one reads the description carefully, one will discover another attribute that is mentioned here—the attribute of the unity. Luther speaks of a "little flock" under "one head," called by the Holy Spirit in "one faith, mind, and understanding." This shows that Luther can easily apply the attribute of unity to the church, too, but again, only if it is understood as the unity of faith, caused by the work of the Holy Spirit.

The same applies to the attribute of catholicity. Luther does not use the term, but in his Small Catechism he speaks of the one, common, true faith. In the word "common," catholicity appears implicitly as the faith common

[28] BC, 437 [47/48].

[29] BC, 437–438 [51/53].

[30] This recalls the famous saying of Irenaeus of Lyon: "Where the Church is, there is the Spirit of God, and where the Spirit of God is, there is the Church" ("*Ubi enim Ecclesia, ibi et Spiritus Dei; et ubi Spiritus Dei, illic Ecclesia*" (Adv. haer. III 24, 1: see *Irénée de Lyon*: *Contre les Hérésies*, 3, 2. Sources Chrétiennes 211. Critical edition by Adelin Rousseau, with Bertrand Hemmerdinger, Louis Doutreleau, and Charles Mercier (Paris: Éditions du Cerf, 1974), 474.

to all. It is again significant that the "common" refers to faith, but not, as Luther says elsewhere,[31] to common rites or church orders.

The attribute of apostolicity, finally, seems to be also included in his interpretation of the third article, even if it is not mentioned directly. For if he states that the Holy Spirit calls the church and keeps it with Jesus Christ in the one common faith, then that is exactly what Luther understood by apostolicity, that the church remains apostolic by keeping the apostolic faith, not by a certain apostolic church order or apostolic succession.

With a view to Luther's understanding of the four attributes, as set out here, what was stated at the beginning can now be confirmed which is that, for Luther, the church plays a central role in the salvific event and is rightly regarded as the one, holy, catholic, and apostolic church. At the same time, however, this is only true for the church in that it depends on the work of the Holy Spirit.

When Luther describes the role of the church in this way, then in the background stands unquestionably his confrontation with the so-called "enthusiasts," against whom it was necessary to emphasize the role of the church as the place and organ through which the Holy Spirit works. For in contrast to the enthusiasts who invoked special revelations of the Spirit, Luther insisted that the work of the Holy Spirit takes place in the church by means of proclaiming the word of God. At the same time, however, he also departed from the papal side which seemed to regard the church as the co-redeemer along with the Holy Spirit. Luther, against this, affirms:

> "The church is responsible in an observable way for proclaiming the Word of God, but it can get the message only as far as the ear. It has no ability to drive into anyone's heart the saving faith that alone can save; for this reason, the Church is the 'co-worker' for salvation, in the full sense, but no one would consider it to be 'co-redeemer' as well."[32]

Conclusion

If one takes a closer look at Luther's remarks on the third article in his *Small Catechism*, it becomes clear that Luther describes a double dynamic in the effect of the Holy Spirit, which manifests itself in view of the individual as well as the church as a whole: the Holy Spirit has called me ... the Holy Spirit calls the church. The vanishing point of this dynamic is the church. The church is the "unique community" in the world, which Luther can also

[31] See Peters, 258–259.

[32] Peters, 291.

compare with a mother that "begets and bears every Christian through the Word of God, which the Holy Spirit reveals and proclaims, through which he illuminates and inflames hearts so that they grasp and accept it, cling to it, and persevere in it."[33]

Luther's pneumatology should, therefore, be treated in much stronger conjunction with his ecclesiology than is often the case. Take as an example the study *De libertate et servitute spiritus* of the Lutheran theologian Martin Timóteo Dietz from Brazil, which was published just a few years ago in 2015. Dietz deals with Luther's pneumatology for the first time on the basis of Luther's treatise "On the Freedom of a Christian" (1520) and comes to the conclusion that Luther had advocated a "cross-theological pneumatology."[34] As Dietz is able to show convincingly, Luther put the cross at the center of the work of the Holy Spirit in several respects: the message conveyed by the Holy Spirit refers to the cross of Christ; the Holy Spirit does not proclaim himself but points away from himself to Christ; the person enlightened by the Holy Spirit is placed in discipleship of the cross; and so on. Therefore, Dietz regards Luther's "cross-theological pneumatology" in a strict contrast to a "triumphalist pneumatology," which emphasizes human abilities and human reason. On the one hand, this is a fascinating analysis that Dietz presents here; on the other hand, the church appears in his work only marginally.[35] According to Luther though, it is precisely the church in which the pneumatology described by Dietz unfolds. Therefore, pneumatology should not be viewed in isolation, but rather finds its goal and direction in ecclesiology.

One might ask now, as Luther does in his *Small Catechism*: What is this? Therefore, in conclusion, a few considerations. The inner connection described by Luther between pneumatology and ecclesiology, between the Holy Spirit and the church, may first lead us to understand the church anew as the place where the work of the Spirit can actually be experienced. That is, not in unusual spiritual experiences, but in the proclamation of the word of God, and the celebration of the sacraments; not in the peculiarity of spiritual revelations, but in the experience of faith that unites us all and elevates no one above the others. The German theologian Notger Slenczka speaks, in this context, of the "miracle of the average," which is to be understood anew.[36]

---

[33] BC, 436 [42].

[34] Dietz, *De libertate et servitute spiritus*, 254. In his research overview, Michael Plathow spoke of a "Pneumatologia crucis," 169.

[35] Dietz, 225–230.

[36] Notger Slenczka, "Das Wunder des Durchschnittlichen: Die systematisch-theologische Reflexion der lutherischen Pneumatologie angesichts charismatischer Bewegungen," in *Yearbook of the Martin Luther Association* 54 (2007), Lutherische Kirche in der Welt, 57–77.

This does not necessarily mean, however, that extraordinary spiritual experiences cannot, and should not, have a place in Lutheran churches. Luther was never concerned with domesticating the Holy Spirit through binding it exclusively to a certain experience.[37] What was more decisive for him was that only that which follows the old Pauline principle can prove to be the work of the Holy Spirit: "So with yourselves, since you are eager for manifestations of the Spirit, strive to excel in building up the church" (1 Cor 14:12).[38]

If there is this inner connection between pneumatology and ecclesiology, then it seems appropriate, from a practical point of view, to raise more awareness of the importance of the work of the Holy Spirit. This could begin, for example, with catechesis. Where are there still families today in which, as recommended by Luther in his *Small Catechism*, not only the Ten Commandments and the Lord's prayer are taught, but also the second main part of the gospel, namely the Creed, and the question "What is this"? At least in my context, this happens, if at all, only in Confirmation classes.

A further consideration would be to look at our liturgical orders to see whether the work of the Holy Spirit, which we connect with certain liturgical actions, is also expressed in an outwardly visible and recognizable way for all to see. In recent decades, there have been developments here which point in the right direction, for example when anointing is again practiced as an element of the baptismal act or epiclesis as an element of the celebration of the Lord's Supper. The question, however, would be whether this is the case everywhere in our churches and to the same extent.[39]

Finally, it remains to clarify what this description of the connection between pneumatology and ecclesiology means for the relationship of the church to the world—what insights can be gained from it for dealing with the political powers of our time, but also for the ecological questions which concern us all. These questions, however, are dealt with in other contributions. That is why I want to stop here.[40]

---

[37] See Plathow, "Der Geist hilft unserer Schwachheit," 163–165. Plathow mentions here, for example, that Luther understood the anointing of the sick according to James 5:14f as the sanative work of the Holy Spirit.

[38] See Luther's sermon on the 10th Sunday after Trinitatis in 1535: WA 41, 391–398.

[39] As an example of a Lutheran understanding of worship that moves in this direction, see Christian Lehnert, "Descent and Ascent: On Lutheran Worship," in *What is Lutheran? Introductions to Theology, Worship, Congregation, Ecumenism and Church Law*, eds. Florian Hübner and Henrike Müller, Lutheran Theology. German Perspectives and Positions 1 (Leipzig: Veröffentlicht, 2019), 63–100.

[40] I would like to give just one reference to a study by the Reformed theologian Michael Welker, in which those issues are dealt with in detail and which gives important ideas: *God the Spirit*, trans. John F. Hoffmeyer (Eugene, Ore.: Wipf and Stock, 2013).

However, I do not want to do this without summarizing the core message which lies in Luther's interpretation of the third article and which may guide us in all our considerations, especially in the process which is initiated with the conference here in Addis Ababa within the Lutheran World Federation. The core message is that for Luther the Creed does not belong to the law but to the gospel; that in Luther's interpretation of the third article he, therefore, expressed the firm confidence ("I believe ...") that the Holy Spirit has not only called each one of us out of the darkness of demonic entanglement, but that he also calls, and daily renews, the church as the community of believers in Christ; that we can be sure that in the church, however small and poor it may sometimes appear to us, we will find the place where salvation is given. As Luther himself formulated in the *Small Catechism*:

> ... everything in this Christian community is so ordered that everyone may daily obtain full forgiveness of sins through the Word and signs appointed to comfort and encourage our consciences as long as we live on earth. Although we have sin, the Holy Spirit sees to it that it does not harm us because we are part of this Christian community.[41]

The Holy Spirit, the comforter, for each one of us as well as for us as the church–that is what Luther wanted to bring to us–the Holy Spirit on whom we may place all our trust. And so, Luther ends his well-known song "Lord, keep us steadfast in your Word" with this verse, with which I would like to conclude:

> O Comforter of priceless worth, /
> send peace and unity on earth; /
> support us in our final strife /
> and lead us out of death to life.[42]

---

[41] BC, 438 [55].

[42] *Laudamus*. Hymnal of the Lutheran World Federation. Gesangbuch für den Lutherischen Weltbund, Budapest ^{5}1984, n. 89. In German: "Gott Heiliger Geist, du Tröster wert, / gib deim Volk ein'erlei Sinn auf Erd, / steh bei un sin der letzten Not, / g'leit uns ins Leben aus dem Tod."

Community of God: Perspectives from the Evangelical Lutheran Church in Botswana[1]

Mari-Anna Auvinen

Introduction

In this short paper, I evaluate Tswana Lutheran identity in light of the community of God. I had the privilege of working and living amongst Tswana friends and pastors in Gaborone while working for the Evangelical Lutheran Church in Botswana as a lecturer in the Woodpecker Theological Seminary between 1996 and 2000. During this time, I felt that my students sometimes understood Luther's theology better than the theologians in my own Finnish cultural context. Luther's idea of the theology of the cross echoed people's life situations, which were not easy, given the poverty and sickness at the time, such as the HIV and AIDS pandemic. In addition, the idea of the church was deeply understood by my students and we were able to share theology in a special way that was relevant for us all. Eventually I became keen to discover the underlying structure of thought that made

[1] There are three different Lutheran churches in Botswana. My research concerns the Evangelical Lutheran Church in Botswana (ELCB). The other Lutheran churches are the Evangelical Lutheran Church in Southern Africa (ELCSA) from South Africa, and a small Lutheran church led by German missionaries, the Lutheran Church of Southern Africa.

this contextual understanding possible and started to conduct interviews and research on Tswana thinking.[2]

When talking about Tswana thinking or philosophy, one needs to be clear that this is not to say that all *Batswana*–people in Botswana–have a homogenous way of thinking. Rather, there is a certain underlying cultural and philosophical structure of thought of which people are aware, and which in this case is helpful in perceiving Luther's theology of the church.[3] Tswana philosophy itself is thousands of years old, with close connections to traditional religious ideas, and this rich inheritance influences people's Lutheran identity. Much like other philosophical systems in Africa, traditional Tswana philosophy is oral in nature and includes principles that are taught to children from an early age. Ruth Finnegan calls this kind of cultural and philosophical structure of thought, and especially its learnt principles, oral literature.[4] It is, however, obvious that modernization and globalization are creating increasing challenges to all cultural traditions. Modernization seems to include a special anthropology that relies on individualism and a dualistic worldview that readily takes on materialistic values, shrinking the idea of a person. This phenomenon is heavily criticized by African scholars and described by Marilynne Robinson as "absence of mind."[5]

To enrich our Lutheran interpretations, it is important to research different traditions and thinking in order to keep our theological ideas lively. In this article, I briefly explain the traditional cosmology and the way of

[2] See Mari-Anna Pöntinen (2013), *African Theology as Liberating Wisdom. Celebrating Life and Harmony in the Evangelical Lutheran Church in Botswana.* Leiden: Brill.
[3] Regarding African philosophy and the structure of cultural philosophies, see: Henry Odera Oruka, *Sage Philosophy: Indigenous Thinkers and Modern Debate on African Philosophy* (Leiden: Brill,1990); Oruka, "Sagacity in African Philosophy"; and Kwasi Wiredu, "On Defining African Philosophy," in *African Philosophy: The Essential Readings,* ed. Tsenay Serequeberhan (New York: Paragon House, 1991), 47–62; 87–110; Pöntinen, *African Theology as Liberating Wisdom*, 64–85.
[4] See Ruth Finnegan, *Oral Literature in Africa* (Oxford: Oxford University Press, 1970); *The Oral and Beyond: Doing Things with Words in Africa* (Oxford: James Carrey, 2007).
[5] See Marilynne Robinson, *Absence of Mind: The Dispelling of Inwardness from the Modern Myth of the Self* (New Haven: Yale University Press, 2010). Concerning criticism, see, for example, Gabriel Setiloane, *African Theology: An Introduction* (Johannesburg: Skotaville Publishers, 1986), 10; Dumie Oafeta Mmualefe, "Towards an Authentic Tswana Christianity: Revising Botho" (MTS thesis, Eden Theological Seminary, 2004), 3; Polycarp Ikuenobe, *Philosophical Perspectives on Communalism and Morality in African Traditions* (Oxford: Lexington Books, 2006), 55; Pöntinen, 193–196.

perceiving a person among the Tswana, and how this thinking influences understanding of the community of God.

Holistic Worldview and Modimo as the Most High

In Tswana cosmology there is no distinction between the spirit and matter; neither is there separation between sacred and secular. European modernization with its Cartesian distinctions did not play a part in forming the Tswana worldview. Cartesian dualism distinguishes between the entities of *res cogitans*, thinking substances, and *res extensa*, dimensional substances.[6] Tswana cosmology, on the other hand, maintains one indivisible cosmological entity in which the metaphysical and the physical are not isolated from each other. This worldview can be called monistic, but not in the conventional European sense; rather, it represents a certain spiritual monism or holism. Holism, as a concept, means an approach which perceives the whole to be more than the sum of its separated fragments.[7]

In order to understand this difference, it is helpful to evaluate the creation narration among the Tswana: In the beginning, *Modimo*,[8] the Supreme Being, created the world by making and furnishing the universe with different items, placing each one in its own place in a certain order. This order includes different categories or levels of being, namely *Modimo* as the Most High, *badimo* (forefathers and mothers of the living), *batho* (the people), then animals, plants, and the rest of nature in a descending order.

All items in their particular places, and in their relations with each other, reflect oneness in a holistic sense; however, everything that exists is dependent on *Modimo* as the Creator, *Mothlodi*. *Modimo* is life itself, the root and source of all that is living. Yet, even if *Modimo* is the Most High, simultaneously God exists in everything that is created in a highly immanent and even panentheistic sense. Panentheism needs to be distinguished from pantheism, since Tswana religion has always been monotheistic by

[6] See René Descartes, Teokset I: Yksityisiä ajatelmia. Järjen käyttöohjeet. Metodin esitys ja optiikka. Kirjeitä 1619-1640, trans. Sami Jansson (Helsinki: Gaudeamus, 2001), 125, 131–133.

[7] Petter Korkman and Mikko Yrjönsuuri, *Filosofian historian kehityslinjoja* (Tampere: Gaudeamus, 2003), 447. For analysis on Tswana holism, see Pöntinen, 153–176.

[8] On *Modimo*, see Pöntinen, 238–262; James N. Amanze, *African Traditional Religions and Culture in Botswana: A Comprehensive Textbook* (Gaborone: Pula Press, 2002), 37–61; Ntloedibe-Kuswani "Translating the Divine; The Case of Modimo in the Setswana Bible," in *Other Ways of Reading: African Women and the Bible*, ed. Musa Dube Shomanah (Atlanta: Society of Biblical Literature, 2001), 78-97; Setiloane, *African Theology*, 21–28.

nature. Rather *Modimo* is the power behind everything and the continuous source of all life. Without *Modimo* nothing exists.

Because of the absence of a dualistic distinction, it follows that there is no "creating something from nothing," *creatio ex nihilo*. Rather, *Modimo* is seen to generate both him/herself and all his/her manifestations continuously. Everything is dependent on this marvelous source of life. Life itself is a gift from God. *Modimo* is seen as a tender mother, *Mme*, and a giving father, *Rre*, to all the living; yet *Modimo* is also *Telo*, a thing or it. The whole universe reflects its creator, God's tenderness for God's children and, simultaneously, God's mysterious and even terrifying power. South African scholar Gabriel Setiloane compares the Tswana God to Rudolf Otto's idea of *mysterium tremendum et fascinans*. He also invites European believers to attend a Tswana school in order to understand God's greatness.[9] I do agree. Dualism seems to weaken the idea of God, separating it from people's lives and the real world.

Person and Community

On the basis of creation, every person is respected in Tswana thinking. A proverb, *motho ke Modimo* (a person is god) describes this phenomenon.[10] An old sage explained to missionaries at the end of the nineteenth century that *Modimo*, while creating, was *diming* (drawing out) himself or herself to a person, much as the missionaries might pour ink onto blotting paper. If you tilt the paper, the ink does not run off, but remains—absorbed. Similarly, the touch of *Modimo* continues to dignify and identify every human person. This traditional explanation is similar to *imago Dei* in the Christian interpretation.

However, *imago Dei* in the Botswana Lutheran church refers rather to the community of people. Thus, according to the traditional idea of a person, humanity or *botho* is a shared quality of all people in a communal sense. The basic principle in Tswana thinking, *Motho ke motho ka batho ba bangwe* (a person is a person because of other people) emphasizes this communal notion.[11] In other words, a person is not a person without other people. Rather humanity as a shared quality indicates community of people and actualizes in relational connections with others. To be a person involves belonging, participation, and interdependence as people under God. In this sense, as Bishop Phillip J. Robinson states, the self is

---

[9] Setiloane, *The Image of God among the Sotho-Tswana* (Rotterdam: A. A. Balkema, 1976), 77, 84–85, 229; Otto 1923, 12–13.

[10] About the proverb, see Amanze, 129; Setiloane, 21.

[11] Amanze, 127; Setiloane, 33; Pöntinen, 178.

incomplete without the other, and therefore people constantly mirror from other faces, who we are in relation to others.[12] According to pastors in the Lutheran church, the African idea of community is also Christian, since community is emphasized in the Bible.

The humanity principle *(botho)* also refers to Tswana ethics. To live according to *botho* is to dignify every human being as equal under God. No one can be said to be more human than any other and oneself is always included among those dignified. Cosmos K. Moenga simplifies *botho* ethics by saying that one needs to see another person as a person and "nothing else." This means that in relations with others, one looks at them without the restrictive lenses of social status, gender, ethnicity, nationality, political opinions, and so on. "We look...[13] Through proper looking and seeing, common humanity actualizes. This leads to feeling and empathy regarding another person's needs. The highest Tswana code in *botho* is to love another person like oneself and respond to that person's needs in solidarity, and with care. *Botho* as an old moral code is similar to Golden Rule in the Bible.[14]

Principles of Theological Thinking in the Lutheran Church

These two principles, the life principle—embracing the Source of Life—and the communal humanity principle, *botho,* permeate theological thinking as a whole in the Botswana Lutheran church. When talking about the holistic and communal approach of African spirituality, Philip J. Robinson points out that this must be taken into account in theological interpretations for the church to be relevant for Batswana people.

However, there are also differences between traditional thinking and Christian interpretations of the life principle. To simplify these differences, it is helpful to evaluate the idea of *vital force.* This notion originates in the research on Bantu philosophy by Placide Tempels[15] who argues that in Bantu traditions—Tswana included—force is an interchangeable concept with

[12] Robinson, 2; Pöntinen, 193. According to John L. Comaroff and Jean Comaroff, *Of Revelation and Revolution: The Dialectics of Modernity on a South African Frontier,* vol. 2 (Chicago: The University of Chicago Press, 1997), the self is not understood in the Tswana tradition to be a state of being, but rather as a process of becoming with the others (381).

[13] Pöntinen, 205.

[14] About communal human existence and *botho* as an ethical principle, see the analysis and discussion in Pöntinen, 176–218.

[15] Placide Tempels, *Bantu Philosophy* (Paris: Presence Africaine, 1956). Even if Tempels is also criticized, his early writings are widely used in African theology.

"being" thus, traditionally, an attribute that is not separated from being. Rather, vitality is seen as a force within all beings who are also capable of possessing force. According to Tempels, the cosmic hierarchy embraces a chain of forces that are capable of possessing vitality and increasing it in other beings by acting as vitalizing agencies. In accordance with this, the Supreme Being in traditional thinking is a self-sustaining force that increases force and vitality in other beings. As noted above, the second hierarchy comprises the ancestors of people, then the people themselves, animals, and plants, in descending vital ranks. It is the higher tiers that exercise vitalizing influence through interactions with the lower ones.[16]

Philip J. Robinson states that Christianity is a new vital force permeating the whole life of the African society. In light of the discussion of *botho* above, it is obvious that, in the Lutheran church, human relations are seen at best as vitalizing interactions. However, it is the relation and interaction with Christ that has a special life-giving nature. This interaction renders a person alive and—even more—Christians are seen to be possessed by Christ. Christ as the life of God flows through human beings, as Lekutlane says, referring to the Pauline statement, "I live, but it is not me who lives, but Christ who lives in me." Since Christ is God, it is *Modimo* who dwells in Christians' inner beings.[17]

This introduces a striking paradox in terms of traditional religious thinking in which *Modimo* as the Most High is unreachable for people and needs to be approached through *badimo* (ancestors) who then vitalize people. In the Lutheran church, it is believed that the Most High descends to the low level of people, incarnating in humanity— "next to a person to be a person." Moreover, Jesus from Nazareth was fulfilling *botho* in its absolute sense. In loving solidarity, he treated the poor and the downtrodden with dignity

[16] Tempels, 51, 58–66. Setiloane, *African Theology* (27–28), much like Vincent Mulago, "Traditional African Religion and Christianity," in *African Traditional Religions in Contemporary Society*, ed. Jacob K. Olupona (Minnesota: Paragon House, 1991), talks rather about vital participation (120). See also Setiloane, *African Theology*, 13–16; Edwin Smith, *The Religion of Lower Races, as Illustrated by the African Bantu* (New York: The Macmillan Company, 1923), 9, 22–23.

[17] Pöntinen, 302–305. Even if possession draws from the Tswana tradition, a similar idea can be found in Luther's thought as well. See WA 17/I, 438: "We are filled with God, and He pours into us all His gifts and grace and fills us with His Spirit, who makes us courageous....His life lives in us, His beatitude makes us blessed, and His love cause love to arise in us. Put briefly, He fills us in order that everything that He is and everything He can do might be in us in all its fullness, and work powerfully, so that we might be divinized throughout." See also Tuomo Mannermaa, *Christ Present in Faith: Luther's View of Justification*, trans. and ed. Kirsi I. Stjerna (Minneapolis: Fortress Press, 2005), 39.

and care. Through the deepest identification with humanity, he took on the destiny of the people and sacrificed himself for the whole of humanity. In Christ, the highest descended to the lowest, the Holy dignified every human person and restored broken humanity with his blood. There is no need for other sacrifices, no need for healers to address fractured harmony. Christ is the great healer, *Ngaka,* and the only mediator between people and God.[18]

In the Lutheran church, the incarnation paradigm forms the third principle of theological thinking. Moenga even talks about the "Lutheran spirit." Firstly, since God, *Modimo,* incarnated to people's social, cultural and political context, theology always needs to be contextual. Secondly, since God, the Most High, descended especially to relate with the poor and undermined, the church needs to follow the same path. Like God, who came to serve the humanity of the downtrodden, the church needs to side with those who are otherwise not able to defend themselves. Since God historically chose to be born in the manger of the poor, God still chooses to be born to the mangers of the poor and marginalized. It is important, as Moenga points out, to understand that the Lutheran spirit needs to be regenerated in the churches to prevent God's name from being used to validate inhuman or exploitative activities, such as payments for healing, which he sees as contemporary indulgences. Philip J. Robinson emphasizes, "God saves his sinful, hopeless and helpless human beings by his grace only."[19]

Community of God

Proper seeing and vitalizing interaction are emphasized in all relationships; however, Moenga states that in interaction with Christ, Christians need to see God and "nothing else." This is parallel, but different, to the moral code in *botho,* which emphasizes that one needs to see a person, and nothing else. Through *botho,* Christ in humanity relates God to people, but it is not enough for people to see only his human nature. Otherwise, there is no Christian spirituality. Thus, people become related to God merely by seeing Christ as God. This is possible through faith, whereas love is the

[18] On the role of Christ as *Ngaka*, the great Healer, Mediator, see Pöntinen; on the role of *badimo* in the Tswana Lutheranism, see Pöntinen, 287–324. It needs to be noted that *badimo* influences the Lutheran identity in Botswana. According to Robinson *badimo* also provides another striking parallel to Christianity as the Communion of Saints.

[19] Philip J. Robinson, *What I hear the Bible Say. To You from Me on my 70th Birthday, July 4, 1940–July 4, 2010* (Ramotswa: ELCB, 2010), 17. About the necessity of contextual theology and the Lutheran spirit, see Pöntinen, 125–152.

driving force bringing the lost children back to the parental God. Through seeing God in Christ, Christ tenderly leads Christians to participate in the Holy Trinity, as partakers in the community of God.[20]

This idea of the Trinity as a community of God differs from traditional religious thinking, yet the approach to the Trinity has connections with the humanity principle. As with humanity, which is seen as a shared quality of people, divinity is a shared quality of the persons in the Trinity. In the holistic perception, the Trinity is more than the sum of individual persons. This communal idea of God places an emphasis on oneness and unity in the Trinity, but also a certain loving interdependence, where God is not seen merely to exist as a community, but also as acting in communion. In this sense, the sender and the sent are always the same.[21]

Moruti Segatlhe explains this mystery by stating that God as the creator is not merely part of the Trinity but, because the Trinity is one and simultaneously three persons, one can say that the whole universe exists "on them." On the other hand, as he states, in Christ the tender mother-heart of God is revealed to people. Meanwhile, it is the Holy Spirit who helps Christians to see God in Christ. Through the Spirit, Christ lives in Christians, who share the divine nature of God as the church, which is a partaker in the Holy Community. In this sense, the church reflects the community of God in the world. Even if the church struggles, and often falls, at the same time it remains holy on the basis of the Trinity, longing for the final liberation.[22] The Holy Spirit, as Moenga emphasizes, "nurtures life in our hearts until the final deliverance when we will enter into its full possession of the glory of God."[23]

However, there is another aspect to the Holy Spirit's work amongst Christians. The Spirit also leads Christians to see other people, in the

---

[20] Pöntinen, 293–296, 343.

[21] See Pöntinen, 338–339.

[22] Pöntinen, 340–349. Cf. Mercy Amba Oduyoye, *Hearing and Knowing: Theological Reflections on Christianity in Africa* (Maryknoll, N.Y.: Orbis Books, 1986), who also perceives the Trinity as a Community, but more as an ethical symbol of communion, which the Church should, but is not able to achieve (144–145). Bishop Moenga, on the contrary, emphasizes the church as partaker in the Holy Community and, therefore, its holiness. It is notable that in traditional religious thought the living reflect the community of *badimo*. Regarding African ideas of the Trinity, see also Mika Vähäkangas, "African Approaches to the Trinity," in *African Theology Today,* ed. Emmanuel Katongole (Scranton: The University of Scranton Press, 2002): 69–84.

[23] Cosmos K. Moenga, "The Role of the Holy Spirit in the Mission of our Churches: A Trinitarian Perspective" (paper presented at Partners' Consultation: Searching for a New Identity; Global Mission in Turmoil, Orivesi, Finland, June 2009), 3; Pöntinen, 349; also WA 17/I, 438.

same way as Christ sees. In addition, the Holy Spirit reveals—and opens people's eyes so they may see—those powers which are used to exploit people and keep them in captivity. Moenga emphasizes that the Holy Spirit is a liberating power. On the other hand, he speaks of another power that seeks rather to benefit—be it spiritually or economically – at the expense of human dignity. According to Moenga, the latter power is clothed in various religious, economic, and political robes, and does not embrace any particular color or religion. Yet it is often the ultimate underlying motif in religious activities.[24] The Holy Spirit also reveals such negative myths[25] as are used to exploit people. It is the Holy Spirit who leads the church to side with the poor and marginalized. In this sense the Holy Spirit instills truthful seeing in interactions and inspires and vitalizes Christians to participate in the mission of God, which always serves humanity.[26]

I end this paper by noting that it is obvious that the holistic perception of the cosmos and *Modimo* as the root and source of life influences theological thinking in the Botswanan Lutheran church much like the communal human principle in *botho*. In this sense, one can emphasize the importance of African spirituality in Lutheran interpretations. However, the incarnation paradigm determines all theological thinking, also capturing cultural and religious principles to explain the life-giving possession in Christ and the Trinity as a communion of persons. Trinitarian theology, as the pastors emphasize, explores the mysteries of love, relationships, personhood, and communion. In relationship with Christ, the Christian spirituality is dependent on perceiving Christ as God. This interaction leads Christians, as partakers, to the community of God.[27]

---

[24] Moenga, "The Role of the Holy Spirit," (5), refers, for example, to some "so called Spiritual Churches" and "how they claim to be empowered by the Spirit of God. They claim that the Spirit empowers them to see visions. To my surprise, they cannot see how the poor Africans who are their members are suffering. Worse still, they contribute to this suffering by charging high prices for the services they render to these poor masses."

[25] Moenga, "Does the Good Samaritan and the HIV/AIDS Victims Meet?" (paper presented at Summer Festivals, organized by FELM and Tampere Congregations, Tampere, Finland, June 2009), 2–3, refers, for example, to the myth of "poor African continent," even if it is a rich continent with plenty of natural resources.

[26] See Pöntinen, 348–360.

[27] Pöntinen, 337–338. Moenga, "The Role of the Holy Spirit," (4), emphasizes the need for African theologians to teach Trinitarian theology in African contexts because of confusions. According to him, "The doctrine of Trinity is neither a teaching about [the] abstract nature of God, nor about God in isolation from everything other than God, but a teaching about God's life with us and our life with each other."

The Holy Spirit in the World

Emmanuel Clapsis

Coping with Pluralism

The increasing pluralism of modern societies and its implications for the self-understanding of the Christian identity are an issue that all Christian churches are currently facing. How should they cope with the inescapable challenge of the cultural, ethnic, and religious pluralism of the present world? Regardless of how extensively and radically the cultural and religious landscape has changed, the identity of the church in the modern world depends on its faithfulness to the Apostolic tradition, the critical awareness of the changing landscape in which it finds itself, and the unswerving belief that in all historical situations and movements God is actively present through God's Spirit despite the ambiguities, conflicts, and destructive evil forces that one finds in them. The awareness of the presence of God's Spirit in history is the basis of the church's prayer for its guidance so it may do the will of God. Turning to God in situations of fear and uncertainty is also emboldened by the assurance of Christ: "In the world you face persecution. But take courage: I have conquered the world!" (John 16:33).

The Particularity and the Universality of the Christian Faith

How can the church remain faithful to the particularity of its tradition and moral practices, continue to claim the universal validity of its beliefs, and at the same time, find room for values and moral perspectives of different people and communities? The question is raised at the end of an era when the emphasis was heavily on finding ways of transcending cultural and religious differences and achieving some universal principles –principles binding on all people, under all or most circumstances. What characterized the communities of that era was their concern as communities, made up of diverse individuals and groups, to find a way to transcend those differences in order to reach consensus on some matters of common human welfare. Now the pendulum has swung and the communities, in light of the homogenized global forces, seek ways to affirm their particularities and reconfessionalize themselves so they can continue to justify their particularity in a plural world. The church, by giving primary emphasis to its particularity at the expense of the universality of the gospel, runs the risk of reducing itself to a sect that is contrary to those communities who overemphasize their universality at the expense of their particularity, and they run the risk of abandoning their specificity. The church is at the same time particular through God's revelation in Jesus Christ and universal in its eschatological orientation. Its faith is grounded in the history of God's revelation that culminates in the coming of God's reign, which is inclusive of all creation.

Discernment of the Spirits

On occasions that the church should judge a conflict between, or among, particular beliefs and moral practices or should choose which particularism it ought to embrace or reject, it will have to seek some universal principle to make that possible. In each concrete situation of life, the church, through prayer, theological reflection, and critical appreciation of its contextual situation, must identify through its judgment the will of God. While doctrinally the church has identified theological and historical criteria that may guide it in discerning in some instances the will of God, it is difficult to interpret the dynamics of the modern world. This can be a highly contested matter if, in light of the advances of human knowledge and science, the church must revise some of its beliefs and moral practices. The difficulties are heightened once the church recognizes the divine presence in other religious and secular communities. How can we discern the active presence of God's Spirit in the ambivalent modern world, and in religious and secular others, without compromising the integrity of the Christian gospel? For Paul, the "discernment of Spirits" is a gift of the Spirit (1 Cor 12:1–11) that has its origins in God ("the same Spirit," "the same Lord," "the same God who activates all of them in everyone") and it is given for "the common good" (1 Cor 12:7). It is the Spirit that makes the church a real foretaste of God's reign, the guide and criterion of discerning the Spirit in the realm of history.[1] The identification of God's Spirit in history with human actions, ideologies, and movements must not overlook the fact that sin and error condition every human act. The Orthodox contribution to the Seventh Assembly of the World Council of Churches (1991) warned that "Given the intrinsic ambiguity of history and the awareness that spirits other than the Holy Spirit may act in the world, we must be cautious not to identify in an absolute manner the Holy Spirit with human progress, actions, social movements, and ideologies."[2] Since the reign of God is an outright gift of the Triune God, we must concur that all human actions in themselves are essentially fallible and imperfect. They contain, despite their claims, hidden elements of evil. This awareness shapes the critical task of the church in the life of the world as the power that unmasks and resists all new and old forms of idolatry and false messianic expectations.[3] The mere existence of the church delimits the claims of any present political organization or movement on the life of its members.

The Mission of the Spirit and the Mission of Christ

It is the mission of the Spirit in the world to bring humanity and creation into unity with the crucified and risen Lord, providing, even in this life, a taste of what it means to live in God's kingdom. What the Holy Spirit does must always be seen with what the Son is doing. Both the Spirit and the incarnate logos act differently but not independently in communicating and doing the will of God the Father. The Holy Spirit cannot be separated from the creative and salvific work of Jesus Christ in God's economy, and neither can Christ be understood apart from the Holy Spirit. The Holy Spirit makes the one Christ into many and the many into one. It distributes Christ to all and unites all into Christ, constituting the body of Christ, the church.

The Holy Spirit is presently active in the world—whenever and wherever people of goodwill transcend their self-interests, self-sufficiency, and containment, and build bridges of communion and communication that lead all into a unity which ultimately brings them into the unity of God in Jesus Christ. He is the Spirit of communion that relates all with Christ and

[1] Gennadios Limouris ed., *Come Holy Spirit, Renew the Whole Creation, An Orthodox Approach for the Seventh Assembly of the World Council of Churches, Canberra Australia, 6-12 February 1991* (Brookline, Mass.: Holy Cross Orthodox Press, 1990), 39.
[2] Limouris, 39.
[3] Ibid., 44.

unites all, empowering people to transcend their individuality and become persons. Wherever the Holy Spirit blows, the boundaries of individualism are transcended, and love and communion emerge. Liberation from individualism in the Holy Spirit results in freedom for others in a community.

The Church as Communion

The Holy Spirit is inconceivable without the community of the people of God, which the Spirit assembles and creates. Being the Spirit of Christ (Rom 8: 9–11), the Spirit naturally creates a Christocentric community, the body of Christ. It makes the church the place where creation liberates itself from self-sufficiency and is offered to its creator as being "God's own." In the Eucharist, it is offered to God by the high priest, our Lord Jesus Christ, and is returned to us as eternal life in the body and blood of our Lord. This whole movement takes place through the invocation of the Spirit (*Epiklesis*) and is significantly called communion. The baptized believers, once they have recognized their limitations and been purified by the Holy Spirit, participate through the Eucharist in God's holiness and thus experience within the Eucharist the fullness of their humanity according to God's will and love. Sanctification and holiness transform the human being into a person who sees God, shares God's glory, and relates to the world with the same predispositions of love that God has for the world.

Once we affirm that the Holy Spirit constitutes the disciples of Christ into a community, the church, and its plenitude, how does the Holy Spirit act beyond the visible boundaries of the church? Here, we must categorically state that although the Triune God is actively present in the church, which is the body of Christ and the temple of the Holy Spirit, we cannot limit God's presence and operation to within the boundaries of the church. God is free to operate in the world in multiple—although incomprehensible for finite beings—ways. The Holy Spirit is as unpredictable as the wind that "blows where it chooses, and you hear the sound of it, but you do not know where it comes from or where it goes" (Jn 3:8). The Spirit's presence is apprehended only from the effects of the Spirit's activity. The Holy Spirit opens up the boundaries of whatever the Spirit touches and brings it in relation with the transcended God. It liberates humanity, and creation in general, from all forms of self-sufficiency and "autonomy" vis-à-vis God. As the other paraclete[4] is "everywhere present and fills all things," it leads all into unity with the incarnate logos. While this unity is transparent within

[4] In John 14:16, Jesus speaks of the Holy Spirit as "another paraclete," indicating Jesus is the first and primary paraclete.

the church, the unity of the world outside of the church is of another nature, realized in different degrees. It depends on contextual realities, human predispositions, and receptiveness of cardinal aspects of the Christian gospel. The unity of humanity and creation with Christ becomes real only in the church since it is the body of Christ in history. In other words, there is salvation outside of the church through the church.

The Holy Spirit Brings the Eschaton into History

History and creation are in the process of becoming what God has expected them to be, and already have become, through Christ and the Holy Spirit. They are open entities that find their fulfillment in God's reign. Their self-enclosure and total alienation from God lead them into disintegration and finally into an existential impasse. The Spirit, through Christ, offers the possibility to humanity and the created world to transcend its creaturely limitations and enter into God's glory (Rom 8:20–21). This movement cannot be realized just through human efforts and desires; it is primarily a gift from God and, for this reason, the church invokes the Holy Spirit (*Epiklesis*) because it believes that the world finds its fulfillment, and transcends the limitations of its nature, only in its unity with God. The church, because of its eschatological nature, resists all immanent ideologies—religious, secular, economic, political, cultural, and ethnic—that imprison humanity into the "iron cage of history." It debunks their claim to be comprehensive interpretations of reality and challenges them to be inter-relational and open to a better future from what humans can imagine, based on its eschatological vision. This critical distance from all anthropocentric human ideologies does not in any way mean that the church should not be open and appreciative of the advance of human science and wisdom under, of course, the presupposition that they do not claim for themselves any sense of ultimacy.

It is the mission of the Spirit to bring the eschaton into history. The Spirit, most notably in the Eucharist, makes the church an icon of God's kingdom. It brings the eschaton into history, albeit not permanently until the second coming of Christ. The new creation is present in history but is not yet history. This new creation will be fully realized when God does away with all our afflictions, suffering, and death. This point is clearly made in 2 Corinthians 1:22 and 5:5 and Ephesians 1:13–14 with the term "guarantee." The Spirit is, as it were, a down payment—the "promised Holy Spirit" of greater gifts in the future (Eph 1:13). The Spirit enkindles something of God's new world even in this world, or as Hebrews 6:4-5 puts it, once we taste the power of God's future. This gift of the Spirit is a "pledge" (ἀρραβών) (2 Cor 1:22; 5:5), a "first fruit" or "down payment" (ἀπαρχή) (Rom

8:23) of what God is offering to God's beloved creation. It is the presence of God in the world, driving all creation and history toward their ultimate destiny, disclosed and anticipated, in the resurrection of Jesus Christ. As a result of God's initiative, it is possible to experience God's glory in this life through the power and enlightenment of the Holy Spirit. The life of the baptized believers and their spirit-filled communities continue to live in history, and their lives are affected by all the fragmentation, evil, and corruption that exists in the world.

The new creation by the Spirit is not a flight by faith into heaven, but rather a recognition of the limitations of the world and a commitment to bring to the world the freedom that the Holy Spirit grants from death, corruption, and evil. The eschatological future is strongly determined by a negation of the negative and by an openness to the development of the positive. The negation of the negative is described in Revelation 21:4, God "will wipe away every tear from their eyes. Death will be no more; mourning and crying and pain will be no more." The further development of the positive condition is reflected in the words "they will be his peoples, and God himself will be with them ... And the one who was seated on the throne said, 'See, I am making all things new.'" (Rev 21:3, 5). God has sent God's word and the Holy Spirit to the world as a foretaste and promise of all that is yet to come.

Eucharistic Spirituality

In the Eucharist, baptized believers who are united with Christ through the Holy Spirit and among themselves because of their unity with Christ, constitute communion. It is in the Eucharist that humanity sacramentally experiences and tastes its future according to God's intention. Wolfhart Pannenberg, in his lectures on Christian Spirituality at Yale University (1977), called the churches of the Reformation to supplant their pietistic and revivalist spiritualities and adopt a eucharistic spirituality. In his estimation, such a turn "may prove to be the most important event in Christian spirituality in our time."[5] He critiques the pietistic and revivalist spiritualties for their primary concern with individual salvation, based on his understanding that the "Body of Christ is more than an association of independent individuals." About Christian humanism, he thinks that it operates with the same individualistic proclivities and is less successful than pietistic and revivalist spiritualities to generate loyalty to religious

[5] Wolfhart Pannenberg, *Christian Spirituality* (Louisville, Ky.: Westminster John Knox Press, 1983).

communities and churches. Noting the unquenched thirst and yearning of people for authentic forms of community and social life, and in light of the failure of modern society to satisfy this yearning, he calls for the rediscovery of the Eucharist primarily as a communal event that actualizes in history God's reign.

He suggests that there is no other place or event in the life of the church where the very foundation of its life can be comparably commemorated and symbolized, as well as reenacted, than in the event of celebration and Communion. Every celebration of the Eucharist reenacts the reality that constitutes the foundation of the church, and that happens not only in the sense of memorial but also in the symbolic power of the Eucharist, where the essence of the church itself is alive, present, and effective. This assumption leads him to the conclusion that the Eucharist, not the sermon, is in the center of the church's life. "The sermon should serve, not dominate, in the church. It should serve the presence of Christ which we celebrate in the Eucharist."[6]

The Eucharist is understood primarily as an eschatological and communal event that could liberate Christians from individualism and provide the church with the universal outlook that is inherent in eucharistic experience and embraces society at large, and all humankind.[7] The Eucharist, in its anthropological implications, and because it embraces the destiny of humanity, encourages and inspires political commitment for the sake of peace and justice. Its eschatological nature, however, cannot put on parity such social and political commitment with what the Eucharist symbolizes as an icon of God's kingdom. What the Eucharist symbolizes "by far exceeds whatever social activities it may inspire: Making it subservient to the actualities of political programs [that] pervert it."[8]

Orthodox theologians agree with the basic premises of Wolfhart Pannenberg about the centrality of the Eucharist for the life of the church. The communal nature of the Eucharist (········) and its eschatological orientation express how the gospel of Jesus Christ can be experienced in life by sustaining and transforming relationships and leading all into God's Kingdom through Christ and the Holy Spirit. The church not only preaches the gospel, but it also discloses to the world its ultimate destiny and authentic being as God has intended.

[6] Pannenberg, 40.

[7] Ibid., 46.

[8] Ibid., 47.

The Challenge of Being a Church of Lutheran Confession in the Context of a Religious Market

Nestor Paulo Friedrich

Introduction

My contribution to this reflection has a definite context, a historical moment, and perspective. It is a partial reading, a reading that contemplates only some aspects of the complex moment we are facing as a Lutheran church in the complex Brazilian context, a reality "soaked in religiosity."

The questions that have guided the reflection in our church, the Evangelical Church of the Lutheran Confession in Brazil (IECLB), include the persistent question about Lutheran identity—the challenge of contextualizing its theology. They also include the question of its viability, sustainability, and the continuity of a Lutheran church with a profile and conditionings in a context of a "religious market" that is extremely competitive, fluid, syncretic, emotional, fast-changing, aggressive, polarized, politically instrumentalized, with promises of power, fame, cures, prosperity, and solutions to all problems. The question is how to translate God's message of grace into a social and religious context that is not at all delightful, which is driven by magic, where the human being is the subject, and God the object? From a religious perspective, these are conditions that empty the world of the holiness that God has given, thus condemning people to a meaningless and empty daily life. I can say from experience, this has not been an easy task.

We Live in a Time When Everything Is Very Intense

The biblical word in 1 Corinthians 12:1-14, which guides our reflection for this sub-theme of the consultation, is a challenge. By the way, the Corinthian community is fascinating. It is an active community. There is movement, they are not lacking in gifts (v. 7). They seek Word and knowledge (v. 5). There is no lack of signs of the gifts of the Spirit. There is no shortage of people to help. I would say, there is an ideal community that persuades.

Paul warns, however, not to surrender to what only our eyes and ears perceive. We must go deeper. The Corinthian community is in danger of disintegration; there is rivalry. There are those who want to project themselves on others. Diversity, the hallmark of the Holy Spirit's sovereign action, may be extinguished. The Holy Spirit is identified only in the extraordinary, thus, spiritual quality is denied to others.

The power to experience gifts of the Spirit, when not used in the service of community building but as an instrument of spiritual vanity and pride,[1] results in divisions in communities as feelings of hierarchical spiritual superiority or inferiority set in.[2] The power granted by the Spirit for Christian witness becomes unilateral when absolutized in the sense of power for success in preaching.

According to Uwe Wegner, Paul gives us a paradigm for evaluating the charismatic movement of that period. It gives us "evangelical criteria of evaluation," beginning with an essential evangelical quality of self-criticism. "Paul shows in 1 and 2 Corinthians that even movements as engaging and attractive as the charismatic cannot be idealized except for a high price."[3]

The Brazilian "religious market" has influenced our communities. The media, especially radio and television, have brought religion into the homes. In 1999, the document "The IECLB at the Gates of the New Millennium"[4] was prepared. The document aimed to outline the church's confessional identity and its specific contribution in the search to promote a more dignified and just life. In the year 2000, the document "IECLB in religious pluralism"[5] was released. This document states that "the multi-

---

[1] Rom 12:3; 1 Cor 12:14–25.

[2] 1 Cor 12:15–20; 21–25.

[3] Uwe Wegner, "Sabedoria de Deus, carismáticos e o esvaziamento da cruz de Cristo em Corinto," in *Profecia e Estado, um Tributo a Milton Schwantes*, eds. Carlos A. Dreher and Outros Orgs (São Leopoldo: Oikos, 2006), 345-346.

[4] "IECLB at the Gates of the New Millennium: Manifesto of the Presidency and of the Synod Pastors," 14 March 1999, luteranos.com.br/conteudo/a-ieclb-as-portas-do-novo-milenio-1999.

[5] "IECLB in Religious Pluralism: IECLB Manifesto," 11 June 2000, luteranos.com.br/conteudo/ieclb-no-pluralismo-religioso-2000.

faceted society, in which anything and everything is allowed, also affects our communities. They feel bewildered in a market of religious pluralism. They find it difficult to articulate their confessional identity and no longer realize what unites them. Against the threats of disintegration, they call for redefining the ethics and conduct of community life and re-reading our confessional identity. The questions that arise are: What is the place of the IECLB in a religious plurality? What is our specific contribution to this widespread hunger and thirst for meaning and direction? Today's society, called "postmodern," is becoming multifaceted to the point of provoking crises of identity, disorientation, and loneliness. Desperation arises in the search for the meaning of life, religious experience, and healing of immediate and individual evils.

This document lists the claims that come from the communities. Among them is the concern with the supermarket-church mentality, the lack of greater liturgical uniformity in worship or ceremonies, liturgies which are often not engaging, and difficult hymns. Young people find community life monotonous and outdated. There are communities that criticize the pastor for taking all the symbols (cross, candles, vestments) from the sanctuary. They find it strange when a pastor presides over services without liturgical robes, adopts the typical costume of Pentecostal preachers (suit and tie), and clumsily tries to imitate successful preachers of neo-Pentecostal churches. Members who do not agree with the "pentecostalization" of worship leave the community—either calling attention to their departure or leaving quietly. On many visits to communities, I have heard outbursts such as "I no longer recognize my church." What these claims reveal is that there is a general abandonment of unifying practices, an imposition of practices that hurt confessional consensus, intolerance for different theological emphases, and difficulty understanding theological diversity as a gift to the church.

The clamor that came from the base of the church led to deep reflection about how to face this reality and to articulate a planned, and intentional, way to face it. In 2000, the IECLB's First Missionary Action Plan (PAMI) was prepared, with the central theme "Recreating and creating congregations together. No congregation without a mission. No mission without a congregation!"[6] In 2008, a second version of PAMI was launched, under the theme "God's Mission our Passion."[7] This program continues today. The

[6] "IECLB Missionary Action Plan," 21 October 2000, luteranos.com.br/conteudo_organizacao/planejamento/pami-plano-de-acao-missionaria-2000-2007.

[7] "IECLB Missionary Action Plan," 18 October 2008, luteranos.com.br/conteudo_organizacao/planejamento/pami-plano-de-acao-missionaria-2008-2012.

fruit of this process of reflection led to seven strategic initiatives aimed at strengthening communities:[8]

1. Follow-up Program for Theology Students
2. Follow-up Program for Ministers
3. Program for Strengthening Community Action
4. Ministry Qualification Program (vicariate)
5. Community Action Qualification Program
6. Communication Qualification Program
7. Functional Qualification Program

The challenges, however, do not stop there. Today, we are living through a crisis in our society that manifests itself in a series of conflicts that impact the church. For example, in Brazil (as in many other countries), we are experiencing moments of intense confrontation. There is a high level of religious intolerance (e.g., destruction of Afro-Brazilian religious temples)[9], political corruption and polarization (accusations like "communist" or "capitalist"), pushback against environmental defenders, and discourse about gender ideology undermining gender justice. Signs of xenophobia and race are growing alarmingly; violence increases (femicide, sexual abuse against children, against LGBTQ people); hate is on the rise. There are many conspiracy theories confusing people's minds, even in the church. In this context, the church is pressured to stand and declare which side it is on. Unfortunately, when moral, religious, political or "truth or purity" tests become the norm, the pursuit of peace is subverted by the goal of eliminating those who are different—either eliminating them physically or symbolically (social networks are evidence of symbolic elimination).

According to writer Eliane Brum,[10] the current confrontation in our society is not a confrontation between right and left, developmentalists and ecologists, rulers and oppositionists, macho and feminists. The present confrontation is deeper and more dramatic; it is between people who think and people who don't think. She concludes: "In a country of widespread anti-politics and anti-education like Brazil, we need to move. (...) dialogue is an act of resistance." In this same article Eliane Brum recalls the phi-

[8] "Management Priorities: Taking Good Care of the IECLB," luteranos.com.br/conteudo/prioridades-de-gestao-2.

[9] Gabriele Roza, "Destroying African Religious Sites is the New 'Holy War' in Brazil," *El Pais*, 3 November 2017, https://brasil.elpais.com/brasil/2017/11/03/politica/1509708790_213116.html.

[10] Eliane Brum, "Congratulations, We Have Reached Maximum Stupidity," *El Pais*, 12 November 2015, https://brasil.elpais.com/brasil/2015/11/09/opinion/1447075142_888033.html.

losopher Marcia Tiburi who says that we live in "a void full of ready-made speech. It is not a silent void, open space to seek the other, the unusual, the surprising. But a noisy void, crammed with clichés, repeated and repetitive phrases, used to protect themselves from thought. (...) the constant invocation of God and biblical laws are used as a shield against reflection. Every effort is made not to have any chance of thought, even a tiny good.

We Live in Times that Conspire against the Gospel of Jesus Christ and Hope

"... we proclaim Christ crucified."[11] To the Philippians, Paul writes, "Let the same mind be in you that was in Christ Jesus, who, though he was in the form of God, did not regard equality with God as something to be exploited, but emptied himself, taking the form of a slave ..."[12]

Today, religious narratives contradict the notion of self-emptying. Preaching about social justice, suffering, pain, the passion of Jesus Christ and, in particular, the cross, does not produce good ratings. What counts is the "show of faith," demonstrations of power, fame, etc.

God's grace and mercy confront the market view in which the human being is reduced to the condition of being a consumer. Marketing makes us believe that we are powerful and that we can do everything individually. These are the principal marks of theologies such as prosperity, positive thinking, and entrepreneurship. They are present in the thinking not only of members, but ministers of the church. While the sixteenth century Reformation had a profound impact on society in its different dimensions, religious proposals today have no impact on change in society, rather, they encourage the church to adapt to it. To what extent was the vision of the "Protestants," heirs of the Reformation, to be assimilated by the logic of the market? God's grace confronts us with the question of sin, both individual and structural.

Historian Leandro Karnal[13] suggests that we are living in what is perhaps one of the most religious moments in human history and that, given the current religious framework and customized religion, the greatest challenge for religious ministers today might be to Christianize Christians again. Isn't it time for us to rediscover the subversive power of God's grace and mercy in a bleak, merciless world?

---

[11] 1 Cor 1:23.

[12] Phil 2:5–11.

[13] This refers to a video by Leandro Karnal, "Deus do Séc. XXI: Religião e a Fé Contemporânea", which was originally accessible at youtube.com/watch?v=nKgCo53uHwk

We Live in a Time that Conspires against Communion

The Apostles' Creed defines the church as "the communion of saints." Unfortunately, this concept does not fit the logic of the market. Especially because the current religious market does not seek communion, but customer satisfaction. This logic dominates our religious market. If the business no longer makes a profit, we put it up for sale:

> SELLING POINT / CHURCH WITH 300 FAITHFUL! R$ 80,000.00
>
> Unique opportunity: I'm selling the church with stage, pulpit, sound, drums and keyboard, 200 chairs and 300 churchgoers with good tithers yielding approximately R$ 7,000.00 per month, plus the rent of R$1400! It all depends on your persuasive power! Photos and more info by WhatsApp[14]

Baptist Pastor Karl Kepler, in light of his research on the "neuroses" of the Evangelical churches, asks, "Why does an institution that could be therapeutic, help to get sick, and why do so many people approaching them get frustrated after a while?"[15] In the book titled *Wounded in the Name of God*, journalist Marilia de Camargo César is no less inditing. She reports cases of spiritual abuse. According to this journalist, "it was not easy to see so many lives shaken precisely in a place that should be synonymous with protection and solidarity: the church of Jesus Christ."[16]

In a world lacking in affection, in human relations, and in safe space, communion and community become miracles given to us by the Holy Spirit in the person of Jesus and the offering he makes us.

The Holy Spirit Makes History

In a fluid context where everything must be immediate, a collective memory that celebrates significant moments of history enables us to rework this memory, re-signify values, update the message and create the sense of community–the "we."

[14] "Vendu ponto/Igreja montada com 300 fieis," 18 May [n.y.], https://me.me/i/vendu-ponto-igreja-montada-com-300-fieis-r-80-000-18-maio-5210269.

[15] Karl Kepler, *Neuroses eclesiásticas e o evangelho para os crentes* (São Paulo: Arte Editorial, 2009), 20–22.

[16] Marília de Camargo César, *Feridos em nome de Deus* (São Paulo: Mundo Cristão, 2009), 15.

The 500th anniversary of the Reformation made it possible to dive back into history and rescue it in a variety of ways including comic books, lectures, theaters, concerts, church days, and special celebrations. It was striking to re-tell this story, recount the work of the Holy Spirit, and rediscover how the gospel freed us from a reality of fear and oppression. It rescued self-esteem. It released us, and that was significant. The symbolic burden of this remembering and celebrating made us look at the past and the present, with a view to the future.

The commemoration of the Reformation makes us realize how the Holy Spirit has acted in our own historical trajectory. Pastor and historian Martin Dreher wrote:

> The history of the IECLB is closely related to the misery to which many European populations were subjected throughout the nineteenth century. ... The nineteenth-century Europe expelled its sons and daughters. ... Germans, Swiss, Dutch, Danes, Norwegians, Swedes, Austrians, Italians, Poles, Spanish Russians, Portuguese and many more migrate to Brazil. Among them are many Protestants: Lutherans, United, Reformed, Waldensians, Anabaptists. Many of them would later form the IECLB. Here we have one of the first characteristics of this Church: a plurality of forms of expression of piety. Its Lutheranism is the result of concessions and discussions, but also of the coexistence and growth of its bases: the communities[17].

This church that is rising brings religiously, economically, politically, and ethnically marginalized groups together in one body. It is a church that lives its life of faith on the fringes of Brazilian society. It represents a Christian presence from the perspective of reform. This is different from the Roman Catholic tradition which was hegemonic in Brazil. This presence came with some tension and difficulties.

The Lutheran presence, despite its marginality, contributed to the slow and lengthy process of establishing religious freedom and a pluralistic society. The first struggles were to secure the right to bury their members with dignity, recognize their marriages, celebrate their faith freely, and be recognized as citizens.

The IECLB community in São Luís do Maranhão, in the northern of Brazil, which emerged in late 2005, was made up of people from different churches, including Pentecostal churches and people without religion. The nameplate of the community on the sanctuary wall reads "IECLB: present in Brazil since 1824" (1824 marks the date of the arrival of the first immigrants in Brazil and the beginning of the Lutheran presence in this country). The IECLB is not "another new" church.

[17] Martin Dreher, *História do Povo Luterano* (São Leopoldo: Editora Sinodal, 2005), 49–50.

The IECLB understands that its mission is to propagate the gospel of Jesus Christ, which unites, includes, and configures different interactions of human living. Living the gospel begins with an open community of faith engaging in dialogue between the Word (the gospel) and its context, and which seeks the liberation and transformation of its society. The utopic vision that challenges and motivates this community is to "be recognized as a church of attractive, inclusive and missionary communities that act in faithfulness to the gospel of Jesus Christ, standing out for the witness of God's love, for the service for human dignity and respect for creation."

Faith in the crucified Christ is an exercise in citizenship. Affirming the grace and mercy of God is foolishness to those who serve, or adapt to the market culture that reduces human beings to mere consumers. It is no coincidence that costly concepts that are central to reform, such as freedom, grace, and mercy, are suppressed. They go against the logic of the reigning religious market. In the face of polarization, fundamentalism, and religious intolerance, we must ask if can we sustain God's compassion revealed in Jesus Christ, especially toward people who do not deserve it, according to our theological prejudices? Are there boundaries to God's compassion and mercy?[18] The answer is, no! There are no boundaries to God's compassion. How then can we justify the religious and sociocultural constructions that deepen processes of exclusion, including by Lutheran "brothers and sisters?"

The celebration of the 500th anniversary of the Reformation made us realize that although we are numerically a minority church, our witness to faith and community life is extremely rich. Our church sustains a huge range of work (including "child mission," women, men, youth, people with special needs, justice and gender, training, schools, pastoral care, Indigenous, education, hospital, and seniors). In the area of diakonia, there is formation, reflection, and the promotion of justice and dignified life. The marks of this community that resist the logic of the religious market, express its life of faith and witness:

We have spirituality with our "feet on the ground." We are not excluded because we are divorced, remarried, drugged or imprisoned. (...) We are actors, we are not secondary characters. (...) At the center of the preaching is the crucified Christ! Our community has experienced that the life of faith is not exclusively a success, but joy despite suffering, such as the loss of a child to death, to drugs, the suffering of the husband, the suffering to parents, children, job loss. The discovery that we are contradictory (*simul iustus et peccator*) is not eliminated with delight (shows, buzzwords or magical conversion) and is not exorcised with buzzwords but gestures

---

[18] Mk 9:11, 13; Lk 15:11-32; Acts 10, 11:1-18; 1 Cor 7: 12-14; Gal 3: 27-28.

in the community. At the center of the gospel is the crucified and risen Christ. In him we see where God looks (Matthew 25) and learn to change the direction of our glance. This generates communion that expresses signs of the Kingdom."[19]

Testimonials like this are key. They inspire, encourage and set the standard for discerning the spirits of the age. They help us to not give in too quickly, without critical evaluation, to recipes of success that do not strengthen the fundamental mark of Lutheran faith: the community experience, "the communion of saints."

We confess that the church is a being of the Word. But what moves us is the continuity of an inherited religious tradition, the visible, institutional church. We are a church backed by Teuto-Brazilian immigration and migration with specific brands. What are the challenges today in this context? IECLB Secretary of Mission, Pastor Pedro Puentes,[20] synthesizes some of the many issues to be addressed for the mission which God has entrusted to us as the reforming church:

- What metaphors will put the text (the Word as law and the gospel) and the context (reality) into fruitful and transformative dialogue, so that the gospel message of justification by grace and faith does not lose its transforming force?

- The post-Pentecostal religious world has changed the cause of sin from personal transgression to the action of spiritual entities. Changing speech also changes the rite bound to it. Consequently, we have moved from confession and regret to moments of rituals employing herbal baths, prayers, and others to rid a person of evil spirits or supernatural entities, as well as ridding a person of deleterious energies. How does this impact religious practice? How do we deal with guilt, sin, and forgiveness that comes from God's love for every human being in Jesus Christ, from a liberating, transformative perspective?

- How can we be a church of communities in a hedonistic, individualistic, and consumerist society, where everything is ephemeral and disposable, in which people feel free for an uncompromising, transient, emotion- and environment-dependent participation?

[19] Norberto Dreher, *Comunidade Jovem, Igreja Viva* - Palestra proferida no encontro da Presidência da IECLB com Pastores e Pastoras Sinodais, 2012.
[20] Pedro Puentes, IECLB e Missão Pós-Fórum, palestra apresentada na consulta com Igreja Evangélica Luterana na Baviera, 2017, 8.

- How can we talk about grace that dignifies, creates belonging to the community of Jesus Christ, and frees through the exercise of love of neighbor, in a context in which people value the merits measured by productivity and consumption?
- How can we talk about the God who incarnates and embraces all humanity and creation in a society in which the current economic and theological models insist on labelling people and life forms as superfluous and disposable?

The Lutheran Charm

The initiative of this LWF global consultation is extremely timely. As LWF member churches in Latin America and the Caribbean (LAC), we are encouraging our shared journey, as well as strengthening the link with the global Lutheran communion at the LAC Leadership Conference. We realize that we can no longer afford to live in isolation. We need to add efforts, faith experiences, capabilities, gifts, and resources, including financial resources. We realize that, at this time, our common challenge is "theological education and formation" at all levels. This theme comes up strongly when we ask ourselves about the mission of the Lutheran churches in the Latin American and Caribbean context. In this context, those who do not have a clear mission project, clarity of identity, clearly defined theology, minimally organized organizational structure, and planning will become increasingly fragile and the mission will be affected. Goodwill, tradition, and history are no longer enough.

In conclusion, I share a word that has always inspired me. Former IECLB President Gottfried Bakemeier, who served as LWF President from 1990 to 1997, in an assessment of "The Feasibility of the Evangelical Church of Lutheran Confession in Brazil (IECLB) - Critical Notes"[21] writes:

> For all these reasons I want to encourage you to (re-) discover the charm of the Lutheran confession. Its charm is not limited to some dogmas and axioms of faith. It concerns a way of being. They reside in biblical hermeneutics that can distinguish between letter and spirit; an anthropological realism that refuses to deify or demonize the human being; a compromised freedom that distances itself from both legalism and permissiveness; in a participatory ecclesial structure that excludes human hierarchy of any kind. The Lutheran confession invites me to faith

[21] Gottfried Brakemeier, "The Viability of the IECLB: Critical Notes," 21 June 2007, luteranos.com.br/conteudo/a-viabilidade-da-ieclb-apontamentos-criticos.

without prohibiting critical reasoning. It asks for "thinking believers," people who know how to judge things, and yet don't remain stuck in criticism. Lutheranism has taught me a certain view of reality that is a little more complicated than many oversimplifications are able to make us believe. To subdivide the world into bandits and good guys, winners and losers, gullible and unbelieving, righteous and sinful. Well, this is the theory of hypocrites or naive ones. It is stupid to oppose the wisdom of the gospel.

Coordinated Formation: Reconnecting through the Active Faith of Children

Christopher Lee McDonald

Introduction

We face a crisis with children on the West Coast of Canada: fewer and fewer are present in our congregations. There may be many ways to explain their absence, but the significance of this loss becomes most apparent when we attend to our physical practices. The need for this approach is obvious, once we acknowledge the social and corporeal requisites necessary for becoming persons. None of us has ever come out of the womb as Cartesian egos, articulate and able to express ourselves as coherent individuals. Some would clarify that we do not enter the world able to do much of anything other than grasp with assistance toward a kind of "joint attention."[1] In other words, we need caregivers and social interaction to become fully human.[2] Likewise, research shows us that close bodily contact is a necessary precursor to any form of human selfhood.[3] As Alison Gopnik articulates the matter, babies are "born knowing that particular facial expressions reflect

[1] Charles Taylor, *The Language Animal: The Full Shape of the Human Linguistic Capacity* (Cambridge, Mass.: Belknap Press, 2016), 66–67.
[2] Stanley I. Greenspan and Stuart G. Shanker, *The First Idea: How Symbols, Language, and Intelligence Evolved from Our Primate Ancestors to Modern Humans* (Cambridge, Mass.: Da Capo Press, 2004), 34–36.
[3] Alison Gopnik, *The Philosophical Baby: What Children's Minds Tell Us About Truth, Love, and the Meaning of Life* (New York: Picador, 2010), 205–209. As she clarifies, "Empathy is intertwined with attachment. It emerges first in intimate face-to-face interactions between babies and the people they love," 208.

particular kinesthetic feelings," and this means that we are primed from birth to link our own physical experiences with those of others.[4] In other words, our social reality is also physical. For these reasons, it seems that we cannot expect to understand, let alone diagnose, the loss of children in our midst, without considering bodies. The corporeal dimension is constitutive of our sociality, and we need to attend to this side of life to reason well about communal crises. In the case of the church, to think correctly about our social, spiritual constitution, especially the loss of those members most sensitive to the affective significance of our movements, we must attend to the bodily dimension of worship, the center from which all Christian work moves.

With this in mind, I have opted to articulate the tragedy of Canadian Lutheran childhood in terms of sedentary bodies.[5] Many who continue to participate in mainline congregations feel helpless to address the problem of children in church. However, those most resistant to the decline tend to be willing to let children have fuller play in the sacred space of the sanctuary.[6] I take from their lead a couple ideas. First, the decline of our churches maps well onto the waning brio in our congregations. Our bodies are becoming inert as we age and lose mobility. At the same time this loss of movement leads us to rely on sedentary practices that reinforce this spiritual ossification. Indeed, we are not just composed of sedentary bodies; we are becoming a sedentary corporate body as well. Second, the way forward is to attend to this sedentary behavior, to develop language that can express the tragedy with appropriate empathy and sensitivity.

I hope to do so both descriptively and analytically. At the descriptive level, I aim to depict the kinds of physical postures that populate our worship services, to provide an image of what it looks like when we join together in praising God. For the sake of time, three practices will occupy my reflections–singing, sitting, and communing. In each case, I will offer descriptions of the outward appearance and coordinate these with phenomenological articulations of what it can be like to participate in these ways.

[4] Gopnik, 205.

[5] When I say "Canadian," I acknowledge the many commonalities that can be seen in broadly white, Western societies, especially in mainline contexts. However, I must limit my analysis to a western Canadian context for the sake of space and accuracy. This paper reflects my local experiences, even though I have seen them mirrored in churches from Oberbalm, Switzerland, to Durham, North Carolina, in the USA.

[6] I want to draw attention to some key names who have embodied this strategy on one level or another: Rob Crosby-Shearer at The Abbey Church (abbeychurch.ca/about), Aneeta Saroop at St. Mary's Metchosin (stmarysmetchosin.ca), and Lyle McKenzie and Lyndon Sayers at Lutheran Church of the Cross (lutheranvictoria.ca/about).

These accounts are not exhaustive by any means, but I intend to capture the spirit of how Lutheran bodies tend to move and experience the space of worship in western Canada.

At the second level, I will move to an analytic account of sedentary bodies and the solution we find in children. The purpose at this point is to provide a cohesive explanation for sedentary worship, what our practices of singing, sitting, and communing all share in common. In particular, it seems to me that our present crisis exposes an old dualism between cerebral and bodily modes of communication. We have become sedentary insofar as we "buffer" ourselves from one another and retreat into our minds. It just so happens that children can resist this tendency because of their cognitive immaturity. It is too much of a strain for them to maintain such an intellectual form of attention. Hence, should we take children seriously in our midst, their corporeal presence can become a resource for liberating us from sedentary practices.

The question that follows is what it looks like to take children seriously. What are some concrete, practical ways forward, given the need to move forward with sensitivity? I want to suggest that we need not disrupt our whole service to incorporate children into our worship. Rather, we can take small steps with the areas in our liturgy most open to change. In particular, we can begin to shift the way we use the "Children's Sermon." Instead of relying on entertainment to carry us through, we can use this time to coordinate the whole congregation bodily, to join our attention together around children. It just might happen that these practices will begin to filter into the rest of our church life. Indeed, the hope is that learning how to incorporate little ones into our liturgy at such key moments will liberate us to worship with one voice again.

Singing

First of all, we Lutherans sing. Hymns and liturgical songs punctuate the service from entrance to closing, and it is clear that they function as a way for members to participate in the theological pattern of the Sunday. The minister often selects (or is involved in selecting) these songs to accent the theme of the day, and this process speaks to the hidden conversation one discovers when working with a liturgical calendar. While patterns are visible in the abstract, song manages to draw us into concrete participation. Hymns are intended to be instruments of physical coordination that bring us into a broader theological service of worship.[7] In a way, they help us to focus our attention on God with one voice.[8]

With such a powerful vehicle of worship, one would think Lutheran churches should be lively, physical places of participation in the adoration of Jesus. And yet, our voices do not coordinate well. Depending on the service, one typically hears a lopsided vocalization. Members in the choir (should there be one) typically sing louder than the rest. With a majority of members being elderly (typically sixty years or older), the rest cannot participate with much volume. There are pockets of bold voices situated around the sanctuary, but the number of people remaining silent can easily outnumber those singing during any given hymn.

To understand how this can be, we must look to the visual cues that characterize participation in hymnody. When people sing, they tend to look down toward their hymnals, scanning the lines so as to keep up with the music.[9] The majority stand slightly hunched with blank faces or furrowed brows. Whether members move their lips or not, they typically remain still, focused on the page before them. Most appear to be uncomfortable with singing, possibly because the musical notation takes too much effort to figure out, and this discomfort shows in their posture and faces. It is similar to the way a choir looks when they are first learning a piece of difficult music. The coordination takes practice, and sight-reading tends to lock them into

---

[7] One may consider Jerome Bruner's summary of Hilary Putnam's position on reference in *Child's Talk: Learning to Use Language* (New York: W. W. Norton & Company, 1983). As Bruner clarifies, "Achieving the *goal* of referring has little to do with agreement about a singular definite referent. It is enough that the parties to a referential exchange know they share enough overlap in their focal attention to make it worthwhile continuing, as Werner Deutsch and Tom Pechmann have noted," 68. The significance of this understanding of reference for worship is that song can direct our attention toward God by establishing sufficient overlap in our focal attention. It is not quite the same as binary conversation in which one partner exchanges in referring to a particular topic. Rather, it draws us into a kind of "joint attention" that can become the condition for further exchange. Perhaps this relates to Robert N. Bellah's suggestions on ritual and language in his magnum opus, *Religion in Human Evolution: From the Paleolithic to the Axial Age* (Cambridge, Mass.: Belknap Press, 2011), 109–116.

[8] "With one voice" functions here as a homage to the North American Lutheran hymnal, *With One Voice* (Minneapolis: Augsburg Fortress Press, 1995).

[9] Some have addressed this problem by installing projector screens on which to show the words and music. This solution has allowed some congregations to wean themselves off a downward orientation toward a book. We see this for example at Peace Lutheran Church in Abbotsford, British Columbia. The solution meets with some success, but there are limitations when this approach is not coordinated with children.

rigid positions full of tension. Clearly, the difficulty of hymnody is part of what complicates physical participation in singing together.

From this description of hymnody, we can discern a couple things. First, it is difficult to coordinate our voices because many do not sing at all. Mouthing the words of a hymn can be an important form of participation for some, but it becomes problematic when more than just a few take part in this way. The loss of volume is painfully apparent, and the disproportionality of vocalization tends to isolate members from one another. Unlike in a choir when one feels the resonance of the rest and thereby can enter into that ambiance with one's voice, the experience becomes that of painful dislocation from others: Either I feel my voice and no one else's, or I feel someone else's voice but not my own.

Second, this loss of vocal mutuality shows up in a series of concomitant bodily tendencies, like rigidity and stooping, which reinforce this lack of coordination. For the majority who lack vocal training, part of the "pain" of dislocated singing is how the process can begin to feel like hard work. The voice cannot blend into a series of other voices as easily because it takes focused effort to feel like one is singing at all.[10] It is the felt isolation from other voices that leads to this pattern of tension in less experienced voices. Some begin to force the sound by tensing the neck and muscling the high notes. Reaching higher pitches becomes a chore, and any pleasure of nestling one's voice into a common thread of sound wanes with the duration of the exercise. Now one's attention has shifted to the physical act of maintaining sound through the verses of the hymn. This shift of focus, in turn, reinforces the felt isolation from others by turning one's act of singing into a kind of performance before an audience. Making a mistake starts to feel insufferably conspicuous because one starts to think about the mechanics of singing rather than the song. Not all may experience the same bodily pressures, especially given the range of registers and vocal abilities in a given community, but the tension visible in how members stoop or grip their hymnals suggests that our singing economy leads to this sort of feedback loop of incoordination.

[10] It may be worth considering here the work of Nathan McDonald, a vocal pedagogue and professional singer in Victoria, British Columbia. One of the questions he asks his students is what the difference is between singing and speaking. Anatomically speaking, they are essentially equivalent, and yet they feel different for us. Nathan locates this difference on the affective planes of the two activities. Singing is more intimate than speaking; it draws us into a closer kind of social space, one that feels particularly vulnerable for most of us.

Sitting

Despite the physical prominence of singing in worship, it is worth noting the way we sit in service as well, because of the "sedentary" pattern of thinking it betrays. In particular, we should note our dependence on the technology of the pew. While sitting need not be problematic for worship—for example, bodily stillness can facilitate adoration and meditation if cultivated in the right way—certain forms of sitting can become an impediment to congregational coordination. We Lutherans on the West Coast of Canada see the problem of the pew and the kind of sitting it cultivates in three ways.

First, the pew has become an impediment to postures other than sitting or standing. Kneeling was a possibility for congregations that developed pews with kneelers, but these have become instruments of the past, either ignored or removed entirely in western Canada. Accordingly, the range of motion available to congregants is severely limited. There is no room for maneuvering from side to side, let alone for exploring the room with one's body. Should anyone need to move more often, especially small children, the experience can be agonizing and claustrophobic. Likewise, should there be a time for coordinating our movements as a community, chairs and pews become awkward barriers that cut us off from one another.

Second, this limitation of posture produces inordinate stress on the quality of worship as performance. When the sermon falters, we notice. When the prayers drone on too long, we suffer through them. When the readers stumble, we judge their execution. This phenomenon of negative attention is related to the way seats encourage us to be a passive audience, a result that echoes the complaints of our Eastern sister churches.[11] In our passivity, we require enough stimulus to carry us through the service. Participation diminishes precisely because we cannot step into the flow of a sermon, reading, or prayer without interrupting it. Indeed, what we commonly intuit in the West to be a kind of problematic power dynamic of preacher over congregation is much closer to a lone voice striving to hold the attention of a fickle public. There is a reason the most successful preachers tend to rely on comedy.

Third, without bodily modes of participation—for example, without some kind of call-and-response dialogue as one might find in the sermons of charismatic churches—our seated disposition becomes cerebral. The flip side of participating in the service as an audience is taking part as thinkers rather than as "pray-ers." In a way, the pew has become for us something closer to a student's chair at a lecture. It facilitates an extended form of

---

[11] See Fr George Lardas, "On the Christian Life: On Chairs in Church," February 2015, stnicholasstratford.org/article_feb2015_chairs.

attention that removes the body from consideration, allowing us to think freely in relation to the sermon, readings, and prayers. This pedagogical aesthetic is not inherently antagonistic to worship, especially given the associations between prayer and theory in Western thinkers like Anselm of Canterbury, Thomas Aquinas, and John Calvin, but most are unable to experience, let alone appreciate, such nuances without a fair amount of theological training. Indeed, without learning how to pray in contemplation, the practice of sitting too easily becomes a sedentary habit prone to distraction or boredom. How many of us, after all, actually recall the sermon?

Communing

Finally, we come to the practice that is in some ways still the furthest from being sedentary for us: Communion or Eucharist. During this practice, a fuller range of movement accompanies the process. While seated, we can sing or remain silent in prayer. When the usher summons us from the pew or row, we rise and line up to receive bread and wine. In some contexts, the baptismal font stands near the altar for members to touch the water and remember their baptisms. A few make the sign of the cross with the water. Most walk by. Nonetheless, during the climax of the progression, nearly everyone cups their hands open to receive the bread. And though not all drink from the common cup, the majority receive wine as well. In other words, we see in this practice a ritual choreography that allows members to enter the space more fully: to walk, to follow, to sing, and to pray with coordinated autonomy.

At the same time, signs of sedentary bodies are visible even in this most robust of practices. Isolation is not particularly apparent, but a lack of semantic coordination accompanies the exercise. Immobility and aging populations are not the problem here. Rather, as with the other forms of Lutheran embodiment in worship–singing and sitting–members struggle to coordinate their movements with spiritual significance. The reigning habits of our broader secular society–habits like lining up, taking turns, or avoiding eye contact–still govern and dominate the unsaid rules of engagement. Anyone can participate in a way, so long as they follow the cues of others and try not to budge in line.[12] On a certain level, this is a

[12] On one occasion at Church of the Cross, guest participants in worship went up to Communion ahead of others, essentially "budging" in line. While doing so did not fully disrupt the process, it was not clear how the congregation should treat this "intrusion." Everyone ignored it at the time, but it was difficult not to feel like they were intruding and messing up something sacred. To leave the matter there, however,

strength of the process.[13] However, this mode of participation does not coordinate us semantically. That is to say, we do not have a common theological language in our movements, and this linguistic absence is visible and has consequences for our participation.

First, the absence shows up in the way the majority stand still during the words of institution. It is rather tedious to maintain an upright posture without a concrete way to participate in the drama of Christ's words to the disciples. When the minister breaks the bread and lifts the cup, the congregation simply stands. It is easy during this time to drift in and out of attention as the words move us into Holy Communion. Such lack of movement contrasts greatly with Eastern Orthodox traditions, in which the sign of the cross accompanies every Trinitarian utterance, and a chorus of bowing meets the elements.[14] Compared to the preponderance of bodily signification available to these Orthodox congregations, we Lutherans are limited to standing without really knowing any better.

Second, this semantic absence in our movements leads most of us to participate thoughtlessly. Many simply do not think to make the sign of the cross or why it might be beneficial to make signs with our bodies when worshiping. Even should we wish to participate more intimately in the practice, we do not register the possibility that movement might help facilitate the process. Indeed, what the practice of Eucharist shows us is that we are physically mute, capable of only the most quotidian movements besides chewing.[15]

---

is to lose out on a moment for deep theological reflection. Guests should be given latitude, surely, but there is also a sense in which the practice of Communion and taking turns in an orderly manner is part of the Christian witness and participation in Jesus Immanuel. Hence, to forgive the act is also to consider prayerfully how this sacred context of respect for Christ's presence with us can be enhanced through the intrusion. Perhaps there is even a sense in which we should celebrate it?

[13] We are able to invite anyone who enters to participate with us in Communion. There are theological disagreements on this point among us, but we need not dismiss the result as a bodily inhibition. Please see the preceding footnote for further reflection on this point.

[14] I attended a Russian Orthodox church in Langley, British Columbia, for a year (St. Herman of Alaska). During this time, I came to see how linguistically articulate the bodies of worshipers could be. Even children showed adroit capacity to kiss icons, bow, and gesticulate.

[15] Here I have in mind the fact that chewing can be a profoundly spiritual practice. Unfortunately, we do not have children asking the question, "How should we chew Jesus?" My father grew up Roman Catholic, and this was one of the questions he thought about during his first Communion. Our failure to ask this sort of question reveals that we do not really experience the Eucharist bodily. What we do with our bodies does not matter, even though we are so intimately communing with the presence of Christ. For Luther, the body mattered. Why then does it not for us?

Sedentary bodies

In summary, our physicality in worship is in jeopardy. When singing, the difficulties of the music and our preoccupation with the hymnal cultivate cautious rigidity in our bodies. Many remain silent, while others struggle on to fill the space with a voice. Accordingly, the song no longer operates as a vehicle to coordinate our voices into a seamless word of praise. Instead, it has become closer to a chore, an exercise less about enhancing our participation in worship and more about ticking the boxes on a theological rubric. Likewise, pews and chairs have become impediments to our bodies. The range of motions possible narrows to sitting or standing, and it is these passive postures that place undue stress on performance and memory. When the minister falters, we notice, but we struggle to remember the lesson. Finally, we face the fracturing of our holy conversation with God in the most robust of bodily practices: Communion. Even in this ritual we are limited because of a linguistic absence. There is virtually no semantic depth to our movements beyond the secular gestures we use to line up, take turns, or avoid prolonged eye contact. It is this absence of spiritual meaning in our movements that reveals to us the presence of sedentary behavior.

To understand why sedentary bodies are so problematic, however, we must dig a little deeper. Discomfort while singing and the tedium of vacillating between sitting and standing does not necessarily explain why the bodily dimension of our worship is breaking down. What do the tensions visible in our singing, the cerebral quality of our sitting, and the semantic absence in our communing all have in common? The answer is deceptively simple–a split between the cerebral and bodily modes of communication.

Many Western scholars would correctly see in this answer an implicit critique of the Enlightenment. As Charles Taylor would suggest, separating the intellect from the body is but one symptom among many of the cultural instrumentalism that runs from Descartes onward.[16] The idea

[16] Taylor, *The Language Animal*, 163–164: "But captivity in distorting pictures is of relevance not only in (bad) philosophy; it also has social and political importance. Certain structuring metaphors have acquired ascendancy in our civilization, which if taken alone will blind us to what is inhuman and destructive in our behavior. Lakoff and Johnson cite the schema 'Time is a Resource': time is something to be used, managed, not 'wasted', and employed to maximum effect. Such an ontology of time, which comes down to us partly through an important theme of Puritan preaching, has become central to our capitalist civilization which privileges instrument rationality. This schema can be extended into the structuring idea that 'Time Is Money'. Under the pressure of this dominant frame, even leisure time becomes a resource, to be used 'to maximum effect' (to recover from labor, to attain maximum enjoyment, to prepare ourselves to work better after the holidays).

that mind and body are two distinct substances goes much further back in some ways (cf. Plato), but the Enlightenment takes this creed to another level by coupling it with a technological, objectifying view of the world.[17] It is the mechanistic image of the body, the notion that we can understand our bodies best as biological machines, that does the damage here.[18] By

---

There is a truth to all this, a truth which has come to be in our civilization; but what this frame can do is occlude other ways of relating to time, devalue them, make them disappear for many people. And this cramps and distorts our lives."

[17] Charles Taylor, *Sources of the Self: The Making of the Modern Identity* (Cambridge, Mass.: Harvard University Press, 1989), 145: "For Descartes, in contrast, there is no such order of Ideas to turn to, and understanding physical reality in terms of such is precisely a paradigm example of the confusion between the soul and the material we must free ourselves from. Coming to a full realization of one's being as immaterial involves perceiving distinctly the ontological cleft between the two, and this involves grasping the material world as mere extension. The material world here includes the body and coming to see the real distinction requires that we disengage from our usual embodied perspective, within which the ordinary person tends to see the objects around him as really qualified by colour or sweetness or heat, tends to think of the pain or tickle as in his tooth or foot. We have to objectify the world, including our own bodies, and that means to come to see them mechanistically and functionally, in the same way that an uninvolved external observer would." Cf. 146: "But this involves more than just the rejection of the traditional ontology; it also does violence to our ordinary, embodied way of experiencing. We have to disengage ourselves from this, for Descartes, irremediably confused and obscure way of grasping things. To bring this whole domain of sensations and sensible properties to clarity means to grasp it as an external observer would, tracing the causal connection between states of the world or my body, described in primary properties, and the 'ideas' they occasion in my mind. Clarity and distinctness require that we step outside ourselves and take a disengaged perspective."

[18] Consider also Greenspan's and Shanker's account of emotions in Descartes: "Descartes viewed emotions as *complex reflexes* that are triggered by internal and/or external stimuli. He believed they consisted of distinctive bodily processes and sensations and are associated with characteristic behaviors and stereotypical facial expressions. In the modern version of this argument, a 'basic' emotion is defined as a complex process consisting of neural, neuromuscular/expressive, and experiential aspects. To qualify as 'basic,' the emotion must be associated with a distinctive facial expression; with certain body movements and postures; with distinctive vocalizations, changes of voice, tone, rhythm, prosody, and stress; and with distinctive sensations and chemical changes in the body.... The emotional responses are treated as a composite form of reflex; namely, a stimulus triggers a neural program that controls a neuromuscular/expressive, autonomic, behavioral, and experiential sequence of events. The essential difference between emotions and reflexes proper is thus seen as a matter of complexity, that is, of how many different elements are coordinated. Hence emotional reactions are, as Descartes

separating body from mind in this way, we have insulated ourselves as thinkers from the rest of the world, including the meanings that inhere in the faces we meet. Charles Taylor describes this state of affairs in terms of the "buffered self," a phrase that depicts the way modern selves resist enchanted perceptions of the cosmos.[19] Much work has gone into resisting this objectifying view of the world from the Romantic era onward, and we have important voices to situate this critique in figures as diverse as Edith Stein, Dietrich Bonhoeffer, and Emmanuel Levinas. Nonetheless, this view of the world has a complicated hold on how we imagine the world. In particular, though we may disagree with the ethical implications of objectification, our sedentary postures in worship reveal a tacit assent to the aesthetic logic of Enlightenment rationalism.[20]

---

argued, unconscious and involuntary, because, like other 'automatic actions,' they operate at a neural/physiological level that is 'beneath the threshold' of introspection and conscious planning," 44–45. To summarize the issue: "emotions constitute the animal side of human behavior: the innate feelings, moods, and mental states that are involuntary and automatic. Reason resides in a completely separate realm of the mind: the part that is independent from emotions, and that, one hopes, comes to govern them," 43. Clearly, the problem with this account of affect and emotions is that they are treated as biomechanically determined stimulus responses. By doing so, one has forfeited entirely the social dimension that invests our affective horizons with significance and meaning. In other words, according to the Cartesian cerebral aesthetic, we are automatons insofar as we feel, and we are human insofar as we rid ourselves of feeling.

[19] Here I have in mind Charles Taylor's arguments about secularity and buffered identities in *A Secular Age* (Cambridge, Mass.: Belknap Press, 2007).

[20] By "aesthetic logic," I have in mind a theory I developed regarding "aesthetic heuristics" in my master's thesis on John Calvin. The major idea is that there are certain aesthetic contours to one's language that can be seen in terminological preferences. By attending to the positive and negative valences of certain habits of description or articulation, one can extrapolate patterns of preference that are both aesthetic and heuristic: namely, they pertain to what one finds beautiful or disgusting in a way that is implicit. In other words, they are basic to the ways we intuit and think through what matters most to us. We can see such terminological patterns arising in many forms of discourse, but they are particularly pertinent in charged discourses (i.e., political, religious, etc.). Essentially, aesthetic heuristics help us to navigate a world of serious conversations without getting bogged down in specifics. At the same time, they can become impediments to empathy by leading us to resist terminological patterns prematurely. We cannot possibly think through the full polysemic range of another's discourse, but reacting with disgust toward certain ways of speaking can also get in the way of understanding. The difficulty is maintaining an open mind while at the same time recognizing the full weight of what is at stake. At this point, I am still working out the theoretical connection between this linguistic horizon of aesthetics and the more tacit, bodily dimensions

Take for example the practice of singing described above. The instrumental body shows up in the way it feels to sing when isolated from others, and we see this disconnection at two levels. First, our bodies cannot harmonize with the semantic contours of the song because of its musical difficulty. What musicians typically take a long time to master—i.e., the coordination of their emotional inflections with the themes and meanings in a given piece—becomes a task to solve with each hymn. The difficulty takes us out of our bodies into a cerebral space of attention. We fail to feel the language of the song, the significance of each line as one follows on the other, because we cannot inhabit the music outside of our minds, outside of a kind of mental effort. That is to say, the task of the song becomes something we experience intellectually, leading us to be in our heads as opposed to in the music. The process becomes inescapably cerebral, if not also boring.

The communal result is an emotively flat engagement that stifles the kind of participation that can effectively coordinate individuals. Notice how the second disconnection follows from the first. The monotone experience of singing while straining removes us from inhabiting the song bodily. We cannot step into the music to move with the meaning of the hymn. Instead, we enter into the mental space of Descartes's *cogito*, which simultaneously buffers us from the presence of others. In the cerebral realm, the play of bodily accents and gestures becomes a distant dialogue. Because we cannot simply be in our own bodies, we cannot enter into the dynamic conversation that gatherings require to coordinate attention. Many of us do not think of the problem in this way, mostly because we experience the process as just another tedious activity, but the boredom of doing something difficult is actually symptomatic of our disconnection. We cannot join together in the common activity of singing because the task is too complicated for the music to be "mutually manifest."[21] Essentially, the lack of musical fluency in our congregations leads to a kind of disjointed attention, precisely the sort of discoordination that alienates children from participating.

---

of aesthetic preference. However, there seems to be some clear evidence in Greenspan's and Shanker's work that co-regulation of emotions leads to the possibility of symbol and language, meaning that though aesthetic heuristics may be most visible in our language, they are actually rooted in our bodily socialization. Hence, the bodily ways we gather can reveal quite substantially our aesthetic crutches, whether we agree with them in theory or not.

[21] Taylor, *The Language Animal*, 265.

The Power of Children

Thankfully, children themselves turn out to be a resource for liberation, precisely because of their sensitivity to sedentary bodies. Most of us who continue to participate in North American congregations are numb to the tedium in our services. Pews and straining to sing have become so normal that we cannot really tell that something is wrong. Membership may be declining, but it is difficult to understand why when we have become so stalwart. Children, in contrast, resist this state of affairs as much as they can. Their little bodies cannot really stay still for the sermon, especially not without some activity to hold their attention. The potential for boredom is so obvious to most of us today that we simply expect children to leave during this portion of the service. Sunday School programming takes place almost exclusively during the readings, sermon, and prayers in our churches, and this separates children from the rest of the congregation for a large portion of worship. We do this because we know children to be particularly sensitive to boredom, especially when bodies must remain sedentary. And yet, by doing so we may also be losing contact with a crucial opportunity. By sending children away, we are forgetting that the presence of children can help us coordinate our attention on God.

It is important at this point not to confuse "sedentary" with "still." Children love being still when playing games, after all. Freezing in place is a common motif in multiple formats, and children love to practice stillness in these ways when it allows them to participate in the joint attention of the group. The problem with being sedentary is the mental effort required to maintain individual focus apart from others. Being in our heads is what is most difficult for children, not so much holding a given position. Hence, their sensitivity to boredom is more of a litmus test for a certain form of cognitive strain than it is for remaining still.

Accordingly, it is not surprising that children feature prominently in biblical depictions of communal coordination. Notice their presence at key moments for describing how Israel should maintain fidelity to God's covenant. In the case of the *Shema* in Deuteronomy 6, Moses calls the people of Israel to remember the Lord's commands and "keep" them "in [their] heart."[22] But the command to "hear" is not limited to the people of Israel as they presently are; rather, it extends to an ongoing family of descendants that incorporates more and more generations into a ritual memory of sacred words.[23] From recitation and conversation to writing

---

[22] Dt 6:6.

[23] Dt 6:2.

and adornment, Moses wants the people to cultivate this memory in all physical aspects of their community.

In a way, Deuteronomy 6 calls the people of Israel to nurture ongoing joint attention, to keep the words of the Lord in collective view throughout their days. As we hear in Psalm 1, happy are those whose "delight is in the law of the Lord, and on his law they meditate day and night."[24] The question is, why are children explicitly part of this project? Why is the expectation that Israel "recite [these words] to [their] children" included in the list of ways the people are meant to cultivate attention toward God?[25] Some may suggest it is simply to ensure that future generations remain faithful to God as well, and this reading seems to be exegetically accurate, but we all know how fickle such an expectation of fidelity would turn out to be. Once children age and become adults, they make their own decisions, and we cannot really force a whole generation to heed our aspirations. Hence, there must be some further reason that children be involved in coordinating this most holy joint attention.[26]

I want to suggest a possible answer lies in the way children struggle to buffer themselves from the rest of the world.[27] This is not just a factor in their sensitivity to boredom; for them, it is also easier for the world to be charged with "the grandeur of God."[28] For children, darkness can be frightening, the cosmos can brim full of spirits, and meanings can inhere in objects and faces. This openness to personal meanings is indicative of their "porous" existence;[29] that is to say, children (especially young chil-

[24] Ps 1:2

[25] Dt 6:7.

[26] I also want to draw attention to Arthur James Murphy's discussion of children in ancient literature in his dissertation, published as: *Kids and Kingdom: The Precarious Presence of Children in the Synoptic Gospels* (Eugene, Ore.: Pickwick Publications, 2013). As he writes, "there is little evidence in Jewish sources of this period that children were valued *as children*," 55. I take from this suggestion that it can be helpful to explore reasons for including children in writing, even when these reasons were not explicitly available or present to the people of the time.

[27] I do not mean this as an answer to an exegetical question in the sense of what the original authors intended. Rather, I mean this as an exegetical possibility which remains hidden in the text and available to us in a day and age that greatly values children as children.

[28] Gerard Manley Hopkins, "God's Grandeur," accessed 20 October 2019: poetryfoundation.org/poems/44395/gods-grandeur.

[29] See Charles Taylor's work on "porous" selves in *A Secular Age*, 35: "Once meanings are not exclusively in the mind, once we can fall under the spell, enter the zone of power of exogenous meaning, then we think of this meaning as including us, or perhaps penetrating us. We are in as it were a kind of space defined by this influence. The meaning can no longer be placed simply within; but nor can it be

dren) are hopelessly present in their bodies, less able to buffer themselves from others.

This ineluctable corporeal presence seems to be key to the power of children. In their cognitive immaturity, children bear the potential to draw adults back into their bodies. In a manner of speaking, it is the physical needs of little ones that evoke our most human, Christ-like ways of living. We know by experience that children draw us into relationships of responsibility. Their physical, emotional, and intellectual needs are unavoidable conditions for being part of their lives. Any parent or caregiver understands the intimacy of this responsibility, the ways that children disrupt the pretense of comfort by making our joy conditional on their joy, our rest dependent on their rest. Accordingly, it is in their bodily neediness that children call us into relationships of coordinated attention, and it is out of necessity that we learn to adjust our bodies to focus along with them on a given moment, topic, or activity.

It is important, then, that children should be included in the *Shema*, even if the significance is only now becoming visible. As Benjamin D. Sommer suggests, "a doctrine may contain the solution to a problem not yet encountered when the doctrine emerged."[30] Their presence in the text may not have been as critical for the people of the time, at least not for the same reasons, but it does bear witness to a crucial need today. What would have been normal then—a sort of vibrant bodily presence in gatherings of worship—has become rare in our churches because of our cerebral aesthetics. Accordingly, it becomes significant to emphasize the presence of children in our midst, not because they should be thought of as fully mature agents

located exclusively without. Rather it is in a kind of interspace which straddles what for us is a clear boundary. Or the boundary is, in an image I want to use here, porous." Cf. 35: "This porousness is most clearly in evidence in the fear of possession. Demons can take us over. And indeed, five centuries ago, many of the more spectacular manifestations of mental illness, what we could class as psychotic behavior, were laid at the door of possession, as in the New Testament times. One 'cure' on offer for this condition was to beat the patient; the idea being that by making this site acutely uncomfortable for the demon, one would induce him to leave." Cf. 36: "But the fuzziness is even greater than that. Even the line between ordinary cases of influence and full possession was not totally sharp. There is a gamut of cases. People spoke of possession when our higher faculties and powers seemed totally eclipsed; for instance, when people fell into delirium. But in a sense, any evil influence involves some eclipse of the highest capacities in us. Only in the case of good influence, for instance, when we are filled with grace, do we become one with the agent/force through what is best and highest in us. Demons may possess us, but God or the Holy Spirit enter us, or quicken us from within."

[30] Benjamin D. Sommer, *Revelation and Authority: Sinai in Jewish Scripture and Tradition* (New Haven, Conn.: Yale University Press, 2015), 97.

without faults, but rather because children bear within them the capacity to draw us closer together. It is their hopelessly corporeal presence that upsets our cerebral pretense. Hence, by bringing children into the bodily conversations and activities that cultivate fidelity to God, we can learn to coordinate our attention on the Lord again with one voice. Indeed, the presence of children allows us to be one in the Holy Spirit.

Concrete Applications

Noticing that children can liberate us from mind-body dualism is important, but we cannot end our reflections here. Without a concrete plan to address the problem of sedentary bodies in our congregations, we cannot really realize the bodily significance of children in our midst. No culture is able to will itself to change all at once. Instead, we must cultivate our imaginations in a bodily horizon, and this means we need to practice in the most pragmatic of senses. Transformation can arise only if we maintain continuity with what has come before while also pressing on toward new horizons. All members of the congregation need to be included in the process, from the youngest to oldest, from the strongest to weakest. Accordingly, real solutions to our crisis will only be manageable should we look to places within our existing liturgies and worship practices that are open to transition.

With this pragmatic approach in mind, I want to identify a place for change that involves relatively little disruption—the children's "sermon" or "message." This time in the service is prime for planting seeds for two reasons. First, adults are more willing to use their bodies when the task is "for the children." What normally feels like an awkward intrusion can become a pleasurable experiment, so long as the pretense of maintaining adult boundaries no longer dominates the activity. Children afford us this opportunity precisely because of their neediness, as argued above. Second, many churches do not use this time well, meaning people are more likely to be open to something new at this point in the service. In most North American contexts, the children's message depends on the showmanship of the minister. If they can entertain both children and adults, people feel like the children's sermon has gone well. However, this success is rare, and it is questionable whether "entertainment" is a good guiding principle for sharing spiritual truths. Many of us feel intuitively that the time is frivolous because little of spiritual substance can be communicated in three to five minutes. Hence, we might say that the children's time is the weakest component in our service, liturgically speaking.

So, what can we do? The trick is to plant the seeds of transformation in such a way as to allow bodily coordination to spread into the rest of the service. A strong approach will take advantage of the opening the children's time provides at two levels. First, one must find a way to incorporate the whole congregation into the children's activity as it unfolds; the process needs to be fully corporate and intergenerational. In other words, the vast majority must have some way to participate bodily in the process, even if some do so only in marginal ways. The sense of "bodily" need not be strenuous here, since the whole point is to coordinate attention. There are many ways to be present with one another, after all. That being said, there must be some form of corporeal engagement that draws the congregation into thinking with their bodies together rather than with their minds separately.

Second, one must develop sufficiently concrete ideas that the congregation and children can explore with their bodies. This means that whoever spearheads the process, or leads the congregation, during this time must learn how to embody the teachings of the church in grand and visible gesture. It is not sufficient to say that God loves us forever, because this kind of verbal abstraction is not accessible to children. Instead, we need to engage these insights by carrying them into our bodies. Extension and duration can be explored to the level of infinity should we allow our corporeal intuitions to play with the ideas. For example, we could ask, "How long can God hug us?" By doing so, we are opening ourselves to the possibility of physically exploring God's everlasting love for us. Accordingly, we must do what children do and begin the physical exchange of hugs (albeit by invitation), perhaps even playing with the idea of how awkward and silly it might be to hug someone forever. The fact that the process can be silly, however, does not mean the question is frivolous. Whether it is right to hug someone without their consent can easily become part of this conversation, meaning significant ethical questions can help anchor our theology of God's embrace. The point is to use this time to open ourselves as a community to the awe and wonder that accompanies any child's physical exploration of proverbial wisdom.

What might this look like? During my tenure as a children's minister, I began a new process with the Anglican congregations of Central Saanich called the "children's song." It took practice and experimentation, but over time this period in the service transformed from a "message" in the conventional sense to a moment for the whole adult congregation to coordinate their attention bodily with the children. Occasionally, I would explore the theme of the day with the children on a physical level prior to singing, but the gist of the practice involved joining together in song. It was important to teach a given piece over a few Sundays, so that members could develop some fluency with the actions and words. However, it was also important to coordinate the repertoire with the Sunday readings. By doing so, we could develop two sides of the song–mastery and theological depth. Over a few Sundays, the congregations could learn a song to the point of knowing it by heart. At the same time, they could explore it in relation to a series of scripture readings, thus solidifying a range of theological connections for the body to explore.

This practice became a staple of our Sunday morning worship, and over time we accumulated a large enough repertoire to evoke a range of theological moods. Often the songs were silly and playful,[31] but there were also moments of still sobriety. When singing "Lord, Listen to Your Children Praying," we sometimes tried it with actions. However, it became most effective for us as a community when we sang it holding hands in a circle. All who joined in, children included, came to cherish this moment of tranquility, perhaps especially because it involved using the worship space in a novel way. The affective nuances of stillness can become especially profound when we combine it with the simple bodily coordination of a ring formed hand in hand. The space a circle opens up proved to be uniquely beneficial for singing because we could feel each other's voices more intimately when we sang face to face. Thus, in songs like this, we came to experience a kind of corporate intimacy only really comprehensible in terms of the Spirit praying in and through us.

Conclusion

At the end of the day, we must heed this possibility for liberation within our midst. For those communities who do not have children, the task is that much more difficult, but healing is not impossible. Indeed, we can learn to be more childlike in our congregations precisely by practicing the kind of bodily presence that children possess naturally. I have seen evidence of this in my own ministry, having worked in a two-point Anglican parish. One congregation stayed roughly the same in size, but the one with only a single child eventually became home to four or five on any given Sunday. At the end of my year-and-a-half tenure, these congregations had a combined twenty-five children actively participating in church. While I provided support at other levels as well, in hindsight one of the most crucial parts of my ministry was training the congregations to join together with children in a bodily way. We did this corporately by transforming the moment in the service called the "children's sermon" into a time for participatory song, as described above. Each song had some physical component,

[31] One song called "Go, We Gotta Go" involved learning the hand jive. Children did not know where this series of movements came from, but many in the congregations were able to recognize the ironic background.

and everyone was invited to join in the actions. Over time, adults began to develop a repertoire of coordinated movement along with the kids. We could explore a whole range of theological moods, from contemplative to praiseworthy, with our bodies.

As a result, we did not merely worship as an adult congregation of individuals, but also as an inter-generational community of joint attention. The physical strain became a prominent refrain for members to tease me about, but they loved the process. They came to experience a kind of union in their attention that is only possible when we coordinate our bodies. The presence of children, along with their participation, enabled us to explore these opportunities without concern. It was not awkward to learn something new when it was "for the children." Accordingly, this growing sense of felt communion began to filter into the other practices of the church. Members began to explore more bodily possibilities in other parts of the service, and a certain Christian camaraderie waxed large. These congregations had experienced a great deal of upheaval and change in the previous five years, and the growing participation of children began to elicit hope once again. Indeed, by learning to coordinate together with children, the congregations began to heal communally; by learning to worship with their little ones, they began to learn better how to live together in faith. My prayer is that we as Lutherans in western Canada would heed this promise of vibrant worship as well, that we would grasp it with outstretched arms and move together in the Holy Spirit once more.

The Lord's Supper as the Call to Community: Conversion to the Lutheran Church in Poland

Sebastian Madejski

Introduction

This paper on the role of liturgy in forming the Lutheran identity in the context of the Evangelical Church of the Augsburg Confession in Poland is the result of my ethnographic research of 100 people via interviews done in 2017. The respondents represent men and women of diverse ages and education levels. The Lutheran liturgy influenced them so profoundly that they decided to join the Evangelical Church of the Augsburg Confession in Poland in the last few years.

The Evangelical Church of the Augsburg Confession is the largest Protestant denomination in Poland. The majority of Polish society belongs to the Roman Catholic Church. However, in the Republic of Poland there are Orthodox, Old Catholic, and Protestant Christians whose churches are represented by the Polish Ecumenical Council. The population of Poland is 38 million people, and the Lutherans in Poland are about 60,000. Therefore, the Lutherans are less than 0.05 percent of Poles.

Every year the Evangelical Augsburg Church of the Augsburg Confession receives about 250 people as new members. These people are from a different background as Catholics represent around 87.5 percent of the population in Poland. Thus, about 75 percent of the converts I interviewed declared that before their conversion into Lutheranism they were Catholics. Nearly seven percent of the respondents answered that before the act of conversion they were "formal Catholics" which means that they did not attend to religious matters until they discovered Lutheranism. About five percent of the respondents used to be agnostics and about three percent used to be atheists. The rest of the respondents were from confessional backgrounds other than the Roman Catholic Church.[1]

I have done research among 100 converts. About 25 percent of them pointed to worship services and the Lord's Supper as the significant elements in their decision to convert to the Lutheran church, which makes conversion and Holy Communion important issues in the context of liturgy and pneumatology.

Liturgy, Metanoia, and Adult Catechesis

One of the respondents said that "the participation in services is my inspiration, enriches me and gives me strength." Lutheran liturgy is, therefore, a particular place where the Holy Spirit works and inspires people to conversion.

The work of the Holy Spirit in the liturgy evokes a change of mind. In biblical Greek, this change of mind is called *metanoia*. The process of changing one's mind is a process which can be short or long. The liturgy plays a very important role in this process. In the liturgy, God's word is proclaimed, and the word motivates a change of life and thinking. However, God's word is not only active in the liturgy.

One of my parishioners, also a convert, said once to me after a worship service, "I was very moved by today's sermon. I've never thought that these services in that particular church could be so important for me... Every Sunday I hear like the sermon is directly to me."

His story is profound. He was baptized in the Catholic Church and didn't think about the rituals and patterns. Once he was driving in his car and the traffic stopped because a Catholic procession on the day of Corpus Christi was passing by. He heard a question on his mobile radio system from another driver, "Is that feast really described in the Bible?" In his heart, that question evoked a very strong need to find out why so many rituals and feasts in his church are not biblical. After some time, his daughter took him to a Lutheran worship service.

God's word is active in the liturgy and Sunday worship. The people gathered in the church are themselves strong evidence of the activity of the Holy Spirit. Many come to Lutheran worship services even when they do not understand the patterns and our liturgical tradition. A cognitive

[1] I collected the above information for the purposes of my master's thesis at the Christian Theological Academy in Warsaw.

understanding is less important during the liturgy because the experience of the Word is so strong. The word of God is proclaimed in the Introit, in the songs, in the readings, in the sermon, and also in the meal (Communion-Ed.) These elements are instruments of the Holy Spirit to work in the hearts of the gathered people. The ministers are only servants who are creating space for this amazing activity.[2]

People who wish to become members of the Lutheran church in Poland normally speak first to the pastor. The ministers report that they welcome people to worship services every Sunday and that the process of catechesis for becoming Lutheran is about one year. However, there are many examples when people have been preparing for many years.

The aim of the preparation is to introduce the person to the doctrine and the practice of the Lutheran church. Potential new members are acquainted with Lutheran liturgy and songs sung in the church. They participate in the life of the church by attending weekly meetings and worship services. Liturgy teaches perseverance in faith and the experience of spirituality.

Therefore, conversion is both a process that occurs in the heart of the person and a public confession and decision to be a member of the chosen church.[3] The Holy Spirit shapes emotions and prepares the soul for entrance to the community.

Catechesis gives confessional knowledge about Lutheranism and is comparable to the course for confirmands. A new confirmation program created by Adrian Korczago and Jerzy Sojka shows that young confirmands have the same questions as adult converts. It is important to add here that the program for confirmands was made on the basis of documents of The Lutheran World Federation concerning confirmation.

The difference between youth confirmation and adult catechesis is the texts quoted from the Bible. In the case of confirmands, the blessing comes from Isaiah 54:10 but for the adult catechumens the verse is 1 Peter 5:10 or 1 Thessalonians 5:23. Also, instead of reciting the Apostles' Creed as the youth do, the adult catechumens say "I believe" after the short description made by the pastor about four elements of Lutheran doctrine–*sola scriptura, solus Christus, sola fide* and *sola gratia*, and *solo verbo.*

I asked in the interviews how the liturgy of becoming a new member was experienced. Agnieszka, one of the converts, described a solemn service during which 13 people converted to the Lutheran church. "The converts had their place next to the pastor–we were in view. After the conversion

[2] *Augsburg Confession*, Article 5, Ministry of the Church: "It is only through these two means (Word and Sacraments) that the Holy Spirit works faith where and when He pleases in only those who hear and do not reject the Gospel."

[3] This data is derived from sociological and psychological research.

ceremony itself, all newly accepted people standing in the front of the altar turned to the congregation and were applauded. Everyone after the service also said goodbye to the congregation with the pastor by shaking hands. To know what I am talking about, you must see it. Conversion in my church is always a great celebration and joy!"

Receiving new members normally happens in a liturgy during the assembly. The aim is to present new people to the community and to encourage the congregation to share their affirmation. Another model is to be received in private with the pastor in an office. One pastor commented, "In my church, I would rather not make public acts of conversion. It seems too scary for them to be in front of all the people. The true testimony that they have to make will be in their family, in the confrontation with the mother-in-law or grandpa who are Catholics."

Liturgy Shapes Identity

The liturgy shapes Lutheran identity. Liturgy inspires and evokes faith. One man who converted to my church said, "The Lutheran liturgy was not the main cause of conversion, but it created a spiritual framework for making decisions that has matured for several years. The liturgy created an inviting starting point through which I could come to other key issues for Lutheran theology—above all, the doctrine of justification."

Elements of the liturgy proclaim the doctrine of justification, which is at the heart of Lutheran theology. For example, songs teach the faith of the church and the church prays through them. They reinforce theological content in the memory of the participants. Even if the sermon is not fully remembered, the refrain of a song might be something that stays after the worship service in the minds of worshipers. The readings recall God's promises. Very often they are set within music. Also, lay people read the readings as a sign of the priesthood of all the baptized.

New members very often do not remember the readings and the question remains whether it is necessary to remember all the details of the readings? Lutheran worship transmits the word of God, which is incomprehensive. Karl-Heinrich Bieritz, German theologian, argued in one of his papers that the reading of words is not intended to achieve particular results, but that the point of reading the texts is so that the Word continues "being read at all—so that the divine Word never becomes silent in this world."[4] Read-

[4] Karl-Heinrich Bieritz, "Auf dass die Stimme Gottes nicht verstumme ... Perikopenordnungen in postmoderner Zeit," *Perikopenordnung in der Diskussion*, GAGF 18, no. 2 (2004): 16.

ings are therefore "a doctrine that does not need to justify anything and nobody, but–as life itself– understands itself. A doctrine with which the church honors the word to which it owes itself."[5]

The liturgy might be uncomprehensive and unexplainable in a certain sense; however, it changes lives. Lutheran liturgy somehow subconsciously shapes a new identity in the frame of these old patterns and symbols. Many new members recognize these words and prayers from Catholic liturgy but, at this time in their life, the words seem to take on new meaning, and the liturgy seems to play a different role. Such a process of shaping and reshaping is God's ongoing activity in the lives of these catechumens. Liturgy should be, therefore, highly missional and inclusive. The question for the church is, how do we promote mission and inclusivity in our worship?

One of the respondents mentioned, "I knew that there are Evangelicals in Poland, but I thought they were Germans. It was from the radio and the websites I learned that there are also Polish Lutherans (...) I heard on the radio an interview with a Lutheran bishop who talked about Lutherans and Good Friday. It moved me very much and I started to search for information on the internet. I quickly understood that it was a sign from God and that this church is the best for me."

In her case, it was not the liturgy that first caught her attention, but the interview with a Lutheran minister who was talking about Good Friday. The liturgical event was an occasion to talk about Christ through modern technology. In this case, the Word came to that person via a radio interview. The respondent noticed that it was divine activity in her life, and this helped her discern that she was in a right place.

One of the respondents said, "I went to the service to the Evangelical Lutheran church and at once I met with the atmosphere of warmth and kindness. There, I get to know people with similar views to mine!"

Another person who I interviewed described his conversion experience as a process that started many years before and reached a final moment with the Lord's Supper in a worship service. "Finally, my decision was made by something like a breath of the Holy Spirit (it appeared with the words inviting to the Sacrament of the Lord's Supper–come and eat everything is ready)."

"The Church draws her life from the Eucharist." These are the words of the encyclical, "Ecclesia de Eucharistia,"[6] of Pope John Paul II. The Second Vatican Council proclaimed that the Eucharist is "the source and summit of the Christian life." Therefore, for Catholics in Poland, the Eucharist is a

[5] Bieritz, "Auf dass die Stimme Gottes nicht verstumme," 17.
[6] John Paul II, Pope. *Ecclesia de Eucharistia*. Vatican City: Libreria Editrice Vaticana, 2003 (English transl. Washington: USCC, 2003).

deeply experiential liturgical moment. Potential converts to Lutheranism are invited to take part in the liturgy and in Holy Communion. However, many of them perceive participation in the Lord's Supper is the highest stage of introduction to the Lutheran community. Very often, converts feel unworthy to participate in it until they wholly acquire the doctrine and the practice of the Lutheran church.

Of course, pastors ensure that everyone in the Lutheran church is invited to take part in the Lord's Supper. However, converts who are still formally Catholic often hesitate to participate. The words in the Roman Catholic eucharistic prayer, "Lord, I am not worthy to receive you, but only say the word and I shall be healed," create a feeling of being unworthy for the Eucharist.

According to Lutheran theology, no one is worthy; however, that fact is not an excuse to exclude people from the Lord's Supper. Only those who feel unworthy are worthy to come to the altar because fear and terror are overcome by God's love and mercy.

The meal of the Eucharist is the place of a joyful "meal," "the heavenly banquet," "the feast of the Lamb," "the service of the new Temple," and "the pure offering rising in all the world."[7] Therefore, the aim of the call to the table is to include everyone who feels unworthy to receive God's grace.

Shaping a New Identity

The Holy Spirit calls them to the table to participate in the Lord's Supper. However, many of them hesitate to participate. This demonstrates how previous religious experience shapes Lutheran identity. This previous experience is not wrong; the sense of multiple belonging in their identity makes our church rich. The identity of the convert is always a creation of the past and the present. Previous spirituality inspires a new one.

Lutheran liturgy is, therefore, highly missional. The Holy Spirit invites people through the words of institution, "Do this in remembrance of me," and through the words "Come because everything is ready, taste it and see how good and faithful is the Lord."[8]

[7] Gordon W. Lathrop, *Holy Things: A Liturgical Theology* (Minneapolis: Fortress Press, 1993), 16.

[8] Translation of Lutheran Agenda which is in use in Lutheran Church in Poland.

The Marks of the Church as Spiritual Practices for Renewal and Revival

Cheryl M. Peterson

There are a number of ways one can bring pneumatology to bear on the question of ecclesial identity. For example, in my own work I have explored this question in terms of the biblical narrative, following the Spirit's missional role in the Acts of the Apostles, and also in terms of the Trinitarian *koinonia* that the Spirit shares with the Father and the Son, which becomes the basis for the church's *koinonia*. The classic "marks of the church" (one, holy, catholic, and apostolic) in the Nicene Creed have long been used to define the nature of the church. In this essay, I explore them pneumatologically – as attributes of the church's identity and spiritual practices for renewal and revival.

Lutherans historically have preferred to reserve the phrase "marks of the church" for the Word and sacrament, rather than for the four "notes" that appear in the Nicene Creed. This is in response to how the Roman Catholic Counter-Reformation apologists used them as distinguishing characteristics, or recognizable marks, by which the true church (meaning the Roman Catholic Church) can be perceived apart from false claimants (meaning the Protestant church).[1] They argued that these marks were empirical and could be seen, as they were firmly and visibly rooted, and

[1] Hans Küng, *The Church*, trans. Ray Ockenden and Rosaleen Ockenden (London: Burns & Oates, 1967), 266.

guaranteed by the ecclesial structures of the church, the office of bishop, the papacy, canon law, etc.[2]

The Reformers had no objection to the marks themselves, but they rejected the idea that they could be used to empirically identity the church. For the Reformers, there were only two outward marks, or signs, for discerning the presence of the true church (and of the Holy Spirit's presence in the church): the pure proclamation of the Word and the administration of the sacraments in accordance with the institution of Christ (Augsburg Confession VII). For Lutherans, these four adjectives in the Creed cannot serve as marks or notes in an empirical or determinative sense. The church's identity is not constituted and marked by a particular ecclesial structure, but by the event of the gospel of justification being proclaimed and the sacraments being administered. One cannot point to anything other than the Word and sacrament to know "where" one can find the church.

In stressing Word and sacrament as the true "marks" of the church, however, Lutherans need not neglect the Nicene "marks" in their ecclesiological reflection. If considered instead as attributes, or as Hans Küng likes to say, dimensions[3] of the church, they can help us think together about our identity as Lutheran churches, especially if we consider them pneumatologically. As dimensions of the Spirit's activity in, and through, the church, these attributes can serve as spiritual practices for renewal and revival, and can offer guidance in the ways we live out God's reconciling mission in our various contexts.

It is important to recognize that these "marks" first and foremost reflect the God who calls, gathers, enlightens, and sends the church out in mission:

1. One – "that they may be one, as we are one, I in them and you in me, that they may become completely one, so that the world may know that you have sent me" (Jn 17:22–23)

2. Holy – "You shall be holy, for I am holy" (1 Pet 1:16)

3. Catholic – "For in him the whole fullness of deity dwells bodily, and you have come to fullness in him, who is the head of every ruler and authority" (Col 2:9); [This one requires a verbal footnote: while the

[2] Since Vatican II, Catholic theologians largely have abandoned the apologetic approach in favor a more eschatological approach, whereby "the four marks are as much future goals of the church, still to be achieved, as they are present realities." See Richard P. McBrien, "The Marks of the Church," *National Catholic Reporter* (8 August 2008), 19.

[3] Hans Küng's preferred term for the traditional marks. See Küng, 8.

word "catholic" does not appear in the Greek New Testament, Avery Dulles has suggested that the term *plērōma* (fullness) is perhaps the nearest biblical equivalent for what we call catholicity.] [4]

4. Apostolic - "As the Father has sent me, so I send you. . . Receive the Holy Spirit." (Jn 20:21-22)

In the following, I will consider each of these in turn, but in reverse order from their appearance in the Nicene Creed. In other words, I begin with the attribute of apostolicity, instead of unity even though it appears first in the creed, perhaps because it was the "mark" that most concerned Constantine, who feared that the debates over *homoousios* were tearing apart his empire. [5] There are two additional reasons to begin with apostolicity instead of unity. The first is epistemological. What is first in our knowledge of the triune nature is not the perichoretic union of the three persons of the Trinity (what we call in theology "the immanent Trinity"), but rather "the divine missions of word and Spirit, which in turn ground our knowledge of the processions and persons of the Trinity" (or what we call in theology the "economic Trinity"[6]). In what Timothy Wengert calls "Luther's reversed Trinity,"[7] it is the Holy Spirit who reveals to us Jesus Christ the Son, who reveals to us the Father's heart, and thus, the self-giving of God. As Luther writes, "We could never come to recognize the Father's favor and grace were it not for the Lord Jesus Christ, who is a mirror of the Father's heart ... but neither could we know anything of Christ, had it not been revealed by the Holy Spirit."[8] This suggests beginning with the mark of apostolicity, that is, with the "sent-ness" of God's own self in the incarnation, life, death, and resurrection of Christ, and the sending of the Spirit at Pentecost who makes Christ known to us.

Second, to begin with apostolicity also makes sense from a specifically Reformation perspective, as it is the mark that refers to the teaching of the apostles, the message of the gospel, the *kergyma*. According to Luther, it is

---

[4] Avery Dulles, *The Catholicity of the Church* (Oxford: Clarendon, 1985), 31.

[5] See, for example, Douglas John Hall, *Confessing the Faith: Christian Theology in a North American Context* (Minneapolis: Fortress Press, 1996), 72-76.

[6] Neil Ormerod, "The Structure of a Systematic Ecclesiology," *Theological Studies* 63, no. 1 (February 2002), 29. See also Stephen Bevans, "God Inside Out: Notes toward a Missionary Theology of the Spirit," *International Bulletin of Missionary Research* 22, no. 3 (1998): 102-105.

[7] Timothy J. Wengert, *Martin Luther's Catechisms: Forming the Faith* (Minneapolis: Fortress Press, 2009), 43-44.

[8] Martin Luther, "The Large Catechism," in *The Book of Concord: The Confessions of the Evangelical Lutheran Church*, eds. Robert Kolb and Timothy J. Wengert, trans. Charles Arand (Minneapolis: Fortress Press, 2000), 439-440.

the proclamation of this gospel message in Word and sacrament that creates the church.[9] As Edmund P. Clowney wrote, "The marks of the church, as developed during the Protestant Reformation, centered on the church as apostolic. The sure sign of Christ's true church is the preaching of the apostolic gospel."[10] Finally, as Darrell Guder has pointed out - speaking specifically to the North American context–starting with apostolicity can help "to restore missional purpose to our theology of the church . . . If we start our Nicene ecclesiology with apostolicity, then we end up defining catholicity and holiness and oneness in rather different ways–in ways closer to the sequence of formation that we find in the Biblical documents."[11]

In what follows, I show this linkage as I reflect on each of these dimensions of the Spirit's activity within the church. I also consider these dimensions in light of the context of the Evangelical Lutheran Church in America (ELCA) in the USA, inviting reflection on which spiritual practices for renewal and revival the member churches of the LWF might adopt to more faithfully cooperate with the Spirit's movement in their specific contexts.

Apostolic

Apostolicity is customarily defined as continuity with, and faithfulness to, the apostolic tradition.[12] As crucial as it is to stress the apostolic origins of the gospel message, Carl Braaten reminds us that it does not mean "constructing an irreducible minimum of apostolic doctrines, nor does it mean linking into an unbroken chain of apostolic offices of leadership; it does mean laying hold of the original eschatological drive of the early

[9] According to Edmund P. Clowney, "The marks of the church, as developed during the Protestant Reformation, centered on the church as apostolic. The sure sign of Christ's true church is the preaching of the apostolic gospel." Clowney, *The Church: Contours of Christian Theology* (Downers Grove, Ill.: Intervarsity Press, 1995), 73.

[10] Clowney, *The Church* (Downers Grove, Ill.: Intervarsity Press, 1995), 73.

[11] Darrell L. Guder, "The Nicene Marks in a Post-Christendom Church," *Re-Forming Ministry*, Presbyterian Church-USA, 27 December 2005, 9-10, pcusa.org/site_media/media/uploads/reformingministry/pdfs/nicene_marks.pdf

[12] This is reflected in the recent international Lutheran-Catholic study document, where apostolic is defined as "an attribute effected by the Holy Spirit who unites, sanctifies, and maintains believers over time in continuity with the apostles' faith, teaching, and institutional order" (The Lutheran World Federation and Pontifical Council for Promoting Christian Unity, *The Apostolicity of the Church: Study Document of the Lutheran-Roman Catholic Commission on Unity* [Minneapolis: Lutheran University Press, 2006], 47). See also Darrell L. Guder, "Missional Connectedness: The Community of Communities in Mission," in *Missional Church: A Vision for the Sending of the Church in North America*, ed. Darrell L. Guder (Grand Rapids, Mich.: Eerdmans, 1999), 255.

Christian apostolate and tracing its trajectory through the discontinuities of time and history."[13]

As a pneumatological dimension of the church's identity, apostolicity also must be understood in this original New Testament sense of being sent out to bear witness to the eschatological future that has broken forth in the life, death, and resurrection of Jesus Christ. Indeed, when we hear "apostolic," we should think "missionary" or "missional." In the Acts of the Apostles, the Holy Spirit blows on the disciples in order to move them from fear to bold proclamation of Christ's death and resurrection, and the new life we are promised through him. The Holy Spirit serves as the church's "mission director," turning disciples into apostles, so that the gospel may be proclaimed to the ends of the earth. As Luther writes in his Large Catechism, it is because the Holy Spirit has not yet gathered together all of God's people, nor has completed the granting of forgiveness, the church has been appointed as the community through which the Spirit speaks and does its work.[14]

In the American context, this is a dimension of ecclesial identity that needs to be reclaimed, and a spiritual practice necessary for renewal and revival. From the arrival of the first Puritans on the shores of North America, the stories of nation and church have intertwined to create a metanarrative of a "Christian America." It is well known that the Puritans arrived in hopes of establishing a Christian society based on biblical laws and spoke of America's election through the covenant, and role in God's providence.[15] The lingering legacy of this cultural, *de facto,* form of Christendom in the United States has shaped the church's identity in problematic ways. For some, it has led to the idea that the church's calling is to "bless" the culture, which can confuse patriotism and discipleship in unfortunate ways. For others, it suggests that the church's calling is to serve as a social club for its own "members" since America is already "Christian." Many congregations in the USA fail to see themselves primarily as communities commissioned, authorized, and sent out by the Holy Spirit to witness to God's liberating good news.

This attribute reminds the church that God does not gather the church for worship, fellowship, and edification; God sends the church into the world to share the gospel with others. The spiritual dimension of apostolicity

---

[13] Carl E. Braaten, *Principles of Lutheran Theology,* 2nd ed. (Minneapolis: Fortress Press 2007), 62.

[14] Luther, "The Large Catechism," *Book of Concord,* 439.

[15] Ernest Cassara, "The Development of America's Sense of Mission," in *The Apocalyptic Vision in America: Interdisciplinary Essays on Myth and Culture,* ed. Lois Parkinson Zamora (Bowling Green, Ohio: Bowling Green University Popular Press, 1982), 64–96; Perry Miller, "The Puritan State and the Puritan Society," in *Errand into the Wilderness* (New York: Harper & Row, 1956), 141–152.

calls the church to be open to the Spirit's empowerment and sending in order to witness to the power of the resurrection to bring new life and hope. Lutherans in the USA need the Spirit's boldness to empower us to share the treasure of the gospel in a context of increasing polarization (along the lines of political ideologies and racial tensions), and in a period of increasing spiritual revival and revolution occurring outside of the churches, to which Diana Butler Bass and others have pointed—especially among those who call themselves "spiritual but not religious."

Two spiritual practices come to mind to help the church reclaim this attribute. The first is that of giving testimony or personal evangelism: to share your faith with someone, to tell them what the life, death, and resurrection of Jesus means to you. Too many American Lutherans prefer to keep their faith private. Many are fearful to share their faith with others, even close friends and neighbors, as they wish to avoid offense. Others are afraid that they do not know enough about the Bible and the faith of the church, but theological education is not required in order to give a personal testimony. As in the Acts of the Apostles, the Holy Spirit will enable our testimony, opening up our voices to share the good news, as well as the ears of others to be able to hear it. The disciples were unable to do anything apart from the Spirit. Until he receives the Spirit at Pentecost, Peter cannot even admit he knows who Jesus is—and then he cannot stop preaching about Jesus (Acts 2:14–36).

The second is "one-on-ones," a tool used by community organizing groups to get to know their neighbors, their hopes, and their fears. Like the disciples, we are called to take the good news out of homes and places of worship, and meet people "where they are." I am not talking here about "cold calling" (knocking on strangers' doors), but simply learning who your neighbors are, and the needs of your wider community. A spiritual practice used by community organizing groups can help the church do this: "one-on-ones" with local leaders and others in your community.[16] This practice begins with listening to the concerns, fears, hopes, and dreams of those neighbors. The focus is on how congregations dwell with their neighbors and accompany them in their struggles, joys, and challenges (as the Holy Spirit or Paraclete accompanies us in ours), working toward the common good with our neighbors, as we share the hope of Christ within us.

What spiritual practices for renewal does this creedal attribute suggest for the member churches that you represent? What challenges do you face in your own context as Lutherans as you live into the spiritual dimension of "apostolicity"?

---

[16] A resource for "one-on-ones" in Dennis A. Jacobsen, *Doing Justice: Congregations and Community Organizing*, 2nd ed. (Minneapolis: Fortress Press, 2017).

Catholic

A church can only be apostolic if it is also catholic, because the scope of the apostolic mission is total and universal. Lutherans have not always been comfortable with this term because of its association with obedience to Rome. Following Augustine, the "catholic church" was defined as the universal church spread throughout the world whose unity is manifested under the authority of Rome. [17] Substituting "Christian" for "catholic" (which is common in many of our churches because of this legacy) does not clarify the matter, since, as Conrad Bergendoff writes, "there can be no question of any other church in the third article of the Creed than the Christian church."[18] More common today is the substitution of the word "universal," which comes closer but still does not capture the full meaning of the term catholic. The word in the original Greek is *kata holon*, which means "according to, or appropriate to, the whole."

In 1968, the Fourth Assembly of the World Council of Churches in Uppsala defined catholicity as "the quality by which the church expresses the fullness, the integrity, and the totality of life in Christ." For German Lutheran theologian Edmund Schlink, "this means that the concept of catholicity is understood in the light of the rich variety of the Spirit's gifts, and, at the same time, of the service to the world which the Spirit inspires."[19] Instead of equating this Spirit-breathed attribute of the church with the universal scope of the apostolic mission (although it includes that), Darrell Guder invites us to think of this attribute qualitatively as well as quantitatively. He proposes "the catholicity of the church is demonstrated in all the ways that the church at every level witnesses to the one gospel that draws all people to Christ."[20] A "catholic" church opens itself to the wind of the Spirit blowing it beyond the limits of particularity in order to embrace the world in its rich diversity, as we see in the Acts of the Apostles. It is the ecclesiastical word for "inclusive."

---

[17] The Lutherans would affirm the catholicity of the church apart from Roman obedience, arguing that there could only be one universal church spreading throughout the world because there could be only one true faith and therefore only one church in which that faith was confessed and believed. The church was catholic insofar as it was faithful to this one gospel attested by Scripture and early Christian fathers. See Dulles, *Catholicity*, 148.

[18] Conrad Bergendoff, *The One Holy Catholic and Apostolic Church*, The Hoover Lectures 1953 (Rock Island, Ill.: Augustana Book Concern, 1954), 51.

[19] Edmund Schlink, "The Holy Spirit and Catholicity: A Report on Section 1 of the Uppsala Assembly," *Ecumenical Review* 21, no. 2 (April 1969): 102.

[20] Guder, "Missional Connectedness," 257.

To be catholic in our ecclesial identity means to consciously point beyond one's own particular ecclesial community to the global church as a fuller expression of the Spirit's work.[21] This includes recognizing that each local congregation is a part of a larger ecclesial whole, but it also means extending ecclesial communion to all socio-economic, racial, and ethnic groups of people, indeed, to all nations. As a catholic community, the church is called to be all-embracing in how, and to whom, it reaches out in mission, in order to reflect the fullness of Christ and the universal salvation offered through his life, death, and resurrection.

Such catholicity suggests the need to call into question the self-interests of members and groups within the church at every level, from the local congregation to the national church and international levels.[22] For the American context, this includes rejecting all attempts to define one's own cultural tradition or theology as normative for the global church.[23] Within the ELCA, it challenges all attempts (intentional or not) of white, European American, middle-class Lutherans to define their cultural tradition as normative for the ELCA, as Lenny Duncan poignantly points out in his book *Dear Church: A Love Letter from a Black Preacher to the Whitest Denomination in the U.S.*[24] In order to claim the ecclesial dimension of catholicity in the USA, there must be an honest acknowledgement of white skin privilege, the racist heritage of the United States, and its continued legacy today—from the criminal justice system to immigration practices. The killings of George Floyd, Breonna Taylor, and Ahmaud Arbery last spring have catalyzed what the media has dubbed a "Racial Reckoning" in the United States, a long-overdue conversation about on-going racial injustice in the USA.

The church has an opportunity to bring the gospel of reconciliation to these issues, but it cannot do so without helping Americans first name the sin and violence that have marred our country—and all of its institutions, including the church—in so many racialized ways.[25] This means exposing racism as "America's original sin"[26] and the "narrative of the lie" of white supremacy on which the United States was founded. Robert J. Schreiter, writing on reconciliation, explains how violence is used to destroy the narratives that sustain a people's identity. "These might be called the nar-

[21] Guder, 257.

[22] Dulles, 180.

[23] Guder, 257.

[24] Lenny Duncan, *Dear Church: A Love Letter from a Black Preacher to the Whitest Denomination in the U.S.* (Minneapolis: Fortress Press, 2019).

[25] Robert J. Schreiter, *Reconciliation: Mission and Ministry in a Changing Social Order* (Maryknoll, N.Y.: Orbis Books, 1992), 34.

[26] See Jim Wallis, *America's Original Sin: Racism, White Privilege, and the Bridge to a New America* (Grand Rapids, Mich.: Brazos Press, 2017).

ratives of the lie, precisely because they are intended to negate the truth of people's own narratives . . . The negation is intended not only to destroy the narrative of the victim, but to pave the way for the oppressor's narrative." [27]

For American Lutherans, this attribute calls us to the spiritual practice of working for racial justice. Here we can draw on some insights from the Gospel of John: the Holy Spirit is not only our Comforter, but also the Spirit of truth, who, as Luther writes in his Sermons on John, "will fill us with a courage that is called a divine, holy, and bold defiance."[28] The Spirit of truth not only teaches us the one who is truth, that is, Christ, but also gives us the courage to stand in it, and to oppose all lies and false gospels, impelling us to testify to that truth.[29] Deanna Thompson appeals to Luther's theology of the cross—calling a thing what it is—for addressing white privilege.[30]

A related spiritual practice for the spiritual attribute of catholicity is radical hospitality, which is more than intentionally welcoming all people into the church. It means offering hospitality in a fundamentally different way. As one denomination puts it, "As a disruption to cycles of brokenness, radical hospitality requires a fundamental shift from a simple practice of offering welcome to an outward movement to stand with others--particularly those who are at society's margins."[31]

What spiritual practices for renewal does this creedal attribute suggest for the member churches that you represent? What are the barriers to a deeper catholicity in your context, and in our global communion, and how can we as Lutherans be more open to the Spirit's leading us to speak to, and resist, unjust ideas, structures, and practices in the world—and church?

Holy

The church is called to be apostolic, to witness to the good news of Jesus Christ and the kingdom of God that has broken into the present through his life, death, and resurrection. In this kingdom, "all belong to the whole" in the fullness of life in his name that is offered through the Holy Spirit,

---

[27] Schreiter, *Reconciliation*, 34.

[28] Martin Luther, *Volume 24, Sermons on the Gospel of St. John, Chapters 14–16*, ed. Jaroslav Pelikan (St. Louis: Concordia Publishing House, 1961), 118. (= *D. Martin Luthers Werke*, Kritisch Gesamtausgabe (Weimarer Ausgabe), 45, 569).

[29] LW 24: 357, 292. WA 46: 52–53; 45:727–728.

[30] Deanna A. Thompson, "Calling a Thing What It Is: A Lutheran Approach to Whiteness," *Dialog* 53, no. 1 (March 2014): 49–57.

[31] Ryan Dunn, "What is Radical Hospitality?", The People of The United Methodist Church, accessed 9 October 2020; umc.org/en/content/what-is-radical-hospitality.

which is to say that the church is also called to be catholic. In order to witness to this in-breaking future, the church is called to be "holy."

This may be the most misunderstood of the attributes, or dimensions, of the church's pneumatological identity. First, holiness must be understood as being "set apart" for this mission in order to engage the world, not to withdraw from it. As with the other attributes, holiness is not an empirical designation that is easily observable by looking at the piety or behavior of its members. As Luther writes in his explanation of the third article of the Creed, holiness is brought about by the gospel and the forgiveness of sins; for Luther, holiness is dependent on the daily experience of the forgiveness of sins–and not moral perfection. In fact, Luther states, "All who would seek to merit holiness through their works rather than the gospel and the forgiveness of sins" separate themselves from the holy community.[32] This blessing is not only experienced vertically, between the individual believer and God, but also horizontally, that is, communally and relationally with other believers. As Luther writes, the Christian experiences new life as "full forgiveness of sins, both in that God forgives us *and that we forgive, bear with and aid one another.*"[33]

This dimension of ecclesial identity needs to be reclaimed as an attribute of the whole church, and not just of its individual members. Holiness historically has been a central focus of the great revival movements in the USA, from the two Great Awakenings in the eighteenth and nineteenth centuries, to the Wesleyan Holiness movement, to revival movements today. Holiness tended to focus more on the individual and the individual's sanctification and perfection, though John Wesley also emphasized "social holiness." The emphasis on empirical holiness in many of these movements frequently led to moralism, with a particular concern for sexual purity.

Following Luther, if holiness is defined by God's blessings of faith and the "full forgiveness of sins," the apostolic mission of the church should include both the proclamation of forgiveness and reconciliation given in Jesus Christ, as well as the witness of living out the power of forgiveness in its own relationships - even if imperfectly. This is a spiritual practice that can help the church live into the attribute of holiness. Too often the church's proclamation of the gospel is hampered by its lack of living according to the same. Christians do not always live by the gift of forgiveness with one another–much less those outside of the church–allowing grudge and resentments to create obstacles to reconciliation. In 2006, the Amish community in Nickel Mines, Pennsylvania, stunned the world with forgiveness when a horrible act of violence against their community left

[32] Luther, "The Large Catechism," *Book of Concord*, 438.
[33] Ibid., 438.

five dead and as many severely injured, because it was such a rare public witness to God's call to forgive.[34] While the church itself is *simul iustus et peccator*, that is, at the same time a fellowship of sinners and a fellowship of saints, Luther reminds that the Holy Spirit is always present to heal and to forgive, making the church "holy," so that it may demonstrate the in-breaking and gracious rule of God, and be an instrument of God's sanctifying and gracious rule for others.[35]

What spiritual practices for renewal does this creedal attribute suggest for the member churches that you represent? How can we, within our member churches and as part of a larger communion of churches, live more fully into the "full forgiveness of sins?"

Unity

As Jesus himself prays in his high priestly prayer in John 17:20–21, unity ought to serve the mission of the church:

> I ask not only on behalf of these, but also on behalf of those who will believe in me through their word, that they may all be one. As you, Father, are in me and I am in you, may they also be in us, so that the world may believe that you have sent me.

The on-going lack of visible unity among the churches remains a serious obstacle to the church's identity and mission. The majority of churches believe that Christians already share spiritual unity through their baptism into Christ and faith, however, it is the healing of historic divisions in the church that enable the church to experience this *koinonia* more deeply and to be a more effective witness in the world. In other words, the work of ecumenism does not create unity, but gives visible expression to the spiritual unity (*koinonia)* that already exists among the baptized in the one body of Christ.

The history of Protestantism has been one of division and merger, and those divisions have been imported from Europe to other countries through missionaries and immigration, including the USA. In addition to the divisions that immigrant Christians brought with them when they came to America, Christians in the USA have split over various doctrinal and ethical issues, including slavery. Many member churches of the LWF, including the ELCA, are committed to ecumenical dialogue to heal historic breaches

[34] Donald B. Kraybill, "Why the Amish Forgive so Quickly," *Christian Science Monitor*, 7 October 2007; csmonitor.com/2007/1002/p09s02-coop.html
[35] Braaten, *Principles of Lutheran Theology*, 68.

and theological differences that have marked the past. For the ELCA, this led to a "full communion" relationship with six other denominations: the Episcopal Church, the Presbyterian Church (U.S.A.), the Reformed Church of America, the United Church of Christ, the Moravian Church, and the United Methodist Church. In another case, with the Mennonites, it led to a public service of repentance and healing.

As stated in its constitution, the ELCA seeks in its faith and life "to manifest the unity given to the people of God by living together in the love of Christ and by joining with other Christians in prayer and action to express and preserve the unity which the Spirit gives" (ELCA Constitution 4.02.f.). In order to more visibly express the "unity which the Spirit gives," a Spirit-breathed church will not be afraid to address both the theological differences that have historically divided our denominations and the issues that continue to further divide Christians within denominations (e.g., sexuality, biblical interpretation), as well as the fact that American Christians continue to segregate themselves by race and class. It also means being open to receiving and learning from other traditions quite different from our own, such as Pentecostalism, where the Spirit may be at work. Spiritual practices that can assist the church in living into the attribute of unity include dialoguing with other Christians—in local contexts as well as at the official denominational level—praying for, and with, other Christians, and when possible, sharing the Eucharist together.

What spiritual practices for renewal does this creedal attribute suggest for the member churches that you represent? Where are we failing to look to see the Spirit at work in other Christian denominations, and what can we learn from them? How can we be open to the Spirit's guidance in addressing theological and other issues that continue to divide the body of Christ and weaken its witness to the transforming power of God's love in Jesus Christ?

Conclusion

In this essay I showed that, though often neglected by Lutheran theology, the four so-called "marks of the church" in the Nicene Creed—one, holy, catholic, and apostolic—offer rich resources for exploring the church's identity, especially when considered spiritual attributes of the church. I explored each attribute theologically from the Lutheran tradition, and contextually as a North American Lutheran. Finally, I suggested some spiritual practices for each that can assist the church in living more fully into these attributes.

Transformed and Freed

Bible Study

"Chloe Told": A Womanist Reading

1 Corinthians 12

Beverly Wallace

> Now there are varieties of gifts, but the same Spirit; and there are varieties of services, but the same Lord; and there are varieties of activities, but it is the same God who activates all of them in everyone. (1 Cor 12: 4-7)

We read this passage after the death of Jesus. A new church was being formed and the people who were called to be the church had to understand anew what they were to be about–things perhaps they had forgotten in their zeal to become who they thought they were to become.

In the letter to the people of Corinth, Paul attempts to assist in this understanding and to help contextualize their understanding of the Holy Spirit.

In this Bible study, "A Womanist Reading of 1 Corinthian 12," I bring in the voice of a woman into this discourse about the Holy Spirit; I've entitled this piece, "Chloe told."

A womanist theological and scriptural interpretation takes seriously the voices of women, especially women of color, and at the same time is inclusive of all–analyzing theological and theoretical issues and concerns through the lenses of race, class, and gender, specifically lifting up the voices of women whose voices are often obscured. Womanist theologians are black women who engage in this enterprise knowing that the personal is political, and it is spiritual.

In this year (2019), which marks the fortieth anniversary of the ordination of women of color in the Evangelical Lutheran Church in America,

I offer this reading that brings the voices of womanist theologians to an exploration of the Holy Spirit.

First, a bit of background. This text was written between 53 and 54 AD which was a time of conflict within the Christian church and the surrounding community. In this context, Chloe was a widow. She was a devout follower in the new church in Corinth. In an earlier chapter of this letter, we see that she writes to Paul. Chloe is mentioned, but often the focus of this text is on Paul. However, Chloe evidently understood the foundation of love and unity that was to be the cornerstone of the church. These were the principles Paul had put forth to guide the church when he originally came to Corinth.

It is clear that Chloe was concerned about the division in this new developing church in Corinth. People were arguing over whose voice had the most authority. There was fighting and quarreling, and the new church was being split a part. And so, Chloe writes to Paul, telling him all that was going on.

Chloe Told

In this passage, we hear the response to Chloe's letter to Paul: "Now concerning spiritual gifts, brothers and sisters, I do not want you to be uninformed" (1 Cor 12:1).

In verse 2, Paul writes, "You know that when you were pagans..." In other translations of the texts it reads, "you were unaware". But here I refer to the translation, "You know that when you were pagans..." Pagans means the "other." It was a word used as an antithesis to who they were. Evidently, defining the "other" was critical to the process of Christian self-identity. Therefore, the meaning of verse 2 is, "But at one time you were the "other."

Paul understood, as he too was an "other." He writes, "when you were pagans, you were enticed and led astray to idols that could not speak" (1 Cor 12:2). Who were these idols that could not speak?

Paul continues in verse 3: "Therefore I want you to understand...." So, what is to be understood? Was there not an understanding of God and the Spirit before the written text and, should I dare ask, before the letters of Paul? Had the people forgotten, or did they not know?

In 1 Corinthians 2:7, Paul wrote, "But we speak God's wisdom, secret and hidden, which God decreed before the ages for our glory." So perhaps it was hidden; there was not only a need for clarification and understanding but perhaps even a need to know and to remember. For there was a time—a time when the people remembered and life was changing—until they forgot.

Linda Thomas, a womanist theologian who is not Lutheran but teaches in one of our Lutheran seminaries in the USA, in writing about the Holy

Spirit and black women, uses an African cosmology to demonstrate why memory is crucially important for the welfare of the community. The community is the crux of ontology, she writes. All creation signifies that which is divine and there is no separation between the sacred and secular.

What I would highlight is that memory is important for the welfare of the community. According to Thomas, who wrote about the Holy Spirit and black women, "the cosmology and the spirituality of our ancestors gave us the abilities to survive".[1] Our foremothers and forefathers, who were taken from this continent, were adults when they were landed in the Americas and the Caribbean. It has been over four hundred years since this happened in Jamestown, Virginia, USA. (What might this say about Lutheranism which recently celebrated five hundred years of the Reformation?) But, as Thomas suggests and I believe, my foreparents had their own religious consciousness regarding the Spirit. They knew the Spirit in deep and complex ways. Black women, Thomas writes, live out of a "memory of the future"[2] led by the power of Spirit.

In one of the seminaries where I taught, we used the metaphor of Sankofa (which can be translated, "go back and get it") as the ongoing theme for our work, our notion of theological education, and our expectations of our students. They had guides—we, their professors, and other staff—and we trusted them to undertake the quest for knowledge. We insisted that—with the help of the Holy Spirit—they go back and "fetch" that from the past which they needed to move to the future as leaders in our church, community, society, and the world. This is what I believe Paul means when he says to the people "I want you to understand...."

So, Paul wrote to the people of Corinth to help them remember, because Chloe told.

Paul wanted them to remember and to understand that one cannot speak (referring to idols who they worshipped, be it Apollo or Cephas or anyone) unless by the Holy Spirit.

Paul also wanted the people of Corinth to understand was there was a variety of gifts.

> Now there are varieties of gifts, but the same Spirit; and there are varieties of services, but the same Lord; and there are varieties of activities, but it is the same God who activates all of them in everyone. To each is given the manifestation of the Spirit for the common good. To one is given through the Spirit the utterance of wisdom, and to another the utterance of knowledge according to the same Spirit,

[1] Thomas, Linda, "The Holy Spirit and Black Women", *Christian Doctrines for Global Gender Justice*. Palgrave Macmillan, 2015. 73-88.

[2] Ibid.

> to another faith by the same Spirit, to another gifts of healing by the one Spirit, to another the working of miracles, to another prophecy, to another the discernment of spirits, to another various kinds of tongues, to another the interpretation of tongues. (1 Cor 12: 4-10)

A Variety of Gifts

Each is given the manifestation of the Spirit for the common good. God has given a variety of gifts for the work in which the community is to engage. Not everyone can do everything. Each member has a unique gift. And these divine gifts of courage and grace were given in the face of evil.

One of the evils the people of Corinth were facing was the loss of a community who were to be followers of the Way. They were followers of the one who went about healing, the one who was unjustly tried, executed, buried in a tomb and who, on the third day, rose from the dead. They were to be followers of one who articulated an understanding of who God was and of how God functioned in a way that was just. They were to be followers of the one who hung out with all kinds of folk, some of whom were deemed to be undesirable. There were those who were oppressed because of gender, ethnicity, class, or even sexual orientation. They were to be followers of one who was social.

According to womanist theologian Karen Baker-Fletcher, "God is Social. God is concerned with who God is in relation to God's self and who God is in relation to creation."[3] God is a divine community whose aim is for authentic community on earth as in heaven. Through God's son, God left the Advocate to comfort, direct them, and gather them.

The Spirit Gathers

Womanist theologians understand this and approach their understanding of God, Jesus the Christ, and the Holy Spirit from a holistic approach that is inclusive of the entire community—both male and female—understanding that God is about the business of healing and wholeness for all. And these gifts are evidence of the indwelling of Spirit.

[3] Karen Baker-Fletcher, *Dancing with God: The Trinity from a Womanist Perspective*. Chalice Press, 2006. ix.

Gifts activated by one and the same Spirit

The Holy Spirit is the power of life. It is the power that brings life out of death. Some scholars question whether we are talking about Spirit or the Holy Spirit. But as an unknown womanist theologian says:

> It is the Spirit of God that the prophets and the Messiah speaks
> It is the Spirit that David sings and danced.
> It is this same Spirit that the apostles and the early followers of Christ are able to use to overcome evil.

Jesus also left the gift of the Holy Spirit. Paul is able to teach the early church by the Spirit. The healing power of God is given in the movement of the Holy Spirit. We are introduced to the movement of the Holy Spirit in Mary, mother of Jesus: Mary, a symbol of courageous, outrageous authority. But who activates her gifts? The Spirit.

Thomas is known to quote the Zimbabwean theologian, Edward Antonio, who says the Spirit is always the Spirit of creation. God's breath is responsible for giving and sustaining life. The Spirit is the heart of God that is Spirit. There is an understanding that God is ever present in creation's struggle for life abundant and for the full realization of freedom, justice, love, and wholeness on earth as in heaven.

Paul seems to be alluding to the fact that God invites and persuades us into healing relations with God, and the rest of creation, to participate in God's creating, healing, restoring, and resurrection activity. This work is activated by the same Spirit. These gifts are diverse in character (with the purpose of collectively working in the community) and have the same origin.

These gifts (and exercising the gifts) were to be engaged by hope, faith, and love—a love that overcomes fear and resists oppression. It is a creative, prophetic, and renewing power of God: resurrection power that begins with the Spirit and ends with the creation of a new thing.

As Thomas wrote about the Holy Spirit, black women, the suffering caused by enslavement, and black women's tenacity to fight for new, sacred life: "This suffering ought not to be; we shall struggle until we have changed the present reality in the just and free and loving community".[4] Thomas says black, enslaved women's survival and resistance are indications of the creative power of the Spirit in their lives. The presence of the indwelling Spirit governs their decision making. They know, as Paul wrote in 2 Corinthians 3:17, that the "Lord is the Spirit, and where the Spirit of the Lord is, there is freedom."

[4] Thomas, 73-88.

These spiritual gifts, or spiritual things, are gifts given of God for the purpose of new life. And this everlasting life is relational.

"For in the one Spirit we were all baptized into one body" (1 Cor 12:13)

The body is the church. The church is a living organism made of mutually interdependent members. "It is the struggle for justice, fulfillment of life, for the building up of loving communities that we may discern the activity of the Spirit."[5] Here Paul talks about Jews or Greeks, slaves or free, saying that, no matter what, we are one. The verse continues.

"And we were all made to drink of one Spirit."

Paul may have been reminding those who read his letter to the people of Corinth not to worship other gods or other leaders (such as Apollo or Cephas) but his focus is on the Spirit—an ancient power—lest they forget. The creative power of the Spirit makes people aware of their own dignity and instills respect for one another. This Spirit is realized and experienced in community. So, we are gathered by the Spirit.

The body has many members

Paul concludes this section by saying in vs. 14, "Indeed, the body does not consist of one member but of many." As another womanist theologian, Eboni Marshall Turman, is quoted as saying "the oneness of the Spirit and its simultaneous multivocality which is the gift of Pentecost is where we hear, experience, feel and inherit one Spirit."[6] This Spirit aids in the suffering and struggling of black women and, I would add, the struggles of all of God's people, including Chloe, who is part of the body.

Chloe and the Spirit of Chloe

Chloe knew that the work of the Holy Spirit is to establish the reign of God. As womanist theologians do, Chloe and her people called on Paul

[5] Thomas, 73-88.
[6] Ibid., 78.

to assist in helping God's people to remember, and understand, the work of the Spirit–the work of God–in the community that was forming. They called to end the divisions and quarrelling about who was right and who was wrong. They called for an end to those things that break community. Chloe was evidently used by the Spirit and–in concert with Paul–assisted in the work of the Spirit.

Could it be that womanist theology, African feminist theology, mujerista theology, and Asian women's theology are gifts of the Spirit? Chloe knew that there was a need for divine involvement: Chloe knew, and Chloe told; and Paul was called. That divine involvement was needed in the past to establish the new, and it is also needed today. And so, the Spirit gathers.

There is a new publication by African-descent Lutheran theologians reflecting on the *Small Catechism*. On the third article of the Creed, it reads:

> The Holy Spirit weaves individual existence into a communal existence. I am because we are and we are because I am. The Holy Spirit blesses us with faith and with diverse gits for equipping the community of faith for participation in a world of crucifixion. And I believe that the Holy Spirt, God's creative gift of love and grace, promises to raise me and join me with the ancestors in eternity. This is most certainly true.[7]

[7] Joseph Bocko, *Luther's Small Catechism with African Descent Reflections*, Augsburg Fortress, 2019.

Transformed, Freed, Empowered: The Spirit's Work in the Gifting and Vocation of All Believers

Veli-Matti Kärkkäinen

Introduction

For Lutherans to consider the work and energies of the Holy Spirit, as we dig deeper into our identity, is an exciting task, for it is far more typical for us to refer such questions to Christ and the Trinity. The turn to the third person of the Trinity is a timely response to the call from our worldwide globalizing community, particularly from the global South, where the majority of Lutherans can be found nowadays. Lutherans in Ethiopia, Tanzania, Indonesia, and elsewhere are reminding us to incorporate pneumatological (related to the doctrine of the Holy Spirit) resources and perspectives in our continuing identity search.

My task in this project is to reflect on the Spirit's work, particularly from an anthropological perspective. I ask: What are some of the ways the Spirit of God is empowering, gifting, and inspiring the people of God in order for them to live out the central Reformation vision of the priesthood of all believers? What is the Spirit's role in our Christian missional vocation?

With those questions in mind, I wish to develop my theme in three interrelated steps:

- The Holy Spirit in Lutheranism: A Reminder
- The Holy Spirit and Gifting: A Challenge
- The Holy Spirit in the World: A Vision

The Holy Spirit in Lutheranism: A Reminder

The many metaphors of the Spirit

What pneumatological resources do we have in our tradition? This question can also be framed in this way, twisting the classical dictum of Tertullian: What has Wittenberg to do with the Pentecost event?

Some Lutheran theologians firmly believe that we do possess Spirit resources and that the Pentecost belongs to Lutherans as much as to other Christian families. For example, in Danish theologian Reginald Prenter's classic, *Spiritus Creator: Studies in Luther's Theology,* he insists that:

> The concept of the Holy Spirit completely dominates Luther's theology. In every decisive matter, whether it be the study of Luther's doctrine of justification, of his doctrine of the sacraments, of his ethics, or of any other fundamental teaching, we are forced to take into consideration this concept of the Holy Spirit."[1]

Though undoubtedly an overstatement, his claims are still worth pondering. For while Lutheranism certainly is not known for a focus on the third member of the Trinity, and though Martin Luther never wrote a separate treatise on the Holy Spirit, he nevertheless had many valuable insights on the Spirit. Particularly important are more than twenty of his Pentecost sermons that were based on various texts supplied by the lectionary. And in his exposition of the third article of the Creed, he notably relates everything to the Spirit: the church, forgiveness of sins, resurrection of the body, and eternal life. Alternatively, we might consider Luther's pneumatology in the context of his Trinitarian teaching, since the doctrine of the Trinity was so formative for Luther, so much so that Bernhard Lohse claims that "[w]ith this constant reference to Christ the Holy Spirit assumed an extraordinarily important place in Luther's theology."[2]

A gifted preacher, Luther often illustrated his sermons and writings with delightful pictures and metaphors. Taking a cue from Acts 17:28, he came up with the idea of calling the Father the "substance" of the Godhead, the Son the "motion" or "movement"–having been sent by the Father, and the Spirit the "rest": "We live according to the Spirit, in whom the Father

---

[1] Reginald Prenter, *Spiritus Creator: Luther's Concept of the Holy Spirit,* trans. John M. Jensen (Philadelphia, Penn.: Muhlenberg Press, 1953), ix.

[2] Bernhard Lohse, *Martin Luther's Theology: Its Historical and Systematic Development,* trans. and ed., Roy A. Harrisville (Minneapolis, Minn.: Fortress Press, 1999), 235.

and the Son rest and live, as it were."[3] In explaining the meaning of the *Paraclete* in John 14-16, Luther compared the Spirit's role to that of the preacher who, like an excellent pastor, reminds the congregation of the dangers of false teachers and of those who boast in human merits. The Holy Spirit takes from Christ's own and shares that with us rather than delivering a "human dream and thought."[4] Particularly inventive is Luther's creative recasting of the creation narrative (Gen 1:2) into a poetic form with analogies drawn from nature:

> The Father creates heaven and earth out of nothing through the Son, whom Moses calls the Word. Over these the Holy Spirit broods. As a hen broods her eggs, keeping them warm in order to hatch her chicks, and, as it were, to bring them to life through heat, so Scripture says that the Holy Spirit brooded, as it were, on the waters to bring to life those substances which were to be quickened and adorned. For it is the office of the Holy Spirit to make alive.[5]

The Spirit's work in word, salvation, and church

Always a Trinitarian theologian, standing firmly on the tradition of the church, Luther made every effort to establish an integral link between the Spirit and Christ. In his exposition of the Creed in the *Large Catechism*, he reminds us that:

> [64] God ... created us ... to redeem and sanctify us. Moreover, having bestowed upon us everything in heaven and on earth, he has given us his Son and his Holy Spirit, through whom he brings us to himself. [65] ... [W]e could never come to recognize the Father's favor and grace were it not for the Lord Christ, who is a mirror of the Father's heart. Apart from him we see nothing but an angry and terrible Judge. But neither could we know anything of Christ, had it not been revealed by the Holy Spirit.[6]

As is well-known, the close and integral relationship between God's word and God's Spirit was a particular concern to him:

---

[3] Martin Luther, *Galatians Commentary* (1519) on 4:6, in *Luther's Works*. American ed. (Libronix Digital Library), ed. Jaroslav Pelikan and Helmut T. Lehman, vol. 27 (Minneapolis, Minn.: Fortress Press, 2002), 290.

[4] Luther, *Sermons on the Gospel of St. John* (1537), chaps. 14–16, in LW 24: 363.

[5] Luther, *Lectures on Genesis*, chap. 1–5, on 1:2, in LW 1: 9.

[6] Luther, *Large Catechism*, Creed, art. 3, #64, 65, in *The Book of Concord: The Confessions of the Evangelical Lutheran Church*, trans. Theodore G. Tappert (Philadelphia, Penn.: Fortress Press, 1959), 419.

> No one can correctly understand God or His Word unless he has received such understanding immediately from the Holy Spirit. But no one can receive it from the Holy Spirit without experiencing, proving, and feeling it. In such experience the Holy Spirit instructs us as in His own school, outside of which nothing is learned but empty words and prattle.[7]

No wonder, then, that the gift of salvation wrought by the Triune God is communicated to us by the Spirit of God. Every confirmed Lutheran knows this passage from the *Small Catechism*:

> I believe that by my own reason or strength I cannot believe in Jesus Christ, my Lord, or come to him. But the Holy Spirit has called me through the Gospel, enlightened me with his gifts, and sanctified and preserved me in true faith, just as he calls, gathers, enlightens, and sanctifies the whole Christian church on earth and preserves it in union with Jesus Christ in the one true faith.[8]

Similarly—and here we come to the center of Luther's pneumatological understanding—it is the work of sanctification, or holiness, that is distinctive of the ministry of the Spirit. Expressing this in an authentic [9] framework, Luther says: "As the Father is called Creator and the Son is called Redeemer, so on account of his work the Holy Spirit must be called Sanctifier, the One who makes holy." Commenting on Romans 8:16 ("[I]t is that very Spirit bearing witness with our spirit that we are children of God") the reformer further reminds us of the testimony of the same Spirit in the heart of the believer.[10]

Yet the Spirit is at work not only in the individual believer's faith and life, but also in the Christian community. Another familiar passage from the *Small Catechism* sums it up: "But the Holy Spirit has called me through the Gospel, enlightened me with his gifts, and sanctified and preserved me in true faith, just as he calls, gathers, enlightens, and sanctifies the whole Christian church on earth and preserves it in union with Jesus Christ in the one true faith."[11] In the *Large Catechism*, Luther elaborates on the various benefits the Spirit brings about in the church, including her calling "together [the church] by the Holy Spirit in one faith, mind, and understanding," and the endowment with "a variety of gifts," in unity.

---

[7] Luther, *The Magnificat*, in LW 21: 299. See also Jeffrey G. Silcock, "Luther on the Holy Spirit and His Use of God's Word," in *The Oxford Handbook of Martin Luther's Theology*, ed. Robert Kolb, Irene Dingel, and Lubomir Batka (Oxford: Oxford University Press, 2014), 307.

[8] Luther, *Small Catechism*, Creed, art. 3, in BC, 345.

[9] Luther, *Large Catechism*, Creed, art. 3, #36, in BC, 415.

[10] Luther, *Lectures on Romans*, in LW 25: 359–360.

[11] *Small Catechism*, Creed, art. 3, #6, in BC, 345.

Indeed, "Until the last day the Holy Spirit remains with the holy community or Christian people" and works out various ministries.[12]

Reflection: Anything missing in our understanding of the Spirit's work?

It is appropriate to pause for a moment and take stock of pneumatological resources and emphases in our tradition. I wish to make four brief comments and then further develop our theme in light of these observations.

First, against the common assumption, or charge, that Lutheranism has ignored the third person of the Trinity, this brief survey, supported by other essays in this collection, tells otherwise. There is in fact a fairly rich repertoire of biblical and theological insights into the many roles of the Spirit in the life of the Christian and the church. Particularly important are the domains of word, salvation, and the church. This is all good and certainly worth preserving.

Second, it is clear that Lutheran pneumatology is almost exclusively focused on the "spiritual" and salvific aspects. It has fairly little to say of God's Spirit outside the personal and communal salvation and spirituality. That said, this is not only a Lutheran liability. Rather, the mainline doctrine of the Spirit, particularly in the Christian West, has concentrated on issues of spirituality, divine word, salvation, sacraments, and some other ecclesial issues.

This has meant, third, that issues having to do with the "public"–or dare we call it, "worldly"? –work of the Spirit have received only scant and occasional treatment. Even though Luther himself invoked a few delightful metaphors from nature, issues related to the Spirit's role in creation have not played a significant role in our tradition. We Lutherans have similarly virtually neglected the Spirit's role in society, politics, economics, culture, entertainment, and the arts and sciences. And we have only very recently even acknowledged the whole issue of the potential role of the S/spirit(s) among religions, even among other Abrahamic faiths (Judaism and Islam).

Last but not least, we Lutherans have neglected, minimized, or outright resisted the ministry of the Holy Spirit in charismatic endowment, spiritual gifts, and dynamic spirituality – all profoundly important themes for the global Lutheran community of the third millennium. The charismatic freedom of the Spirit has been a contentious issue among Lutherans, and more often than not there have been attempts to "limit" the Spirit's work. Despite all this, the charismatic element is a key asset for cultivating and facilitating vocation among the whole people of God and we neglect it to the detriment of our ministry and spiritual health.

[12] *Large Catechism*, Creed, art. 3, in BC, 416–417

Let us now unpack these observations and relate our reflections and insights into the gifting, vocation, and the ministry of the whole people of God, for the sake of the Triune God's mission in the world.

Holy Spirit and Gifting: A Challenge

Why do we struggle with the charismatic element?

Another way to title this subsection would be to ask of ourselves: "What has Wittenberg to do with Charisms?" Why are we Lutherans so often wary of speaking too much, or at all, of spiritual gifts and empowerment? There are a number of reasons. I begin with the most obvious ones.

The roots of our charismatic suspicion go far back in Christian history, at least to the second part of the second century, when a powerful Spirit movement named Montanism emerged. It challenged the authority of the church and her hierarchy, particularly that of the bishops. Under the leadership of Montanus, this movement claimed to receive direct messages from the Spirit of God (unmediated by the church), and hence a divinely granted authority over existing ecclesiastical powers. In later history, even after the mainstream church defeated Montanism, charismatically endowed, and usually prophetic, movements arose over and over again, particularly during times of spiritual awakening and refreshment. For example, in the medieval period, there were many such movements in the church catholic.

By the time the Protestant Reformation emerged, this ancient suspicion towards free-spirited groups and leaders had grown deep and wide. The mainstream church considered them a threat. Yet, this charismatic vitality did not die out.

Enter Martin Luther who had to fight simultaneously on two fronts. On the one hand, this former Augustinian monk had become critical of his own catholic church's reliance on the hierarchy and human leadership over the Spirit and word. At the same time, counterintuitively, the Church of Rome, particularly among its numerous monastic orders, had developed a long and varied tradition of cultivating all kinds of mystical, spiritualistic, and charismatic phenomena, from healing and exorcism to prophetic word and other charisms. Luther thought that at times the Church of Rome gave these phenomena authority over the written word.

On the other hand, he had to face the Reformation era's version of the Montanists, that is the Anabaptists (of various sorts) and other "left-wing" reformers, whom he (mistakenly and pejoratively) called the "Enthusiasts." Rightly or wrongly, Luther assumed that they claimed a "direct," unmediated spiritual experience and so undermined the sacraments and the Word.[13]

This fear of the spiritualists resulted in what theology calls "cessationism." From the English word "to cease," it simply means the idea of coming to an end of the charismatic phenomena and miracles after the closing of the Christian canon in the fourth century. Why? The reason, so cessationists surmise, is that whereas before the biblical canon was in place divinely granted spiritual "signs" were needed to ascertain the authenticity of the ministry and teaching of a leader or a community, no such guarantees were required once the written word was available to serve as the criterion. The Lutheran Reformation subscribed to this view. An example is Luther's distinction between two comings of the Spirit: first, "In the primitive church ... in a manifest and visible form...with visible signs" including speaking in tongues and thereafter, including his own time, "without a visible form, namely...through the spoken Word" into our hearts.[14]

I have suggested that there might be two categories of cessationism: first, what might be called "soft-core" cessationism, according to which there is no dogmatic denial of charisms even after the closing of the canon, but rather a wondering of why they seem not to be happening now. In my understanding, Luther himself probably represented this interpretation as, even after having left his religious order, he, for example, testified and was open to what seemed to be miraculous healings. The second category could be dubbed "hard-core" cessationism, typical of some movements much later than Reformation, including the American Reformed fundamentalism of the turn of the twentieth century. Benjamin B. Warfield's *Counterfeit Miracles* (1918) showcases this interpretation: since spiritual gifts have ceased, should you encounter a claim to one, it must be counterfeit.

There are other reasons that have contributed to the Lutheran suspicion towards the charismatic element. These include a biased, careless interpretation of some doctrinal formulations and emphases which, rightly used, are essential for the Lutheran understanding of faith. For example, a programmatic Lutheran insistence is that under normal circumstances the believer may encounter the

[13] In hindsight, and in fairness to the Anabaptists, with the exception of the extremes such as the followers of Müntzer, by and large left-wing Reformers did not want to get around the written Word. On the contrary, in current terminology they were fundamentalists who wished to take literally the biblical teaching, including pacifism. Similarly, even with regard to the sacraments, they did not necessarily want to undermine them, even if their theological understanding of them was radically different from the Catholics and mainline Protestants. In their desire to go back to the believers' baptism, they appealed to the Bible and they were deeply concerned about widespread nominalism among the church folks who seemed to practice sacraments as a more or less automatic way of earning salvation.

[14] Luther, *Galatians Commentary* (1535), in LW 26: 374–375.

Holy Spirit and the Spirit's work in the context of Scripture and the sacraments. While this does not have to mean an absolute rejection of the Spirit's freedom to move elsewhere, it is a pastoral-theological safeguard. A well-known prescription from *Schmalcald Articles*, penned by Luther himself, states:

> In these matters, which concern the external, spoken Word, we must hold firmly to the conviction that God gives no one his Spirit or grace except through or with the external Word which comes before. Thus, we shall be protected from the enthusiasts–that is, from the spiritualists who boast that they possess the Spirit without and before the Word and who therefore judge, interpret, and twist the Scriptures or spoken Word according to their pleasure...Accordingly, we should and must constantly maintain that God will not deal with us except through his external Word and sacrament.[15]

The same general rule is echoed in Luther's exposition of Psalms with regard to a pastoral situation in which a person needs the Spirit's touch for encouragement: "We must not, as the sectarians do, imagine that God comforts us immediately, without His Word. Comfort does not come to us without the Word, which the Holy Spirit effectively calls to mind and enkindles in our hearts."[16]

This tight linking of the Spirit and word and sacraments can be a precious and comfortable Lutheran rule. But when its contextual and occasional nature is forgotten–namely that it was a polemic reaction against what the reformers regarded as an extreme spiritualist bent among the Anabaptists–and when it is used carelessly against every claim for the reception of spiritual experiences, gifts, and manifestations, then the rule becomes counterproductive and even harmful. Our history knows too many such regretful instances. Furthermore, it may border on an attempt to curtail the freedom of God's Spirit by human means, an effort doomed to failure.

Another significant obstacle to the embrace of the charismatic gifts and manifestations has to do with numerous and varied pastoral-theological problems among those who claim to be charismatics, whether in the Lutheran community or beyond it. They are so obvious and so well-known that it suffices to merely list a few of them:

- abuse of gifts
- pride and a sense of superiority
- prosperity gospel
- "counterfeit" and false claims of the miraculous
- divisions and splits in the community
- strange and awkward claims, such as that (little) children serve as healers and exorcists

---

[15] *Schmalcald Articles*, part 3, art. 8, #3, 10, in BC, 312–313.

[16] Luther, *Selected Psalms III*, in LW 14: 62.

And finally, there is no denying the fact that Pentecostals of various stripes, people who often identify themselves as the custodians of the Spirit, have regrettably contributed to many prejudices against even authentic charismatic manifestations. Too many strange and unhelpful things have been done in the name of the Pentecost and the Spirit. On the other hand, Lutheran and other mainline constituencies are often envious of Pentecostals' success in gaining attention, drawing people, and expanding their ministries.

Now, having reflected on some of the main reasons for the Lutheran reservation against the charismatic element, let us attempt some constructive explorations into the significance and benefits of the Spirit's gifting and empowerment for the sake of the vocation of the whole people of God.

Charismatic gifting and the ministry of the whole people of God in one body

Let me begin with a somewhat provocative statement, namely that "normal Christian life is charismatic." To illustrate and deepen that claim, I lay out the following five short "theses" and further develop their meaning and significance for our topic:

- The charismatic is not an "exception," it is the norm.
- The charismatic does not compete with Christ and Word.
- The charismatic and the character belong together.
- The charismatic is not (typically) wild and uncontrolled.
- The charismatic is for all believers–for vocations.

So, what does charismatic gifting mean? What are we talking about when we speak of charisms? Since our confessional texts do not address this issue constructively, we go first to the New Testament teaching. Biblical texts are clear that charisms range from the more extraordinary (miraculous works, healing, exorcism, words of wisdom, prophetic words) to the more "mundane" (teaching, exhortation, giving generously). A quick look at the following New Testament passages offers evidence: 1 Corinthians 12:8-11, 28-31; Romans 12:6-8; and 1 Peter 4:10. In other words, the domain of the charisms is broad. At the same time, charisms are manifold and diverse; there is no fixed "list" in the canon, as if only particular ones were normative.

According to the New Testament witness, all believers are given gifts. In that sense, all believers are charismatic: "To each is given the manifestation of the Spirit for the common good." (1 Cor 12:7). Each of us receives "gifts that differ according to the grace given to us" (Rom 12:6). These gifts are not assigned, let alone brought about, by human persons, not even by the leaders of the community. Rather, charisms, spiritual gifts, and endowments are distributed sovereignly by the "Spirit, who allots to each one individually just as the

Spirit chooses." (1 Cor 12:11) Yet this does not make void the Christian's active embrace, and even pursuit, of gifts. Paul instructs us that notwithstanding the divine sovereignty, the faithful are "[to] strive for the greater gifts." (v. 31)

Importantly, the New Testament emphasizes that the gifts and endowments are not meant for boasting, to create sense of superiority, nor for selfish enjoyment. They are meant "for the common good" (v. 7), for service and ministry, that is, for vocation. This central principle is brought home vividly and robustly in Paul's teaching in 1 Corinthians 12. The rough outline alone makes this clear. Drawing from the body analogy (the church as the body of Christ), the chapter reveals three interrelated principles, at the center of which is the vocation, or ministry, of the whole people of God, through the empowerment and gifting of the Spirit:

- 12:1-3 The Lordship of Jesus Christ
- 12:4-11 The Diversity of Gifts, by One Spirit
- 12:12-27 The Unity of the Body in Service

Over against Lutheran fears that by opening ourselves up to the wide and rich charismatic energies of the Holy Spirit, our focus on Christ and Trinity might be thwarted, Paul reminds us first of the lordship of the Head of the Body. Pleasing to the Triune God is only such charismatic ministry that is based on an uncompromising lordship of Christ. There is no place for human pride and selfish motives; rather, charismatic gifting is about lifting up Christ and his name. Based on Christ's lordship, in an integral Trinitarian logic, "there are varieties of gifts, but the same Spirit; and there are varieties of service, but the same Lord; and there are varieties of working, but it is the same God who inspires them all in everyone" (vv. 4-6). And all of that is for the united, concerted ministry of the whole people of God, for the sake of the unity of the body in which everybody needs one another, and everybody may contribute to each other.

Knowing that the ultimate aim of the charismatic gifting and endowment is to facilitate our vocational capacity in ministry of the whole people of God, I turn now to consider in more detail the nature of the church's ministry.

Ministry as Charismatic-Diaconal Vocation of the Whole Community

Although the terms "ministry" and "minister" are commonplace in ecclesiastical English, it might come as a surprise that a single corresponding word is difficult to find in the New Testament. Instead, there are two terms that denote what we mean by the term "ministry." The first one is *diakonia*, a word with several interrelated meanings and usages in the canon, but which, for our purposes, simply functions as the placeholder for ministry. An illustrative example is Paul's statement in 2 Corinthians 4:1 where he talks about his ministry [*diakonia*] "by God's mercy" (so also,1 Pet 4:10). From the Greek word meaning "lowly service" (initially referring to table service by the slaves), it communicates humble service for the benefit of others and a lowly status, rather than a privilege.

Another term more or less synonymous with our English word *ministry* is the aforementioned *charisma*, meaning "graced" endowment or capacity from God. The root of the term *charism* lies in the Greek term *charis*, meaning grace. This reminds us that all gifts, endowments, and capacities are given to us with no consideration of our own merit. Such gifts stem from divine grace and benevolence. Hence, there is absolutely no place for pride or feelings of superiority. Therefore, charisms, rightly understood, have nothing to do with the "theology of glory": how can one boast who submits to the lordship of Christ (1 Cor 12:1-3), putting himself or herself willingly in a lowly place of serving others (*diakonia*), and receives charisms by the grace of God?

Who, then, are the ministers—the charismatically gifted and endowed diaconal servants—of the church? The answer is simple and profound: the whole community is the "minister" of the church. Not a few select individuals or groups, but the whole church, every member of the body. This is the crux and essence of the Lutheran principle of the priesthood of all believers. There is not only one center or locus of ministry in the church, there are many, and they all contribute to the common good. In the words of the Episcopalian theologian Miroslav Volf, the Christian church is a "polycentric community" with the participation, gifting, and responsibility of all members instead of the traditional "bipolar" model in which those in office do the church's work and the laity observes.[17]

But what about the role and significance of the ordained ministers, pastors, bishops, and others? Yes, they do have indispensable work to do, but they are first and foremost a part of the community and serve alongside it. The ordained are there for the sake of the "order"[18] and diaconally-charismatically serve the community. The ordained are not above, but rather in the community. One of their key tasks is to train others for the ministry (Eph 4:13). As with every member of the community, they are accountable to the community and to her Lord. [19]

A stunning description of the early church in the Book of Acts, in the aftermath of the Day of Pentecost, gives us an example in every age:

---

[17] Miroslav Volf, *After Our Likeness: The Church as the Image of the Trinity* (Grand Rapids, Mich.: Wm. B. Eerdmans, 1998), 224-225.

[18] *Augsburg Confession*, 14, in BC, 36.

[19] See also Veli-Matti Kärkkäinen, "Missional Existence as the Charismatic-Diaconal Ministry," in *Hope and Community*, A Constructive Christian Theology for the Pluralistic World, vol. 5 (Grand Rapids, Mich.: Wm. B. Eerdmans, 2017), 400-420.

> ... [And] many wonders and signs were being done by the apostles. All who believed were together and had all things in common; they would see their possessions and goods and distribute the proceeds to all, as any had need. Day by day, as they spent much time together in the temple, they broke bread at home and ate their food with glad and generous hearts, praising God and having the goodwill of all the people. And day by day the Lord added to their number those who were being saved (Acts 2:43-47).[20]

Just consider the amazing balance and richness of this particular community, gifted, freed, and empowered by the Pentecostal Spirit. United in fellowship, including both the regular teaching of the Word and the celebration of the sacraments, as well as the social-diaconal caring for each other's needs, they witnessed manifold charismatic phenomena and manifestations, and their outreach to people around them resulted in steady growth. What a pattern to imitate!

Having now inquired into Lutheran pneumatological resources with regard to the gifting and empowering of the ministry of the whole people of God, the third main section of the essay expands and enriches our vision of the work of the Spirit. Above, I noted the Lutheran lack of attention to the Spirit's role outside the church and personal salvation. This lacuna has to do with the "public" work of the Spirit in creation, the sciences, society, politics, economics, culture, entertainment, the arts, and other faith traditions.

The Holy Spirit in the World: A Vision

The Spirit "blows where it wills"

This Johannine Jesus statement (Jn 3:8) reminds us of the sovereignty and absolute freedom of the Spirit of God in the world that the Triune God has created. As we re-imagine our Lutheran identity at the beginning of the third millennium, it is well worth asking the following kinds of questions with regard to our conception of the freedom of the Spirit:

- What is the special ministry of the Spirit in creation? What kinds of resources can we find for discerning the Spirit in creation drawing on our tradition's robust creation theology, typically conceived of through the lens of the first article of the Creed?

- What might the sovereign Spirit have to do in society, outside the church? Are there particular domains of human society in which the

[20] Emphases added.

Spirit's role might be more prominent: perhaps in the arts and culture; in economics and work; in science and education; and so forth?

- Is there any connection between pneumatology and the secular-scientific framework in understanding the world and ourselves? Or are these two ways of explanation totally disconnected?

- What could we say about the reality and meaning of the "spirits," spiritual powers, power encounters, exorcism, and similar topics? While these questions are heard more frequently among Lutherans living in the global South, in the global North Lutherans routinely ignore or even blatantly deny them. Should we just leave these topics to Roman Catholics (who have recently reinstituted the ancient office of the exorcist, for example), to Pentecostal-Charismatics, and to some Evangelicals? Or should we instead help Lutheran communities drink from our own spiritual-theological wells?

- What, if any, is the ministry and role of the Spirit of God among living faith traditions? How would pneumatology inform and guide Lutheran communities and believers living in diverse multireligious contexts?

- And what about secularism? Alongside religions, secularisms in various forms are growing and flourishing. Does pneumatology inform our understanding of what secularism might represent?

One way to inspire and construct a more truly global vision of the Spirit's work and domain is to speak of the "spheres" or "layers" of the Spirit. What if the Spirit of God is at work:

- in *creation*, as the Spirit of life, bringing about, nourishing, and enlivening creation, with an invitation to a careful engagement with natural sciences as well as with green-environmental efforts?

- in *cosmos*, as the divine Spirit (among other spirits), spiritual powers, and spiritual energies, with a call for a faithful and wise discernment of the spirits?

- among *religions*, as the Spirit of the Triune God among the spirits of other religions, with the invitation into mutually enriching, comparative theological work?

- in *society*, as the Public Spirit, in politics, economics, social structures, arts, and entertainment–leaving "not a square inch in the whole domain of our human existence" (A. Kuyper) untouched by the Triune God?

- in the *church*, as the Ecclesial Spirit, creating the temple of the Spirit, a charismatically empowered, guided, sanctified, renewed, and unified community in the service of the world, including spiritual, diaconal, socio-political, and environmental tasks?

- in personal *salvation*, as the Salvific Spirit, in all aspects of the *ordo salutis*, including not only the "spiritual" domain (election, new birth, sanctification, and so forth) but also mental-physical healing and charismatic endowment and gifting?[21]

A Final Challenge

This last section of the essay is by far the shortest–and intentionally so. At the moment, we have fairly little to report. For this is only the beginning of our exploration, a widening of our vision. Where this journey takes us, we have yet to see.

In the meantime, let us be challenged and energized by the passionate words of Robert W. Cummings, a former generation's missionary to India, a Presbyterian turned Pentecostal. His call is to all Christian churches and communities, including to ours:

> Shameful neglect of the Holy Spirit is the great sin of the Christian Church, and it is the greatest sin of the average Christian. We forget that when the Church came into being at Pentecost *every* member, the *least* as well as the greatest, was supernaturally filled with the Holy Spirit.... We have told the men and women of our own day who have had great experiences to keep them in the background lest ordinary Christians... should get the idea that they, too, may have such wonderful experiences. We sum it all up when we piously sing, "I ask no dreams, no prophet ecstasies; no sudden rending of the veil of clay; no angel visitant, no opening skies." So we get none.[22]

[21] For details, see Veli-Matti Kärkkäinen, Part 1: "Spirit," in *Spirit and Salvation*, A Constructive Christian Theology for the Pluralistic World, vol. 4 (Grand Rapids, Mich.: Wm. B. Eerdmans, 2016), 7–22.
[22] Robert W. Cummings, "Unto You Is the Promise: A Personal Testimony" (Lucknow, India: Lucknow Publishing House, 1941), 1–2.

We Believe in the Holy Spirit: Global Perspectives on Lutheran Identity

Yacob Godebo

This paper pays particular attention to three points: how Lutheran theological identities are formed; the contemporary significance of Lutheran theological identities; and how Lutheran theological identities inform the Lutheran sense of vocation and ministry. I will begin by addressing how Lutheran theological identities are formed.

Lutheran churches know very well that their theological identities are formed and rooted in three divinely appointed means of grace (the word of God, Holy Baptism, and Holy Communion); faith in Christ that receives salvation and justification through these means; and the gift of the Holy Spirit, who works through these means towards believers' transformation and sanctification. These features were delivered to the world by the divine person, Jesus Christ. Scripture shows how Jesus instituted and delivered these features to the world.

- **The word of God:** Jesus declared that anyone who keeps his word will become his disciple and will never see death.[1] He asserted that those who do not want to hear and hold his word will be judged by that same word on the day of the last judgment.[2] This indicates that Jesus' words, and all the teaching of the gospels, are capable of saving and condemning, and thus are the decisive element for salvation. Paul acknowledged that the word of God builds up the life of believers and

[1] Jn 8:31, 51.
[2] Jn 12:47–48.

places them among those who are sanctified by faith in Christ.[3] Similarly, Luther acknowledged that "God's Word contains and conveys all the fullness of God."[4] Therefore, whoever has the word has everything that is required for salvation.[5] Lutherans commit themselves to this word as the decisive means of salvation.

- **Holy baptism:** Jesus declared that "no one can enter the kingdom of God without being born of water and the Spirit."[6] He insisted on this birth as the primary requirement to be met in order to belong to the kingdom of God. When this baptism is conducted by church with the visible element of water, God baptizes the candidate invisibly with the Holy Spirit. The two elements—visible natural water and invisible Holy Spirit—together yield one result: rebirth in the Spirit for new life. Paul perceived this fact and affirmed that God justifies the sinner in this baptism[7] and that those who are baptized are those who have put on Christ and are new creatures.[8] In baptism, divine life is mystically imparted to the sinner who is given a new identity in Christ and eternal life. Baptism, therefore, for Lutherans, is God's work[9] through which God brings the "dead back to life" and shares eternal life, which is "life of the Trinity" with them.[10] It "brings all God's grace;"[11] "gives forgiveness of sins . . . and the Holy Spirit with His gifts;"[12] and "initiates a new relationship with God."[13] Therefore, for Lutherans, post-baptismal life means a new life—a shared life with the Trinity—with far-reaching differences in the character and quality of life. Lutherans acknowledge this to be the objective work of God and commit themselves to this life identity.

[3] Acts 20:32.
[4] Paul Althaus, *The Theology of Martin Luther*, trans. Robert C. Schultz (Philadelphia: Fortress Press, 1966), 353.
[5] Althaus, 350.
[6] Jn 3:5.
[7] Rom 6:4-7.
[8] Gal 3:27.
[9] *Large Catechism* IV: 4, 8, 31, 35.
[10] Carl L. Beckwith, *The Holy Trinity*, Confessional Lutheran Dogmatics, vol. 3 (Fort Wayne, Ind.: The Luther Academy, 2016), 233.
[11] David P. Scaer, *Baptism*, Confessional Lutheran Dogmatics, vol. 11 (St. Louis, Mo.: The Luther Academy, 1999), 11.
[12] *Large Catechism* IV: 41.
[13] CA, Apology II. 35-37.

- **Holy Communion:** Jesus declared that he is "the bread that comes down from heaven, so that one may eat of it and not die. ... the bread that I will give for the life of the world is my flesh. ... Those who eat my flesh and drink my blood will have eternal life ... [and] abide in me, and I in them."[14] At the last supper, he instituted the means to eat his flesh and drink his blood.[15] He asserted that divine life is mystically imparted to those who share in his flesh and blood.[16] Paul assures this by saying that believers are justified by the blood of Jesus. Therefore, Jesus' life is mystically imparted to them: they become children of God – co-heirs with Christ to live by the Spirit of God.[17] In and through his flesh and blood, a believer's soul is united with Christ's soul and becomes an equal partner of eternal life. His flesh and blood, therefore, is "the medium through which the atonement is applied to each communicant."[18] Herein lies the mystery of incarnation and Emmanuel. Here again, Lutherans find their assurance and identity in the objective work of God and commit themselves to this life identity. For Lutherans, faith is the means by which they receive and hold the salvific benefits gained through these means of grace.

- **Faith in Christ:** Jesus declared, "For God so loved the world that he gave his only Son, so that everyone who believes in him may not perish but have eternal life."[19] After his ascension and glorification, Jesus revealed himself to Saul (later Paul) on the road to Damascus and declared to him that those who believed in him receive "a place among those who are sanctified by faith in me."[20] These sayings assure believers about the value of faith in Jesus. It is on this theological and biblical foundation that Lutherans assert that God's love displayed on the cross of Christ is not conditional and does not require human efforts for salvation: It just requires believing in God. They assert that our salvation is accomplished by God and delivered to us by God through faith in Christ who is appointed by God. This is where the Lutheran doctrine of justification by faith, "the article with and by which the

[14] Jn 6:41, 50–51, 53–56.
[15] Mt 26:26–28.
[16] Jn 14:20; 17:23.
[17] Rom 5:9; 8:14.
[18] John R. Stephenson, *The Lord's Supper*, Confessional Lutheran Dogmatics, vol. 12 (St. Louis: The Luther Academy, 2003), 191.
[19] Jn 3:16; 6:29, 40.
[20] Acts 26:17–18.

> church stands and without which it falls," is rooted.[21] For Lutherans, this is the doctrine on which both the church and individual believers "stand or fall."[22] Thus, Lutherans assert that faith in Christ is the means in and through which God delivers his saving and gracious acts to the world.[23] This is why they emphasize God's gracious initiative in salvation as opposed to any subjective effort to achieve salvation and reject any boasting about individual effort in the salvation enterprise.[24]

From this scriptural evidence, it can be noted that Jesus assured his followers that the word of God, holy baptism, Holy Communion, and faith in Christ are an end in themselves for salvation and for attaining eternal life. Added to these, as we will see shortly, is God's gracious gift of the Holy Spirit who indwells and guides believers and seals their salvation and sanctification. As God instituted these means of grace and works in, and through, them to bring salvation and sanctification to sinners' lives, the Holy Spirit, too, works through them because the Holy Spirit works what God works.[25] Hence, the word of God, holy baptism, Holy Communion, faith in Christ, and the gift of the Holy Spirit are theologically rooted and pneumatologically applied as the absolute means of salvation and sanctification. God has laid specific salvific mandates on them. Therefore, they are essentials and mandatory for Christian theology and life. They are normative for salvation and are both parameter and paramount for Christian belief, teaching, life, and mission. This is a two-thousand-year theological identity of Christianity as a whole and a five-hundred-year theological identity of Lutherans in particular. Lutheran theological identities are formed on this theological and biblical reality. Their faith, doctrine, confessions, spirituality, mission and vocations are founded and rooted in these divinely destined and divinely delivered features. This is a Lutheran theological characteristic and forms the eternal Lutheran theological identities and, thus, their dogmas. Once again, we acknowledge, in agreement with Luther, that here we stand. This, I think, can be the answer to the question of how Lutheran theological identities are formed.

When it comes to the question of the contemporary significance of the Lutheran theological identities, without any doubt and any compromise, their significance is expressed from Hosanna to Maranatha. Worship and

---

[21] R. C. Sproul, *Faith Alone: The Evangelical Doctrine of Justification* (Ada, Mich.: Baker Books, 1995), 67–68.

[22] Sproul, 70.

[23] Althaus, 211–220.

[24] CA, XX. 11–13.

[25] CA, V.

liturgical structures and mission and evangelization approaches may differ from region to region, or country to country, depending on a given contextual situation: however, basic theological identities that are rooted in the elements previously mentioned are never subject to change. As long as Lutherans live and witness to these core features of Christian identity, they can comfortably articulate a coherent and shared narrative that helps them recognize each other in this existing and lasting Christian identity, and accept each other as brothers and sisters of one living family in Christ.

With regard to the question of how Lutheran theological identities inform the Lutheran sense of vocation and ministry, it is unequivocal that the Lutheran sense of vocations and ministry is rooted in the word and work of God. We shall see this later in this paper.

The second document I focused on is the concept note for this consultation. It contains many evolving issues from which I picked only three due to the limits of my presentation. The concept note states that, "Some churches of the LWF call for renewal by reviving spirituality, and some churches struggle to understand the myriad expressions of spiritual gifts that call into question their experience of faith in the Lutheran Church." It then puts a question: "What can we say about the work of the Holy Spirit?" In order to duly answer this question, the LWF wants to "engage member churches and theologians in theological reflection on the work of the Holy Spirit," beginning with the theme "We believe in the Holy Spirit - Global Perspectives on Lutheran Identity." It adds that the aim and objective of this consultation is to "create a framework for understanding the person and work of the Holy Spirit that can be deployed in future regional gatherings and frame contextual engagement."[26] This requires answering the question: What can we say about the person and work of the Holy Spirit? The sole and core answer to this question is that we keep on believing and saying what the scriptures teach us, and how the creeds and confessions guide us in our understanding of the person and the work of the Holy Spirit. If more clarification is required, then, a few points may be drawn from the scriptures and historical situations:

1. In the Old Testament, the Spirit of God (the equivalent of the New Testament's Holy Spirit) was presented as the giver and sustainer of life and the giver of supernatural gifts and acts. The Spirit was presented as a divine agent through whom supernatural wisdom, knowledge, power, skills, prophecy, ecstatic utterance, special visions and dreams, renewal and transformation were delivered to God's people. Throughout the post-Mosaic period down to

[26] The Concept Note for the LWF Global Consultation, "We Believe in the Holy Spirit: Global Perspectives on Lutheran Identities," Addis Ababa, 23–27 October 2019, 2–3.

Malachi, the covenant community knew God's manifestations and actions only through the Spirit of God. God was assuring the people that God acts among them neither by might nor by power, but by the Spirit.[27]

2. In the New Testament, Jesus declared at the beginning of his earthly ministry that the Holy Spirit was upon him, anointing him to preach good news and to rescue people from bondage and deformity.[28] Near the end of his earthly ministry, he promised to equip his followers with power from on high which would be realized in the coming of the Holy Spirit. He pledged that the Holy Spirit would empower them;[29] would be with them forever (in them and dwelling with them); would teach them; and would guide them into all truth.[30] This promise was fulfilled at Pentecost when the Holy Spirit came upon Jesus' followers, accompanied by some audible and visible charismatic manifestations. Therefore, the pouring out, indwelling, gifting, empowering, illumining, and guiding of the Holy Spirit became the nature, life, and identity of Christianity. Lutheran theological identities contain this reality and Lutherans acknowledge this reality with the Large Catechism.[31]

3. The New Testament also indicates that during and after Pentecost, manifestations of the Holy Spirit were sometimes connected with, and resulted in, audible and visible charismatic manifestations. The Book of Acts, in particular, indicates that beginning from the day of Pentecost when the Holy Spirit pours upon people, the Spirit gives them audible and visible charismata as indications of the Spirit coming and working among them. Sometimes when audible and visible charismatic manifestations occurred, they occurred along with, or following, the coming of the Holy Spirit. When viewed through the lens of the Book of Acts, the Holy Spirit seems to manifest the Spirit's coming, presence, gifts, and activities through charismata.[32] In the early church, the Holy Spirit, which is invisible by nature, manifests through these charismata. It seems that it was understood that the coming, presence, gifts, and operations of the Holy Spirit were bestowed through the charismata. This seems to be the reason that Paul declared such gifts as speaking in tongues, discerning of spirits, signs, wonders, miracles, exorcising, compassion, leadership, and

[27] Zec 4:6.

[28] Lk 4:18–21.

[29] Lk 24:49.

[30] Jn 14:16, 17, 26; 16:13.

[31] *Large Catechism* II: 37–39.

[32] Acts 2; 10; 19; cf. Joel 2: 28–30.

administration, etc. as the gifts and works of the Holy Spirit.[33] In both the Old and the New Testaments, these charismata and their manifestations and dispensations are presented as tightly connected to the manifestation and activities of the Holy Spirit. Having given them such gifts, the Holy Spirit moved people in power and initiated subjective experiences. From the perspective of the scriptures therefore, it seems that the objective reception and subjective experience of the Holy Spirit remain central presuppositions of the doctrine of the Holy Spirit. Lutheran churches are founded and rooted in this foundation. So, what can Lutherans say today about the work of the Holy Spirit? Can they acknowledge this theological and biblical reality of the objective reception and subjective experience of the Holy Spirit as part of their theological identity?

Nevertheless, the subjective experience of the Holy Spirit did not get much attention in the history of Christianity for at least two reasons. First, the subjective experience does not appear to be mandatory for salvation, the church's life, or ministry. It happens only when God wants to intervene, introduce something new, initiate salvation or act. Since salvation, worship, and ministry are possible without it; subjective experience cannot be made a mandatory practice.

Second, historically the subjective experience has not been promoted in Christian experience for these reasons:

1. The subject of the subjective experience of the Holy Spirit came to church's attention more clearly through the Montanist movement. However, as the movement was considered a heretic threat to the church, it was condemned. Major tensions resulting from the concept of subjective experience formally began with the Montanist movement.[34] As the church continued to be anxious to avoid sectarian movements, it declined to integrate such experiences into the life of the church. This remained the basic reaction of the church to movements with similar tendencies throughout church history.[35] Thereon both the institutional church and charismatic groups continued to associate the Holy Spirit with subjective experience and the

[33] Rom 12:3–8; 1 Cor 12:1–11

[34] Paul Tillich, *A Complete History of Christian Thought*, ed. Carl E. Braaten (N.Y.: Harper and Row Publishers, 1968), 40. See also W. H. Griffith Thomas, *The Holy Spirit of God* (Grand Rapids, Mich.: Kregel Publications, 1986), 80–82.

[35] Louis Bouyer, "Some Charismatic Manifestations in the History of the Church," in *Perspectives on Charismatic Renewal*, ed. Edward O'Conner (Notre Dame, Ind.: University of Notre Dame Press, 1975), 114.

two contradicting views, institutional and charismatic, of the doctrine of the Holy Spirit formally took roots in this historical event.

2. The Second Ecumenical Council's formulation of the doctrine of the Holy Spirit emphasized only doctrinal belief and did not consider the issue of the subjective experience. Thereon, the Holy Spirit became only an object of faith. This played a role in creating a division between objective doctrinal belief and the subjective experience of the Holy Spirit, which lasted through the centuries down to the present.

3. When the church moved from the patristic period to the medieval period, in addition to the two historical reasons mentioned above, the church of the medieval period adopted some non-biblical traditions through which it replaced the place and role of the Holy Spirit in the church's life and ministry.[36] Thereby, not only has the subjective experience, but also the objective reception concept of the Holy Spirit seem to have been ignored in the medieval church.

4. Subjective experience of the Holy Spirit was not part of the emphasis in the teaching and practice of the sixteenth century Reformers. However, they emphasized that the Holy Spirit works in, and through, the preached word and Holy Sacraments. In particular, Luther placed his emphasis on the far greater invisible miracle wrought through the preaching of the gospel and the administration of sacraments.[37] As we have noted above, the Reformers' conviction and position were based on the existing theological and biblical foundations of Christianity. The radical wing of the Reformers, however, played a significant role in bringing the subjective experience of the Holy Spirit to prominence. Their emphasis on subjective experience continued to influence individuals and groups within Protestantism and produced a number of movements with similar convictions in the period between 1600 and 1900. The twentieth century Pentecostal movement was viewed as a result of that continued influence and an offshoot of the radical Reformers.

---

[36] Yves Congar, *I Believe in the Holy Spirit: The Complete Three Volume Work in One Volume*, vol. 1, trans. David Smith (Chestnut Ridge, N.Y.: Herder and Herder Books, 1997), 161–163.

[37] Martin Luther, *Lectures on Isaiah 1–39*, Luther's Works, vol. 16, ed. Jaroslav Pelikan and Helmut T. Lehmann (St. Louis: Concordia Publishing House, 1969), 302. See also vol. 24, *Sermon on the Gospel of St. John 14–16*, eds. Jaroslav Pelikan and Helmut T. Lehmann (St. Louis, Mo.: Concordia Publishing House, 1961), 79, 192; Jean Calvin, *Institutes of the Christian Religion*, vol. 1, ed. John T. McNeill, trans. Ford Lewis Battles (London: Westminster John Knox Press, 1960, repr. 2006), Book I: ix:1–3.

In the 1960s, after several centuries of neglect, the concept of the subjective experience began to receive attention again. As a result of the influence of the charismatic movement, the situation has changed, and subjective experience has become an almost common experience throughout Christendom. The prayerful call of "Come Holy Spirit" represents a longing for the Spirit to come with power to work and renew the whole creation, and equip and empower the church for life, worship, and mission.[38] Evidence for this emerges from two different World Council of Churches (WCC) consultations.

The first was the WCC consultation on the significance of the charismatic renewal, held in Bossey, Geneva, in March 1980. The theme of the consultation was "Towards a church renewed and united in the Holy Spirit." Phillip Potter, WCC general secretary at the time, presented a paper titled "Charismatic renewal and the World Council of Churches."[39] The second was WCC's Seventh Assembly, held in Canberra, Australia, in February 1989 with its theme "Come Holy Spirit: Renew the Whole Creation." The report adopted by the assembly contained this statement: "We are built up through the gifts of the Spirit into a people empowered to do God's will, to share the good news, and to become a community of sharing.... Indeed, the Spirit lifts up our vision and points us to the renewal of the whole creation."[40] The WCC cry seems to stem from a renewed understanding of, and longing for, the coming and working of the Holy Spirit within the church and the whole creation. This by itself seems a renewal and transformation of Christendom's perspective about the subjective experience of the Holy Spirit. This renewed ecumenical interest offers an ecumenical view and common understanding of the presence, power, and workings of the Holy Spirit in the church, as well as in the whole creation.

In light of this, when the LWF asks what it can say about the person and works of the Holy Spirit that engages member churches and theologians in a fresh discussion on this subject, does this imply building a new Lutheran pneumatology or is it an expression of longing similar to that of the WCC (cited here)? Is it a hunger and longing for genuine openness and the renewing, gifting, empowering, transforming, and equipping work of the Holy Spirit within Lutheran churches? If the latter is the case, then no doubt remains that this is an ongoing process of the church that

---

[38] C. Samuel Storms, "A Third Wave View," in *Are Miraculous Gifts for Today? Four Views*, ed. Wayne A. Grudem (Grand Rapids, Mich.: Zondervan, 1996), 175.

[39] Arnold Bittlinger, *The Church is Charismatic* (Geneva: WCC Publications, 1981), 75.

[40] World Council of Churches, *Come Holy Spirit: Renew the Whole Creation*, Six Bible Studies on the Theme of the Seventh Assembly of the WCC (Geneva: WCC Publications, 1989), 7–8.

continues to inspire a new sense of vocation. In light of this, Lutherans can always ask "Come Holy Spirit: renew our life, worship, mission, ministry, relationships and vocations."

The concept note states that "contemporary discourse about spirituality is frequently driven by individuals who claim to have spiritual gifts (*charismata)* via special revelations of the Holy Spirit." It says that this type of spiritual narrative "can be exclusionary, and often underwrites anthropological, social, and political narratives ... and create anxieties about Lutheran identity." These features, from the LWF's point of view, call for a framework for addressing such fundamental spiritual and practical issues in Lutheran churches.[41] This statement seems to refer to the challenges resulting from the influences of the charismatic movement. As mentioned above, this has been a common problem in almost all the established churches since the 1960s. If this is the case, then can this consultation "provide a framework for addressing such fundamental spiritual and practical issues in Lutheran churches?" Of course, the consultation may provide a framework as expected. Yet the question is whether this will avoid or integrate charismatic spirituality?

The challenges resulting from the influence of charismatic spirituality may leave Lutheran churches with a critical choice. On the one hand, as they are bound by the theological values of the Reformation and maintain a high regard for the doctrine of justification by faith, they may not want to encourage their congregations to engage in any kind of enthusiastic subjective experience relating to charismatic spirituality. On the other hand, as the church of Christ they cannot, I think, teach and guide their congregations to reject charismatic spirituality in case God comes to them, wants to give them particular charismatic gifts, and use them. For example, if Lutherans agree with the idea of longing and praying for the continued coming of the Holy Spirit, and renewing of their life, worship, mission, ministry, relationships, and vocations, what if the Holy Spirit responds to their longings and prayers by manifesting audible and visible charismata among them? If this happens in their congregations, can they advise their congregations to say "No thank you! Pass me by God! I am alright with what I have (referring to the means of grace and faith)." Or should they guide them to remain open to how God wants to speak to them, endow them, and empower them; to remain open to God working in expected, and unexpected, ways, through special and fresh manifestations of the Holy Spirit? This is what perplexes me. Will the framework that is to be provided by this consultation consider this and help solve such perplexities?

---

[41] Concept Note for the LWF Global Consultation, "We Believe in the Holy Spirit, 3.

If the consultation succeeds in providing the anticipated framework, then my church may benefit from it. One may ask "how" and "why" questions. The influence of the charismatic movement has become one of the troubling current trends affecting the EECMY's theological identity. The movement has introduced EECMY congregations to some traditionally neglected aspects of the doctrine and practice of the Holy Spirit. What the congregations traditionally learned about the Holy Spirit was the single phrase in the third article of the Apostles' Creed, "I believe in the Holy Spirit," which is recited at regular Sunday worship. Since 1991, the time when religious and worship freedom was declared in Ethiopia and charismatic experiences invaded the country's non-Pentecostal denominations, congregations have rediscovered the person, power, gifts, and workings of the Holy Spirit, and engaged in personal experiences of these features. Traditionally it was believed that the Holy Spirit carries the Spirit's work of regeneration, renewal, sanctification and healing through faith, confession, absolution, the word, sacraments, and forgiveness of sins. Accordingly, any appeal to miraculous divine intervention was neglected in traditional worship and liturgical structures.

However, due to the impact of the charismatic movement, congregations have been taught that the Holy Spirit acts without, and beyond, these formal features. They have been taught that the Holy Spirit endows them with charismatic gifts regardless of their gender, age, and level of literacy. This made them hungry to receive and realize charismatic gifts. Accordingly, many have been motivated to fast and pray in the expectation that the Holy Spirit will endow them with these gifts. Many people, including those who are illiterate, have been endowed with gifts such as prophecy, revelation, healing, discerning spirits, and working miracles. They have demonstrated these gifts in public sessions. Thereby, receiving these gifts and experiencing Pentecostal or charismatic forms of worship have become common experiences in the churches of non-Pentecostal denominations in Ethiopia, including the EECMY. These experiences are attributed to the new and special revelation of the Holy Spirit.

Some genuine experiences of visible charismata have spoken to a very real hunger in congregations for a deep spiritual and charismatic life in which they experience an intervention of God in their daily heartfelt needs. Physical healing has become the most significant feature as it touches people at a point of desperate need and draws their attention to divine power and action. Accordingly, conducting weekly healing prayers has become common practice for almost all congregations of non-Pentecostal denominations. This is a very different experience to that of traditional worship. In addition to physical healing, charismatic experiences have contributed to significant changes in other social features such as breaking down religious and social barriers and creating relationships between peoples from different denominations; introducing changes to traditional perspectives on women's role both in church and society; and moral and ethical healing in the lives of some church members. It has also significantly contributed to the current rapid and impressive growth in EECMY membership, finances, and geographic structure. Overall, the situation seems to indicate that a practical pneumatological release has happened and that this release from traditional limitations has led congregations to experience the power and gifts of the Holy Spirit.

Hence, comparing and contrasting traditional worship and liturgy to the effects they enjoy from charismatic worship, congregations seriously criticize the traditional worship structure which is unable to provide them with resourceful and meaningful spirituality. As time passes, this may cause a painful crisis in the church's theology and principles of *sola scriptura*. In addition, there are many heartbreaking and distressing counterfeit experiences, tensions, conflicts, divisions, and splits in congregations which relate to, and result from, charismatic experiences. The EECMY has been able to handle all these problems and is successfully maintaining and preserving its Lutheran identity. Yet, the influence of the movement has caused a considerable identity crisis in worship and liturgy. The framework to be provided by this consultation may provide input and new insights that will help the EECMY to act pro-actively.

The concept paper states that, "Contemporary constellations of economic and political power, legal challenges, scientific and technological discoveries, and new psycho-social developments continuously call for new expressions of Lutheran distinctives."[42] This sentence seems to express the cry of a threatened church body. It raises the question of how and why these features challenge Lutheran theological identity and call for new expressions of Lutheran distinctives. It also leads to the question of what is meant by "new expressions of Lutheran distinctives." The search for answers to these questions helps us to answer the question of how Lutheran theological identities inform the Lutheran sense of vocation and ministry.

It is obvious that the church of Christ is to continue the tradition of the ministry of Jesus in which the divine holistic approach ministry to humankind was demonstrated. The mystery of the foundation and existence of the church in the world is to extend this theological tradition. Lutheran churches believe that they are meant to serve human beings in the way God would serve them.[43] Lutheran existence, faith, missional and spiritual principles and actions, emphasize that salvation involves both a

[42] Concept Note for the LWF Global Consultation, "We Believe in the Holy Spirit," 3.
[43] Mt 7:12.

person's spiritual and social welfare dimensions. This is where Lutherans strive to apply their spiritual gifts and the vocation of the priesthood of all believers.[44] Therefore, Lutheran theological identities can be summed up as being instruments of God's holistic approach of mission to the world.[45] This is what Luther understood when he asserted that the priesthood of all believers is drawn from, and rooted in, Christ's priesthood. Therefore, priesthood is not merely standing in a good relationship with God but standing before God on behalf of our neighbors and the world.[46] This is how Lutherans carry out God's mission and purpose for the world and enact their theological identity through social action. For Lutherans, it is in and through this fact that the social presence of the divine can be displayed. In this way, the new kingdom of God can be demonstrated and practically delivered to the world and many be drawn into it. This is the reason social transformation is a strong aspect of the LWF's commitment and why the LWF has become a prominent and influential mission organization working toward transforming the social conditions of millions.

While striving to fulfill this mission, social, cultural, political, economic, scientific, and technological developments emerge and challenge Lutheran theological distinctives in one way or another. For example, we are learning that there are numbers of former mission organizations that have been struggling with membership and economic decline; a decline in mission vision and zeal for evangelization; the loss of their former power, influence, and effectiveness among contemporary societies; and the state of spirituality which constitutes a pressing need for the renewing, reviving, and transforming power and works of the Holy Spirit. The most bitter struggle, however, is between avoiding and embracing new cultural developments which are incompatible with Christian theological convictions and evangelical commitments. These include seeing biblical moral and ethical laws through the lens of contemporary spiritual cultures; secular humanism and individuals' unreserved freedom; the culture of letting people be free to enjoy everything created by God; homosexuality; transsexuality; freedom to have abortions; and racial and tribal conflicts (xenophobia). These cultural developments have permeated, and had a bad influence on, contemporary Christians worldwide. The result is a crisis in traditional social and religious rules, systems, orders, worship and liturgy structures, and authorities and dogmas. Moreover, we are aware that some of these developments have provided grounds for splitting the unity of Lutheran

[44] Althaus, 304–310.
[45] Ibid.
[46] Ibid., 314.

churches: some favor embracing and blessing these cultural changes while others curse and avoid them.

Given that Lutherans are being shaken by religious, social, and cultural changes, and lack a proper response to them, the question is whether these challenges require new expressions of Lutheran distinctives? What do the new expressions of Lutheran distinctives imply? To my mind, these challenges do not require any new expression of Lutheran distinctives. Rather, they remind Lutherans of two main things. First, they remind Lutherans to stand firm and defend their five-hundred-year-old theological distinctives which are based on Scripture's authority. Second, they remind Lutherans to ask what they can say about the person and work of the Holy Spirit when the church is attacked by the effects of current cultural developments?

My conclusion is to remind Lutheran churches that the Holy Spirit—the impossibility specialist—is on the boat and answers every concern and confusion encountered there. When we call upon the Spirit in faith, we are given many incomprehensively impressive answers by the power with which the Spirit solved Peter's riddle of eating or avoiding something unclean and unusual.[47] Therefore, let Lutherans not try to struggle to respond to challenges with their own resources, but long and pray for divine resources that may be supplied by Pentecostal power and charismatic manifestations. Let Lutherans keep calling the Holy Spirit by saying "Come Holy Spirit: Renew our worship, mission, ministry, relationships, and vocations; and give us unity, wisdom and insight to overcome our current acute challenges.

May God give Lutherans the prophetic insight of seeing the direction and status of their faith life. May God's light lead them. Come Holy Spirit: renew the whole creation in the direction God agrees with and stands on. May God's might help them now and forever!

---

[47] Acts 10:9–20.

The Vocation of the Priesthood of All Humans: Toward a Wider Understanding and Meaning of the Lutheran Teaching

Sofie Halvarsson

The Holy Spirit in Creation

"We believe in the Holy Spirit."

I read that claim and ask myself: What does this really mean? I am not asking how to explain it in a dogmatic formula; but rather, I am asking how this belief expresses itself in our daily lives?[1]

Everything I will present in this paper emerges from the definition of the Holy Spirit as something that is present in creation. God's Spirit–*ru'ach*–וּרַח moved over the waters in the beginning[2] and is the source of life and the breath of humankind.[3] We believe that God created every human being in the image of God and that God is constantly seeking ways to reach us.[4]

---

[1] Throughout this article, I will use the pronouns *we* or *our/ourselves*, mainly to mean us Lutherans, or Christians, or more broadly, everyone interested in living the Christian life I am referring to.

[2] Gen 1:2.

[3] Gen 2:7.

[4] This is clarified in *Together Towards Life: Mission and Evangelism in Changing Landscapes* (Geneva: World Council of Churches, 2012), 12. https://missionstudies.org/wp-content/uploads/2015/06/Together_towards_Life.pdf.

When people witness this breath–the Holy Spirit–they experience God. We can have these experiences in different ways: in the Bible, through interpretation of the scriptures; in traditions; and–my main point–in our daily lives. I want to emphasize something here that has been forgotten or under-emphasized–all human beings can experience the presence of the Holy Spirit.

I believe that Scripture is based on experience, tradition is formed by experience, and– since I believe the Holy Spirit makes itself known to every person–that every human voice has something important to say about God. Thus, if we want to learn more about God, we must embrace the vocation of the priesthood of all believers or–more broadly stated–the priesthood of all people.[5]

The Holy Spirit in the Scriptures

As a Lutheran, I embrace *sola scriptura.* But what does this mean? What are the scriptures? Scripture is based on experiences and stories about how God acts in people's lives. The stories have become words, but from the beginning they were historically situated experiences: feelings, thoughts, senses, and relationships. The stories are more than words on paper: experiences surpass the limitations of language. There is always more to know about God–more that is beyond.

Someone who believes himself or herself to have had an experience of the Divine can easily understand this: it is not easy to tell the story of a personal experience of the Holy Spirit because no one can relive another person's experience. Someone who recounts your story will not do it justice, even though it needs to be heard. It is the same with the stories and experiences in the Bible. The stories about how people have experienced God need to be understood as something that surpasses words. These stories are so important that we cannot take them literally, because words do not do justice to encounters between people and the Holy Spirit.

Theologian Rosemary Radford Ruether says that theological discussion goes wrong when it discusses "experiences" as something connected with, and unique to, for example, feminist theology or liberation theology. She believes instead that women's experiences form one part of the range of hu-

[5] Origin of vocation: Middle English *vocacion* from Ecclesiastical Late Latin *vocatio,* a calling from L, an invitation, court summons from *vocare,* to call from *vox,* voice. Priesthood is a term that can be interpreted in many ways. When I use priesthood here, I mean it as a task to witness and point at God's work.

man experience.[6] I agree with her when she says that theological discussion has sometimes treated the Bible as something objective whereas Scripture and tradition reflect collective human experiences: human experiences mark the beginning and the end of the hermeneutical circle. She describes these experiences as an interactive dialogue between the Divine and individuals and communities.[7] For Radford Ruether, the uniqueness of feminist theology is in seeing women's experiences as part of the scriptures and traditions which are collective human experiences.[8] By this, she means that feminist theology exposes "classic theology"[9] as based on male experiences rather than on universal experiences. Therefore, her main point is that the "classic theology" should not be seen as something that has universal authority.[10] Radford Ruether's approach allows us to identify overlooked experiences.

The Holy Spirit in tradition

People have always found ways to interpret transcendent experiences and structure them within religions and traditions and so, when we attempt to interpret the message for today in stories told in the Bible, we use the constructions of systematic theology. The danger is that, in trying to understand experiences described in the Bible, we might lock the gospel into a few specific interpretations.

As a Lutheran, I believe it is important to be true to the gospel by embracing *sola scriptura*. This means that we should not reduce the gospel to only some experiences or lock it into dogmatic interpretations: that would make the gospel into something fixed in stone—not alive. I understand God as life itself and believe that we must distinguish which images set us free and embrace life, and which do not.

God and Images of God

Christian tradition encompasses a complex of ideas and ways of interpreting and imagining our world. It is important that we distinguish between

---

[6] Rosemary Radford Ruether, *Sexism and God-Talk: Toward a Feminist Theology* (Boston: Beacon Press, 1983), 13.
[7] Ibid., 12.
[8] Ibid., 13.
[9] By classic theology, I mean teachings and interpretations within the theology which have been considered the most normative ones.
[10] Radford Ruether, 13.

images of God and God: these do not necessarily always correspond. Images can help us to relate to God but are not God. God is greater than the images. For example, God came into this world in an unimagined way, as a poor man. By becoming human, God, through Jesus, gave us a recognizable image through which to relate to God: but at the same time God transcended our preconceptions. God is both within and beyond our images. When God becomes manifest, it is not always in ways that we humans have pictured before us.[11]

It is not wrong to have images of God. They are necessary for us in relating to God. The problem is when we hold to certain images and preach about them as if they were the only valid ways of relating to God, and when we use them as a means to proclaim to others that they have got it wrong. When we frame how we rationalize God's being and work, it can be helpful for us, but we must understand that God does not fit into a frame.

Once, when I was visiting a church, I got into a theological discussion with the preacher. We each had different ways of interpreting the Bible. I saw from how he interpreted the Bible text that he hurt a friend of mine, so I asked him: "What if Jesus were to come back and go to this person and hug him and say that he is beloved and should not be judged, but rather be respected as the person he is and how he is living? What would you say then?" The preacher replied: "But that will not happen." When I asked him why not, he said: "Because it says that in the Bible." I said: "Who are you to decide what God will and can do?"

This example shows how easy it is for people of faith to confuse their images of God with God. I would say that an image of God always includes other things than the character of God: it includes how we think God wants us to live our lives. I would also say that, in our attempt to be loyal to the gospel, we have a tendency to go back and borrow old images from the Bible or tradition instead of embracing how the Holy Spirit speaks to us today.

There are many ways of understanding the nature of sin, but I would say that we often hang on to old images and interpretations of sin so tightly that we miss how sin shows itself today. The task of living a Christian life is to be open and to interpret how sin takes form in our lives today. I would say that, in order to understand old images of sin, we need to understand why an act was considered as sin in that context: That act may not always be sinful. For example, if I talk to someone and make that person feel bad, we may consider that a sin. However, it would be wrong to never use the act of speaking again. The point is that, in doing so, we must be careful not to abuse our power or harm others. We need to be aware of this when

[11] From the Swedish monograph *Bildfaktorn*, by Magnus Malm (Skelleftea: Artos & Norma Bokförlag), 52.

we read the Bible. We should not collect all the acts in the Bible that were considered sinful in that time and context, and proclaim them today. Instead, we should look for the underlying message. This might lead us to conclude that sin is whatever demolishes life or when people are harmed. The Bible offers examples from the times in which it was written. If we simply take these examples and proclaim them today, I do not think that we are being true to the message, to the gospel, to the Holy Spirit, and to God's will. Therefore, we must constantly be open to the Holy Spirit and wherever it takes form and embraces life. At the same time, we need to be open and see what destroys life. To be contextual and to change is to be true to the gospel and to our Lutheran identity. If we are not open to seeing that the Holy Spirit blows wherever it wants, then we are worshiping images instead of God.[12]

The Holy Spirit in You and Me: In All Humans

I believe it is important for my future work as a Lutheran pastor to not reproduce these locked-in interpretations and tell people that these are the only valid experiences. Instead, I want people to understand the vocation of the priesthood of all believers or, as I see it, all of humankind.

Since I believe that God is life itself, and that the Holy Spirit is within every human being, I mean that we can know God through our experiences today as well as through the scriptures and tradition. This is a possibility for everyone, because we are all created in the image of God. God is life and becomes alive through our daily experiences, not only through books or texts. God, or the Holy Spirit, is in everyone. The problem is that not everyone believes that their own feelings, experiences, and relation to God are valid. This limits our understanding of God to long-accepted images rather than seeing God in the contemporary experiences of women, men, children, and young people in different contexts. I believe that our experiences today are not a threat to the gospel: they are necessary ways to stay true to the gospel. If we believe in the Holy Spirit and the promise of Pentecost, we must embrace the understanding that God did not stop meeting us after Jesus Christ. The same spirit that created the earth and filled Jesus is present in our lives today.

[12] This can also be argued for from the first of the Ten Commandments, "You shall have no other gods before me" (Ex 20:3), in the way that we should not let our images of God become the goal of our worship; rather we should be open to the understanding of God as beyond images. Even if God may be within image, God is also beyond them.

This is why I want to open up a wider understanding and interpretation of the vocation of the priesthood of all believers. I believe everyone has something to say about God, even if they do not think so themselves, because I believe the Holy Spirit is within everyone: God is already there, whether we count ourselves as believers or not. As the World Council of Churches writes in its document about mission, *Together Towards Life*, "God is there before we come (Acts 17) and our task is not to bring God along, but to witness to the God who is already there."[13]

It is my firm belief that the Holy Spirit is present in our lives. However, because we have created images, frameworks, and rules about how this Holy Spirit expresses itself, we are missing some people's experiences. Yet, every human being has something to say about God. There are so many lost stories, so many of God's manifestations in our lives which are not being heard, because the person who experiences God does not think that these experiences are valid.

I read in a book about a woman who was struggling with her faith and went into a chapel and found peace. When her counsellor asked her why, the woman said she felt released because she understood that God does not exist. After some time with her counsellor, she realized that what had released her was not that she had stopped believing in God, but that she did not believe anymore in the demanding image of God that she had imagined. Saying no to her image of God was not the same as saying no to God: it was the other way around. Letting go of an old image of God was to say yes to the true God.[14] If, when we meditate or pray and try to hear where the Holy Spirit is leading us, we reject everything that does not conform to other people's experiences or traditional answers, then it is easy to miss when God speaks to us.[15] In other words, when God does not fit the frame, we think it wasn't an experience of God. I say that we should allow ourselves to see that the Holy Spirit often works in mysterious ways which are beyond our imagination.[16]

This does not mean that tradition, or other people's experiences or images should be rejected. I mean that we need to discern which ones carry the gospel and which do not. Tradition is an important contribution to our understanding of God; however, it can be problematic if we see the tradition as the only valid explanation of the scriptures. Christian tradition has been good at representing only some experiences: often these are presented by privileged men with influence and power. The experiences of women or

[13] *Together Towards Life*, 34.
[14] Malm, *Bildfaktorn*, 93.
[15] Ibid., 52.
[16] Lk 1:34–35; Jn 3:8; Acts 2:16–21.

marginalized people have not been presented enough. If we do not share the stories of these experiences, we will limit our understanding of God.

But how do we recognize the Holy Spirit? In Sweden, where I come from, the self has been seen in Lutheran tradition as something bad and sinful. My experience is that the self is often considered by Lutherans as something in contradiction to God. I believe that this negative view of the self has made us afraid of listening to ourselves. We have been led not to believe in our own thoughts, as that might get in the way of doing good things for others. I do not agree with this. I believe in being thankful that we are created in the image of God and that the Holy Spirit lives in us. However, not everything we humans feel or think corresponds to the work of the Holy Spirit, so it is important to define how the Holy Spirit expresses itself in our lives.

The question is: How do we recognize the Holy Spirit? How do we recognize it within ourselves? How can we recognize it within someone else? I once asked my classmates: How do I separate what is the Holy Spirit and what is not? I asked this question because I had recently been in a situation where people were claiming that they were doing the work of the Holy Spirit, yet I knew that there are always people who do terrifying and harmful work in the name of God. One of my classmates shared my concern and answered: "I never think the Holy Spirit relates to me in a terrifying way. If something doesn't feel good, if it makes me feel bad, then it is not the Holy Spirit."[17] Another one of my classmates said: "Jesus does not make himself known by telling other persons his name. He makes himself known by acting like God." Even though these were spontaneous reflections, I think there is some importance within them:

We discern the Spirit of God wherever life in its fullness is affirmed and in all its dimensions, including liberation of the oppressed, healing and reconciliation of broken communities, and the restoration of creation. We also discern evil spirits wherever forces of death and destruction of life prevail.[18]

Humans who proclaim they are doing work in the name of God and are filled by the Holy Spirit, but who do not act as such, must be questioned. The Holy Spirit is not made visible in labels or images. The Spirit is seen in life-affirming acts.

---

[17] This also corresponds to the words repeated through the Bible when God addresses humans: "Do not be afraid."

[18] *Together Towards Life*, 11.

> We believe in God, the Holy Spirit, the Life-giver, who sustains and empowers life and renews the whole creation (Gen 2:7; Jn 3:8). A denial of life is a rejection of the God of life.[19]

Simone Weil, a French philosopher and mystic, shows us how to be open to life and the Spirit:

> It seemed to me certain, and I still think so today, that one can never wrestle enough with God if one does so out of pure regard for the truth. Christ likes us to prefer truth to him because, before being Christ, he is truth. If one turns aside from him to go toward the truth, one will not go far before falling into his arms.[20]

From this we can understand that by seeking the truth, we will also find Christ. If we embrace actions and situations where the true identity of God shows itself, we will find God. This truth surpasses our images and expresses itself in unexpected ways:

> Another perspective emphasizes that the Holy Spirit is the "Spirit of Truth" that leads us to the "whole truth" (Jn 16:13) and blows wherever he/she wills (Jn 3:8), thus embracing the whole of the cosmos; it proclaims the Holy Spirit as the source of Christ and the church as the eschatological coming together (synaxis) of the people of God in God's kingdom.[21]

So, where does the Spirit blow today? Do we experience the Holy Spirit wherever it blows? Do we affirm life and truth wherever we encounter them? Or are we too restricted by our images of how God acts and what God can do? It is time that we open ourselves to expressions of the Holy Spirit in our lives.

We Must Listen for Silenced Voices

If we believe that experiences of God did not end with the Bible but are living through us today through the Holy Spirit, we should embrace the vocation of the priesthood of all believers and of all humankind. This will affect how we look at our neighbor. If we believe God is in everyone, we realize that we can learn about God from children, the homeless, and all the people we do not usually listen to. It means that these people should

[19] *Together Towards Life*, 4.
[20] Simone Weil, *Gravity and Grace*.
[21] *Together Towards Life*, 9.

not be seen as objects of mercy, but as carriers of the gospel. Without these people, we cannot see the whole story of God. Their stories help us broaden our understanding of God. If we want to understand God, we need each other and each other's experiences.

Where are the lost voices? Whose transcendent experiences have not been heard? Where has the Holy Spirit breathed? Which voices that affirm love and life have been neglected because of our limited views?

I believe that Christians need to look around to see the people we don't listen to because they don't match our reading of Scripture. If we believe in the Holy Spirit, we must believe that God talks through people today and that this has consequences for us:

> The churches are called to discern the work of the life-giving Spirit sent into the world and to join with the Holy Spirit in bringing about God's reign of justice (Acts 1:6–8). When we have discerned the Holy Spirit's presence, we are called to respond, recognizing that God's Spirit is often subversive, leading us beyond boundaries and surprising us.[22]

This is not something new. Jesus did this. He met the poor, the sick, and marginalized women—people who believed themselves to be unworthy. But Jesus went to these people and affirmed them: he showed them, and others, that they have a relationship with God. Perhaps it was not a coincidence that he sent these people out to bear witness. Let us not stop listening to their stories in the scriptures. Without these marginalized people in the Bible, we would lack a diverse understanding of God. However, let us also look at our own context and see who these people are today: let us welcome the Holy Spirit wherever it blows.

This might mean listening to the child who says, "I don't know anything about God, but I believe God loves me;" listening to the LGBTQ person who says, "I believe God loves me as I am;" or listening to myself saying, "It's my firm belief that I am something good, created in the image of God, and that I deserve to be loved." It might mean:

> The affirmation of God's mission (Dei) points to the belief in God as One who acts in history and in creation, in concrete realities of time and contexts, who seeks the fullness of life for the whole earth through justice, peace, and reconciliation. Participation in God's ongoing work of liberation and reconciliation by the Holy Spirit, therefore, includes discerning and unmasking the demons that exploit and enslave. For example, this involves deconstructing patriarchal ideologies, uphold-

[22] *Together Towards Life*, 11.

> ing the right to self-determination for Indigenous peoples, and challenging the social embeddedness of racism and casteism.[23]

Let us come back to Radford Ruether who says that human experiences are both the end and the starting point in the hermeneutical circle.[24] The silenced experience, which we discover today, may give us new perspectives for reading and interpreting the Bible and tradition. This will lead us to new insights. These are not only experiences of the Divine, but also of engaging in an interactive dialectic with the world. This interactive dialectic includes the Bible and tradition.[25] Within, and beyond, these experiences, the Holy Spirit makes itself known. If we embrace the vocation of the priesthood of all believers, or of all humankind, it means that we must listen to, and include, all voices which affirm life and truth. Experiences have been lost in translation and to tradition. As disciples of Jesus, we need to find what is lost. We need to draw attention to voices which have been silenced. We need each other and each other's experiences: if we miss one story about God, we miss a bit of the whole story of God.

---

[23] *Together Towards Life*, 17.

[24] Radford Ruether, 12.

[25] I am aware that I am also within this interactive dialectic. I am a product of my time and context, of the tradition and society I am standing in. I am considering myself to be making claims from a neutral position, but I am aware that I am myself a product of a theology.

A Mourning Grace: Bataknese "Andung-Andung" as a Theological Aesthetic in the Experience of Trauma

Novriana Gloria Hutagalung

Experience as a reflection of faith is one of the theological sites that have a role that is as important as doctrinal debate. Trauma studies criticize theology that always puts forward the intellectuality of theology, which is described as intact and unbroken, by witnessing to experiences of people with trauma that show the fragility of humans and even of creation. Trauma destroys an identity that is known and shatters this identity that is attached to the person who experiences it.

The question that will be asked in this paper is how to remember sexual violence as self-historicity that is no longer embarrassing and avoided? How does theology respond to the wounds caused by traumatic experiences? How can we give voice to the perspective of the people who are living with trauma in theology?

I will interpret Luther's theology of grace in light of the Toba Bataknese traditional way of mourning. In a society that expects us to always put on a happy face, I suggest that we can mourn in the aftermath of trauma, as mourning is an act of grace.

Trauma: A Death That Remains

There is no single definition of trauma. In *Trauma and Recovery*, Judith Herman correlates the relationship between trauma in the public sphere that occurs in war veterans (men) and trauma in the private sphere that occurs in the household (women and children). Similar symptoms or syndromes can be found in victims of sexual violence, domestic violence, and war veterans. Herman highlighted that women who were raped experienced insomnia, nightmares, dissociation, and numbness and were easily shocked.[1] Trauma always returns and haunts the victim at an unexpected time.[2] People who experience trauma cannot avoid this reality and experience it again and again. Trauma becomes the center of one's self-identification.[3]

In *Spirit and Trauma*, Shelly Rambo interprets trauma as suffering that remains.[4] Trauma studies focus on powerful experiences that continue in the present, return, and influence the present and future of the person. She radically interprets trauma as a direct encounter with death. Death here is not interpreted literally. Rambo interprets death as an extraordinary event that destroys all one's knowledge about the world and the surrounding environment, self-identity, self-epistemology, and one's self construction. A person who experiences a traumatic event cannot return to live "as usual" or return to the period before the event occurred. According to Rambo, "the storm is always present."[5] Life and death are impossible to separate. For people who live with trauma, there is no past or future, only the present. The linear concept of time also becomes problematic. According to Rambo, this linear concept of time understanding is somewhat dangerous. Trauma opposes the statement that time heals. In fact, in trauma distortions in time constitute the wound.[6] The experience of trauma makes a person unable to remember the past and to clearly see his or her future because the trauma is so haunting that it destroys that person's view of time.

The experience of trauma can be understood as the experience of death. However, the reality of death does not end, instead it remains. The traumatic experience inspires theological discourse beyond the experience of the cross as a symbol of suffering, and then reinterprets life after death.

Trauma is a story about a storm that never ends. Trauma is the story that never left.[7] The Holy Spirit is bound to, and through, what remains. Rambo also proposes redemption from the middle. She states that every redemptive hermeneutic must depart from the realization that death and

---

[1] Judith Herman, *Trauma and Recovery: The Aftermath of Violence from Domestic Abuse to Political Terror* (New York: Basic Books, 1992), 31.

[2] Cathy Caruth, *Unclaimed Experience: Trauma, Narrative, and History* (Baltimore, Md.: John Hopkins University Press, 1996), 4.

[3] Caruth, 8.

[4] Shelly Rambo, *Spirit and Trauma: A Theology of Remaining* (Louisville, Ky.: Westminster John Knox Press, 2010), 15.

[5] Ibid., 4.

[6] Ibid., 19.

[7] Ibid., 143.

life are bound to one another; death remains and haunts.[8] Rambo also talks about how to feel alive again through imaginative practices that are embodied. When speaking about trauma recovery, the physical connection to the world needs to be restored as well.[9]

In *Sites of Violence, Sites of Grace,* Cynthia Hess states that trauma as a form of violence can attack and destroy a body.[10] Trauma fragments and disrupts the victim's ability to integrate memories; destroys personal narratives that have been held; prevents victims from building healthy interpersonal relationships; and deconstructs the victim's vision of his or her future.[11]

Traumatic events are events that shake one's life violently, not because they rarely occur, but because they exceed human ability to adapt. Traumatic events confront humans with terror, extreme helplessness, loss of self-control, and intense fear.[12] The greatness or the severity of a traumatic event cannot be measured by one single dimension because trauma affects the brain's nervous system so violently.

The social context can influence how victims remember traumatic events.[13] Child victims of sexual abuse are more easily subjected to dissociation, especially because society does not recognize that sexual abuse is a human catastrophe. Society often avoids the fact that sexual abuse occurs. Shame arises when personal trauma happens. If people realize and recognize that personal trauma occurs, and, therefore, provide compassion in people with trauma can be lessened. However, if the community does not acknowledge personal trauma, the possibility of dissociation will be greater. Traumatic memories are not forgotten. Trauma studies say that the body remembers. Although the mind forgets, the body remembers.

Flora A. Keshgegian is one of the many theologians who construct memory as a theological category.[14] The process of remembering can help a person restore a sense of self which has been fragmented due to trauma. The process of remembering is not merely historical; remembering is also a theological and ethical practice that aims to provide impact and change. Keshgegian states that the process of remembering is both an individual and a communal process. She refers to the memory of the incarnation, life,

---

[8] Rambo, 156.

[9] Ibid., 162.

[10] Cynthia Hess, *Sites of Violence, Sites of Grace: Christian Nonviolence and the Traumatized Self* (Lanham, Md.: Lexington Books, 2009), 3.

[11] Ibid., 34.

[12] Herman, 33.

[13] Hess, 45.

[14] See Flora A. Keshgegian, *Redeeming Memories: A Theology of Healing and Transformation* (Nashville, Tenn.: Abingdon Press, 2000).

death, and resurrection of Jesus Christ who redeemed God's people and re-members the people as followers of Christ. Therefore, when we gather as a church, it is as a community of remembrance, engaging in a multifaceted practice of remembering for the sake of redemption.

The community—both church and society—has the potential to help people who are traumatized to experience recovery. Herman notes that the process of healing personal and collective trauma tends to be similar. This is due to the syndrome shown by survivors of personal and collective trauma that has similarities. Herman noted several basic healing stages including maintaining security, reconstructing trauma narratives, and restoring connections between victims and their communities. People with trauma narrative need a social context that affirms and protects the victim and is a witness to the trauma and violence experienced by the victim. For individual victims, social connection occurs by restoring relationships with friends, lovers and family. For the larger community, social connection is created by political movements that give voice to the disempowered.[15] Group therapy has shown great promise for trauma recovery because groups can offer such a powerful antidote to the shame and social isolation that afflict trauma survivors. The therapeutic community also helps people with trauma develop self -compassion and acceptance.[16]

If a person with a trauma experience puts the story in a narrative framework, then that person can experience reorientation of time, which Hess calls re-temporalization. People with trauma can stop sinking into the past, and participate in the present, by strengthening their lives in a transformative community such as the church.

The church as an eschatological community can contribute to, and participate in, re-temporalization of trauma survivors by offering a view where they can claim a communal future that differs from their traumatic past.[17] People with trauma can heal their trauma by reshaping identity through participation in the communal identity of the church because everyone has a personal and communal identity as part of the body of Christ. Human beings are profoundly broken, even as they are regenerated by God's grace. Hess does not deny that the brokenness of humanity and of creation will not disappear even though God renews everything. In this life, we are both fragmented and whole, broken and redeemed.[18]

---

[15] Herman, 9.
[16] Ibid., 273.
[17] Hess, 130.
[18] Ibid., 143.

Witnessing to trauma can be an instrument in efforts to prevent future violent events.[19] The involvement of trauma survivors in the eschatological community can help them develop a vision of hope for their future. This reality deepens their understanding of God's love as manifested through the community and will enable them to flourish and resist being overwhelmed by the brokenness of the world. Christian community both engages in the present and hopes for the future; it embodies this future, although it has never been in an unbroken form.[20]

Re-Membering Ourselves through Andung-Andung

As I have mentioned before, Keshgegian uses memory as a theological category. She puts forward a new paradigm about remembering, especially remembering trauma and dangerous memories ("dangerous memory" as discovered by Johann Baptist Metz). She states that by transforming memories of traumatic events, a person can recover from trauma. With the process of remembering, a person whose identity is fragmented due to a traumatic event can be re-integrated. She says, "In the beginning is the remembering, which leads to re-membering."[21]

The church is a community of remembering. Remembering, then, is both a practice of self- and community formation. It is through a practice of remembering that Christians constitute their identity as a faithful people and as a community embodied as Christ's own.[22] Suffering and loss must be remembered and mourned. Mourning means allowing oneself to experience the harm and the hurt, to accept the irretrievable nature of the losses, and to grieve. Although the loss is never forgotten or restored, mourning eventually allows the pain and losses to be less dominant.[23] It plunges the survivor into profound grief. But mourning itself is a strategy of resistance to the totalizing effects of the abuse. Mourning entails facing the truth of what happened and accepting the injury fully, at the core of one's being. It involves the reality of the losses. As a survivor mourns, she finally lets go of the pain and the loss, even though scars of the injury will remain forever.[24]

---

[19] Rambo, 24.
[20] Hess, 134.
[21] Keshgegian, 24.
[22] Ibid., 26.
[23] Ibid., 121.
[24] Ibid., 42.

Along with Hess, Keshgegian states that a person's future is greatly influenced by how she remembers the memories of her life. A victim of sexual assault can bury these memories and never make them public. This can be because she is afraid and ashamed of her memories. Keshgegian also states that a flashback is a response that occurs when the body remembers, even when the mind refuses to remember.[25]

A traumatic memory not only recalls the feelings that arise when an event occurs, but also the pain and betrayal caused by the lack of protection from the people around. The process of remembering is not only personal and interpersonal, but also social and political. Bearing in mind that recovery can only occur in a society that has accepted and acknowledged the reality of sexual violence, this process of remembering influences the community and the narrative identity of the community.[26]

The process of remembering traumatic events ultimately leads to the process of mourning and reinterpreting the past. The victim mourns all the traumatic experiences she feels psychologically and physically. The act of mourning makes the victim feel extreme sorrow and sadness. However, mourning is also a defense or a way to resist the effects of sexual violence. Mourning means facing and accepting the reality of the violence and accepting the wound fully and totally in one's core. Mourning means making room for past wounds.[27] When the victim mourns, the victim also releases the pain and loss she feels, even though the wound will remain forever. The wound is a memory of the suffering, but the wound no longer has the ability to hurt the victim.[28]

As someone who was born to a family who adheres to the traditional values of the Toba Bataknese, I explored an available way for trauma recovery by returning to my traditional roots as the eldest daughter of a Toba Batak family. Like Keshgegian, I see mourning has a healing dimension. Mourning means expressing the wound, without having to expose the wound itself.

Mangandung[29] is a process of mourning in the Toba Bataknese culture. *Andung-andung*, or lamentations, are usually sung when someone dies. In addition, andung-andung is also sung to express the sadness or suffering of life experienced by a Toba Batak. Andung-andung is a type of oral literature

[25] Keshgegian, 37.

[26] Ibid., 45.

[27] Ibid., 160.

[28] Ibid., 42.

[29] *Mangandung* (verb); *Andung-andung* (noun).

that contains an outpouring of feelings to mourn someone's life and death.[30] Andung-andung is referred to as literature because the use of words is different from the words Bataknese use daily. In the andung-andung that I attach below, there are examples of this special use of language: *rumondop ari* which means a rainy day; *sambor ma nipiku* which means my dream is gone; and *lungun lungunan* which means lonely but also, isolation.

I propose that andung-andung can be an alternative to trauma healing, particularly in the Toba Batak church. It can relieve the horrible atmosphere of losing loved ones. One forgotten side of andung-andung is that it does not only apply in the event of loss. It is also echoed when someone experiences an unfortunate event, namely a traumatic experience. I explore the trauma healing dimension of *mangandung* by using Keshkegian's opinion that mourning is needed by people who have experienced trauma as an effort to recover from their trauma. I imagine victims of sexual abuse, especially within the Bataknese church, practices the beauty of mourning, both traditionally and liturgically.

Andung-Andung: A Grace of Theological Aesthetics

The good and beautiful points to God's gracious presence and activity.[31] In the aftermath of trauma, andung-andung is the beauty that points to God as we cry and mourn over our brokenness as human beings. The main point that I want to make in this paper is that mourning is an act of grace. Andung-andung is an art of trauma healing, an art of crying, and an art of releasing one's agony. Through the theology of re-membering offered by Keshgegian, I can see that andung-andung is truly a spiritual gift that is found in the Protestant Christian Batak Church (HKBP) in Indonesia.

In Luther's Trinitarian theology, the grace of God is operative in earthly, as well as in spiritual, matters. That human beings cannot find the grace of God in creation does not mean that the divine gifts of grace are not present in the world of creation.[32] The human person is born into a world of abundant life, from the beginning, immersed in a network of relations.

---

[30] Julyo Armando Hugo and Ilona Situmeang, "Penafsiran Makna Lagu Tradisional Batak Toba Andung 'Saur Matua Ma Ho Inang': Analisis Semiotika Ferdinand de Saussure," *Semiotika* 10, no. 1 (2016): 2.

[31] Laurie Cassidy and Maureen H. O'Connell, eds., *She Who Imagines: Feminist Theological Aesthetics* (Collegeville, Minn.: Liturgical Press, 2012), xiii.

[32] Niels Henrik Gregersen, "Grace in Nature and History: Luther's Doctrine of Creation Revisited," *Dialog: A Journal of Theology* 44, no. 1 (February 2005): 20.

In Luther's sermons on the Gospel of John, he makes clear that the understanding of the eternal being of the divine word of God in the heart of the Father is not rationally discernible, for only the Holy Spirit can create listeners.[33] The "how" of divine action is incomprehensible, not because God is far away from creation, but because God is so fully woven into the fabric of creation. For the presence of the Father, Son, and Holy Spirit is so intimately woven into the texture of creation that creation itself becomes a text. This text of creation communicates law as well as of the gospel, signs of death as well as signs of grace and love.[34]

God is not sitting at a specific place but is operative all over. If the divine transcendence signifies that God cannot be contained in time and space, the divine immanence means that this one-and-only God is radically immanent in space as well as in the smallest conceivable events, including in the event of grieving or mourning. In the event of listening, sounds and voices are transformed into messengers of meaning and sensual-spiritual presence.[35] In the event of mourning, tears and wounds are transformed into grace. God's grace without us receiving grace is not of any worth. The grace of God is the primary agent in salvation. In relation to the remission of sins, the role of the human being is one of "complete passivity."[36]

Happiness is always seen as the highest ideal (in addition to basic needs) that can, and even, must be achieved by humans. Contrary to this, sadness is interpreted as a form of negative emotion that must be avoided and eliminated. People who experience trauma tend to experience depression as a prolonged impact of the deadly tragedy experienced. However, the public stigma of sexual violence forces people who experience trauma to choose to hide these emotions. However, instead of trying to analyze traumatic experiences that have different effects for everyone, I want to invite us to mourn, to grieve the wounds and pains we experience. I invite us to express our sadness by crying, by lamenting.

Aesthetics have the capacity to shape and change human thought patterns.[37] Aesthetics can restore a sense of significance, something that is lost when someone is traumatized. Through aesthetic experience, one can rebuild subjectivity and self-identity. Fragmented self-identity can be

[33] Gregersen, 23.
[34] Ibid., 28.
[35] Ibid., 24.
[36] WA 4, 487, 19–20, as quoted by R. L. Grace, "Luther's Doctrine of Grace," *Scottish Journal of Theology* 18, no. 4, (2009).
[37] Tone Roald and Johannes Lang, eds., *Art and Identity: Essays on the Aesthetic Creation of Mind* (Amsterdam: Rodopi, 2013), 7.

rebuilt when one's self experiences an encounter with art, because art is always connected to its environment.

Beauty is tied closely to the way one lives and acts –a practice and not an idea.[38] Andung-andung is a way of the Toba Bataknese, in particular, to live and practice their traditional beauty. When someone does *mangandung*, she or he is practicing the beauty of grieving. Aesthetics is not only about art; more than that, aesthetics is a process of creating meaning that can be the starting point for recovery from trauma. They are ways of encountering the beauty of God in both expected and unexpected places.[39] We encounter the beauty of God through sadness and grief. In our tears, God's grace transforms our wounds and heals them. Therefore, mourning is now not restricted to what we have known; it is instead to practice beauty.

Mourning is truly a grace of God for the church, which is sometimes forced to show only happiness and joyful emotions, hiding her vulnerability and fragility, hiding her wounds that are still bleeding. Andung-andung is also truly a grace of God, particularly for Batak churches in Indonesia. It is a call to embrace sadness and grief–even death. I am inviting all of us here to look at our inner self, where we hide all of our scars and untold stories–facing these things that are often covered by our happy masks. We are called to face our wounds with love. As an eschatological community, we are invited to create a safe space where everyone feels like they belong, along with their painful and traumatic experiences.

THE HOLY SPIRIT MOURNS WITH US

Recovery from trauma is possible. The time needed is different for each person. Recovery requires a community that is willing to share the wounds suffered by people who have experienced trauma. Recovery needs a community that is willing to remember the wounds. The process of remembering traumatic events ultimately leads people with trauma to the process of mourning. Mourning is the most difficult process in trauma recovery because it requires a person to fully and completely accept the pain in the deepest part of the self. Mourning is the most difficult process because it requires us to accept the fact that wounds will always leave their marks. Through the word of God, the Holy Spirit connects faithful remembering to proclamation, opening up and relating human existence to the reality of

[38] Susan A. Ross, "For the Beauty of the Earth: Women, Sacramentality, and Justice," in *She Who Imagines*, eds. Cassidy and O'Connell, 12.
[39] Ross, 14.

divine speech through the act of proclamation.[40] Through andung-andung, our traumas are proclaimed in silence. As the apostle Paul said in Romans 8:26, the Spirit prays with us, even in unspoken words. The Spirit sighs in us in the midst of terror. The Holy Spirit begins to cry in our heart. The Holy Spirit helps us in our weakness, intercedes for us with sighs too deep for words, and bears witness to our tears. The Holy Spirit mourns with us. The Holy Spirit cries with us. She transforms our wound and heals it.

Andung-andung ni Boru na Hansit
(The Lamentation of a Wounded Woman)
Amang (Father)
Tangihon ahu Amang (Listen to me, O, Father)
Ale Amang na marasiroha (O, merciful Father)
Ale Debata na mardenggan basa (O, gracious God)
Di rumondop ari, tangis au Amang (As the rains fall, so are my tears)
Maila au Amang, lam bernit sitaonon (I'm ashamed, everything feels too much to bear)
Sambor ma nipiku, sungkot ma ngolungku (My dreams are gone, my life has ended)
Alusi ma tangishon da Among (Hear my cry, o, Father)
Asi rohaM pasaor ma tu au on na dangolon (Have mercy on me, for I am miserable)
Alusi ma Among (Answer me, Father)
Lungun-lungunan manogot tu botari (I cry all day long)
Martua au, sai urupi ma (Bless me and help me)

[40] Paul S. Chung, *The Spirit of God Transforming Life: The Reformation and Theology of the Holy Spirit* (New York: Palgrave MacMillan, 2009), 7.

Youth Leadership in South Africa

Kagiso Harry Morudu

Introduction

As I was writing this paper, there was much discussion in social media about the role of young people in the Evangelical Lutheran Church in Southern Africa (ELCSA). As we try to unpack the role of young people in the church, we need to remember that the church is only a microcosm of society. Therefore, we cannot forget the role of young people in fighting a government that segregated people according to their skin color such as the actions and struggles of youth in the 1940s, and those represented in the Muziwakhe Lembede & Mangaliso Sobukwe generations. The Soweto uprising speaks to this. The struggle did not stop there. Today there is a #Feesmustfall movement, which is about stopping the increase in university fees and a call for the government to increase bursaries in universities so that more young people can be assisted. South Africa's young people are agents of change and are not relegated to the back during times of struggle.

The Youth League of the Evangelical Lutheran Church in Southern Africa

We can see that young people are active members in the church: they have programs such as Bible studies, singing, leading worship services, doing outreach programs, and holding cultural days. Even with minimal resources, members of the church's youth league organize their own fundraising activities. According to statistics about South Africa, youth between the ages of 15 and 24 are the most vulnerable: In the first quarter of 2019, the unemployment rate in this age group was 55.2 percent.[1] The ELCSA Youth League Constitution designates "young people" as those between 12 and 35 years of age. Most league members are still in high school or university. This means that the Youth League is one of the groups that is struggling financially. Most parishes, including those that are financially viable do not have budget provisions for the league despite the fact that most members are unemployed or still in school. Youth should be the responsibility of the "parents, the Sunday school teachers, the elders, the deacons, the membership as such, as well as the responsibility of one another as youth themselves. This responsibility is inalienable and untransferable."[2]

The Experience of Church for Young People

Jones says that understanding church ministry depends solely on our understanding of what the church is.[3] In my interaction with youth in the Eastern Circuit, their experience of church is both positive and negative. They say that the church is supposed to be a place of comfort where they can forget about their problems. Yet, they feel it is run more as a money-making scheme where church dues known as *Makgetho* take precedence over spirituality. In some parishes, if a youth member owes church dues, there are penalties. This may include refusing to baptize their children or denying young couples the use of church facilities for their weddings.

The other challenge is that the Youth League is seen as a "stepping-stone" toward other organizations in the church.[4] In other words, the Youth League is treated as a transactional league. This is, perhaps, linked to the understanding that youth is a transactional period between childhood and adulthood. Hence, the Youth League becomes a preparatory organization that trains young people for other leagues such as the Prayer Women's League, Prayer Men's League and even eldership. In my view, all ministries are equally important.

Jones's definition of church goes beyond the place of worship. In the New Testament, the Greek word *ecclesia* is used for "church"—a word that

[1] Department of Statistics, Republic of South Africa, "Youth graduate unemployment rate increases in Q1:2019," accessible at statssa.gov.za/?p=12121

[2] Malan Nel, *Youth Ministry: An Inclusive Missional Approach* (Cape Town, Aosis, 2005), 79.

[3] D. Jones, *Ecumenism* (Cluster Publication,1999), 71.

[4] Nel, 57.

means "a called assembly."[5] Jones argues that the New Testament defines church as the body of Christ (1 Cor 12:27).

A church is a community of individual living members (1 Cor 12:20) and also a community which trusts in the one and true God, Christ Jesus.[6] However, Jones thinks that this definition is too spiritual because usually this is not what people see in the church:

All we see are all-too-human organizations divided from one another by walls of mutual suspicion and bitterness built over centuries of prejudices, misunderstandings and the failure to be truly Christian towards each other.[7]

What Jones says clearly reveals that the church is run by sinful human beings and cannot be perfect. It is due to our sinful human nature that the church is not immune from sin. Althaus reminds us what Martin Luther says:

> The Church is not wood and stone by the group of people who believe in Christ. Whoever seeks the Church should join himself to them and observe what they teach, pray and believe. For they certainly have Christ amongst them.[8]

This shows that the church is a Christocentric community. It is Christ who is present in the faith of the church.

Jones speaks of church as both a human institution and a sacrament.[9] It is a human institution because it is a gathering of human beings with their flaws. Therefore, "the institutional model stresses the cohesion of the church as an organization, with a divinely sanctioned hierarchy and a divinely guaranteed orthodoxy".[10] Putting Christ at the center creates an understanding that the church is also a divine institution.

However, the model of the church as a human institution with a hierarchy poses a theologically creative tension. It represents classism within the church as the clergy is customarily considered superior to the laity, making the latter to be seen as passive.[11] Everything centers on ordained ministers because they are perceived as authoritative: the laity is expected to obey. A clergy-centric model kills the spirit "of the priesthood of all believers." With this model, clergy may be thought to be more powerful than all the believers in the community of faith.

---

[5] Jones, 71.
[6] Ibid.
[7] Ibid., 72.
[8] Paul Althaus, *The Theology of Martin Luther,* (Fortress Press, 1966), 287.
[9] Jones, 71.
[10] Ibid., 77.
[11] Ibid.

This model, therefore, results in the laity becoming lax and passive to the point that they are not empowered to discover and unleash their gifts for ministry.[12] This is why Youth League members feel they are not recognized by the church. Their role is relegated to singing during services and, whenever there are events, they are expected to do the cleaning.

In fact, the body of Christ should be actively involved in the ministry of the church. Surely when every baptized member in the assembly of God participates fully, God's kingdom grows rapidly. In the assembly of God there are no spectators: every member in the assembly is called to play an active role in God's ministry. God's ministry is inclusive and involves men, women, youth, and children. God's ministry within the church is not for a few chosen individuals. Even if there are different titles within the church, all members have an equal role to play in the church's ministry.

Jones further sees the church as sacramental because it is located in the inner and outer spiritual spheres. Jones says the inner spiritual sphere is where one recognizes the Holy Spirit and the outer spiritual sphere is where the Spirit is made visible in the work of Christians.[13] Long before Christians become involved in the ministry of God, the Holy Spirit is at work among the people of God. The ministry of the church is empowered by the Holy Spirit: without guidance of the Holy Spirit, there cannot be church ministry.

Both the institutional and the sacramental understandings of "church" have something to offer to the understanding of church ministry. Contrary to the institutional model, the sacramental understanding of church sees ordained and lay people as equals. Jones argues this model emphasizes that the church is sacramental and hence its entire ministry is effective in communicating grace. The church must be transformative, enabling, and united. It should be a community that allows its members to utilize their God-given gifts.[14]

The spirituality of laity emanates from this model because all members are empowered to discover their gifts. This is unlike the institutional model, which creates a dichotomy between the clergy and laity (Jones 1999: 76). As the role of the ordained minister in the sacramental model is to motivate and equip all members, Jones concludes that such a model finds its expression in the servanthood of Jesus Christ (1999: 76). In Jesus Christ, every member is important: no one is higher than the other. That is why gender barriers are destroyed, allowing both men and women to play a critical role in building the kingdom of God.

---

[12] Jones,100.

[13] Ibid., 76.

[14] Ibid.

Youth Leadership in the Bible and Now

The Bible is a powerful reference tool and can be used to either oppress or empower people. This has led to many debates about whether the Bible is the inspired word of God. The Bible has been used, taught, and preached in the church largely from a male perspective. Wallace suggests that problems of Biblical interpretation relate to the reason and skill of the interpreter (Wallace 1999: 46). This is because "we can use it to intrude our own thoughts upon God's word or we can use it to subject our thoughts to God's word."[15]

The Bible has been used as a tool to hinder women and young people from obtaining leadership positions in the church. Conradie argues that the Bible has become the church's book of reference when constructing church norms, values, and ethics.[16] Hence Pierre argues that when theologians interpret scripture, it is crucial that they look at three hermeneutical approaches of interpreting scriptures: authorship of the text, the context in which the text was written, and the audience for which the text was written.[17] This approach helps today's readers understand the cultural gap between us and the first readers of the text. Nonetheless, "No one enters a text without presumptions as we are finite human who inhabit a particular culture and a specific society."[18] Nel thinks that in the processing of understanding the role of children and youth in the Bible, it is important to not use the Bible in a fundamentalistic way.[19]

Therefore, we should be careful when selecting biblical texts. In the Bible we can identify stories of God entering into a covenant with children and youth. What is clear though, is that children are seen as a reward, or blessing, from God (Ps 128). Furthermore, God wants to have a special relationship with children as God is the God of their parents: God wants to be their God as well (Gen 17:7). God calls young people to ministry: Josiah was a king at eight years old. His mission was to bring a rebellious nation back to God. The prophet Jeremiah was only seventeen years-old when he was called to minister to Judah (Jer 1: 4-8). Samuel was also called between the ages of twelve and thirteen years, and David was called when he was a teenager. In the New Testament, Jesus confirms the importance

[15] Ronald S. Wallace, *On the Interpretation and the Use of the Bible*, (Scottish Academic Press, 1999), 46.
[16] Ernest M. Conradie, *Angling for Interpretation: A first introduction to public, theological and contextual hermeneutics*, (Stellenbosch, Sun Press, 2008), 3.
[17] Simone St. Pierre, *The Struggle to serve: The ordination of women in the Roman Catholic Church*, (Mcfarland and Company, Inc., Publishers, 1994), 52.
[18] Thomas R. Schreiner, *Two views on women in ministry*, (Zondervan Publishing House, 2001), 178.
[19] Nel, *Youth Ministry*.

of children to a society that seemed to have lost this insight. It is through the ministry of Jesus, that we come to realize the full revelation of God's relationship to children. Jesus' ministry affirmed children and protected their rights against those that saw them as unimportant (Mt 18: 1-14, 19:13-15).[20] According to Acts 21:9, even unmarried daughters received their gift of prophecy, and children were active participants during services as they are directly addressed in Ephesians 6:1 and Colossians 3:20.

Despite such biblical references, the Youth League has always felt neglected, even by their pastors. The reason for not supporting youth events is normally based on finances. The Youth League is unable to book expensive accommodation during conferences or even receive a token of appreciation from pastors. The Youth League feels that pastors support leagues that are financially viable. Indeed, in the documentation of ELCSA Church Council 141 it was noted that "outstanding financial challenges are still ongoing. The church council will assist to resolve the matter."

Transformational Leadership as a Model for Youth Leadership

There is no doubt that youth identity and culture has been formed by youth in isolation from the dominant culture, as exclusion has forced youth to create their own spaces (Nel 2005:14). The undermining of women and youth results from the definitions of leadership and power by some scholars. For example, Deventer defines leadership as "one or other form of dominance where the subordinate more or less has to accept the commands and control of another."[21] Due to gender stereotyping, a woman who leads with the same authority and power as a man will be judged unfairly and called bossy, rude, bitchy, bully or "pheke"—a Tswana name, which means that she acts like a man or she wants to wear men's trousers.

According to ELCSA' constitution, Youth League leaders form part of councils at all levels, however, they are considered non-voting members. It is sad that women and youth who support the church are not part of key strategic positions (e.g., in the decision-making bodies of the Eastern Circuit and the Central Diocese where only men have voting rights). All bishops in ELCSA are male and the executive council of ELCSA's Central Diocese is also a male club. Clearly, women and youth are voiceless in the decision-

[20] Nel, *Youth Ministry.*

[21] V. Van Deventer & M. Mojapelo-Batka, *A Student's A-Z Psychology,* (Cape Town. Interpak Books, 2013), 1.

making bodies of ELCSA. An emancipated ELCSA will only be possible when women and youth join hands to ensure that their voices are heard.

Youth in the church are considered to be the "church of tomorrow." As they are the church of tomorrow, they end up being relegated to the background today. I vividly recall that in the parish where I am serving, there was a vacancy in the Financial Planning Committee. We had to second someone and there was a suggestion of selecting a young person. The constitution of the church is clear that we need to have someone in that role with the requisite skills. This young person had financial accounting skills, but this was not the reason she was co-opted. She was co-opted because she is young, and they wanted to train her for future church leadership. The problem is that this young woman and other young people are being prepared to be leaders tomorrow instead of empowering them to be leaders today.

Lee suggests that Christian leadership has two dimensions. The first dimension concerns individuals and nurturing their faith. The second dimension concerns the whole community and calls on individuals to focus on the needs of other people through the ministries of evangelism, outreach, and service.[22]

Hewitt says that present-day leaders fail to read the signs of the times or to discover the gospel of our Lord and savior, here and now.[23] Further, he suggests that the church and its leaders should be aware of fundamental shifts in basic values and lifestyle (1989: 17). For these reasons, the church is in need of transformational leaders. Young people can be agents of change.

Transformational theory can be detected in both the Old and the New Testaments. In the Genesis creation stories, we see a God of transformation who changed chaos into order (Gen 2). Furthermore, we hear of prophets such as Amos who aimed to transform the thinking and caring patterns of people. Their message was to repent and change behavior and thoughts.[24]

In the New Testament, we encounter Jesus as a transformative leader when he challenges the status quo and calls for radical renewal, morality, and faithfulness (Lewis 1996:7-8). The call to transformation is clear when he says, "you have heard that it was said ... but I say ..." (Mt 5:21-22). It is clear that those words were a challenge to the people and their leaders. Jesus was calling for a radical change or renewal or morality and faithfulness.[25] The commissioning of the disciples to the world was a sign of transformative leadership.

---

[22] Harris W. Lee, *Effective Church Leadership*, (Augusburg Fortress, 1989), 28.
[23] R. R. Hewitt, *Transforming Leadership*, (United Kingdom, Streets Printers, 1996), 17.
[24] Philip V. Lewis, *Transformational leadership: A new model for total church involvement*, (Zondervan Publishing House, 1996), 7.
[25] Lee, 32.

It is clear that transformational leaders, like Jesus, are agents of change: they are not caretakers or keepers of the status quo. Jesus challenges the order of the day as we read in Matthew 5:38-42.[26]

Patriarchy in Church and the Changing World

The word "patriarchy" can be defined as "the rule of the father": it is a system which elevates and normalizes the idea that men should be in power at home and in church, society, politics, and the economy. In other words, this is a form of system, which gives men dominance over women and children. However, Rackozy argues that it is not all men who are privileged to have dominance such as those who are gay or poor.[27]

The patriarchal system in both Greek and Roman societies put men in the role of the head of the women, children, slaves, and concubines in the household. Simply put, patriarchy is an oppressive mechanism exercised by husbands, political leaders, and employers. This influences boys to dominate girls. In the Jewish culture, society valued the family. It too, was a hierarchical system that placed a husband at the head followed by his wife, the children (boys first followed by girls) and the slaves. The boys' upbringing influenced their treatment of women.[28]

Durrheim argues that patriarchy can be expressed as androcentrism, exclusion, and forceful subjection.[29] It is due to androcentrism that the world tends to center on men: many cultural values and norms favor males more than females. These norms and values have excluded the women's worldview through silencing their contributions and perceptions.[30]

Women are often named or defined in relation to the men in their lives—father, husband or children.[31] This is because these women are perceived as having no personal rights. They are treated as the property of the men: this limits their contributions as human beings. In our present context, women who are pastors and married to male pastors are called *mma moruti* (pastor's wife) but a man who is married to a female pastor is never named as *Ntate Moruti wa Mamoruti* (a pastor who is married to a pastor).

---

[26] Lee, 32.

[27] Susan Rakoczy, *In Her Name: Women Doing Theology*, (Pietermaritzburg, South Africa, Clusters Publications, 2004), 78.

[28] S. J. Achtemer, in *Ministry in three dimensions*, (Great Britain, Longman and Todd Ltd, 2001), 288.

[29] Terre Blanche, Durrheim, Painter, eds. *Research in Practice: Applied Methods for Social Science*, (Cape Town, UCT Press, 2006), 102.

[30] Ibid.

[31] Ibid.

In some situations, women are not even allowed to speak for themselves: men speak on their behalf. For example, during a Batswana funeral it is always a man who gives a vote of thanks. In a case where the men in the family are not comfortable speaking in public, the family will ask a man who is close to the family to offer the vote of thanks. Such practices encourage the oppression of women.

However, the world looks at the South African constitution as a guide because of the way it encourages and promotes equality for all citizens: "The state may not fairly discriminate directly or indirectly against anyone or more for any reason, including race, gender, sex, pregnancy, marital status, ethnic or social origin, color, sexual orientation, age, disability, religion, conscience, belief, culture, language and birth".[32] In addition, the country's bill of rights emphasizes equality for all. This equality for all citizens is all postulated in the Bible when Paul writes, "there is no longer Jew or Greek, there is no longer slave or free, there is no longer male and female; for all of you are one in Christ Jesus" (Gal 3: 28).

Through baptism we are joined to the ministry of service to God and others. Baptism is a transforming event that empowers all the baptized to participate in God's ministry. God gives the mandate to ministry for God's people. There can never be a body without various parts and therefore the church will not function properly without these parts. Hence Paul argued that "the eye cannot say to the hand, 'I have no need of you'" (1 Cor 12:21). This makes the point that both the old and the young need each other, and expresses the notion of mutual empowerment.

The constitution of South Africa is superior and cuts across all other constitutions, including that of the Evangelical Lutheran Church in Southern Africa. Despite such a powerful tool, it seems patriarchal tendencies still prevail in church and society. I know this to be so because I grew up in a context where girls and boys had different roles e.g., a girl's place is understood to be in the kitchen and a boy's place is understood to be outside in the garden. Kisembo notes that "The man who helps his wife out with the house chores has no dignity and everyone, men and women, often have grave reservations about such a one."[33] Such mentalities are still prevalent: the saying *Mosadi o goga monna ka nko* literally means "she pulls him by the nose" and figuratively means that this man is inferior which is why he can be led by his wife.

[32] Chapter 2 of the Constitution of the Republic of South Africa, 1996.

[33] Benezeri Kisembo, *African Christian Marriages*, (Jeoffrey Japman Publishers, 1997), 121.

Sexism in Worship

As I have noted, this topic is both theological and practical. Theology is born from the life of the people: Senn says that "theology is concerned with language because God communicates with people in, with, and under the languages in use" (visible words as well as spoken words).[34] He goes on to say that liturgical theology needs to look deeply at how we address God and one another in liturgical assembly. In our congregation, God is addressed as "He" and Sunday school children usually see God as an old man with a beard. Our sermons and liturgies present a male God. For example, when celebrating Holy Communion, the celebrant will say in the *praefatio*, "who on the tree of the cross did give salvation unto mankind." "Mankind" should at least be "humankind." During worship services, all congregants, including women, are addressed as "brethren." There are also songs such as "Faith of our Fathers," which should be changed to "Faith of our parents (or ancestors)." The idea of God as male has led to men being considered more like God unlike women and consequently, women should be submissive to men.

In our attempt to understand the motherhood and fatherhood of God, it is important to note that the language used in the Bible is both symbolic and metaphoric.[35] However, Sumner asserts that these biblical metaphors should not be completely disregarded as they are meant to tell us something about God. We cannot avoid the fact that we will never understand God adequately.[36]

Referring to God as either father or mother should not make one think that God is either female and or male: God is not a biological being. Some traditionalists have turned a blind eye to texts that evoke God as a mother. Their focus is on the maleness of God as they believe that God is entirely masculine. Their standpoint is that the Bible usually expresses God in male terms such as Lord, King, he, abba.[37] It is disingenuous though to suggest that there are no texts that show the divine motherhood of God. God is expressed as the one who has given birth (Deut 32:18), a mother comforting her child (Is 66:13), and as a woman looking for a lost coin (Lk 15:8-10).[38] Nonetheless, we should not dismiss that Jesus addressed God as father:

[34] Frank C. Senn, *Christian Liturgy: Catholic and Evangelical*, (Augsburg Fortress, 1997), 40.

[35] Sarah Sumner, *Men and Women in the Church*, (InterVarsity Press, 2003), 115.

[36] Ibid., 116.

[37] Wilhelm Adolph Visser't Hooft, *The Fatherhood of God in an age of emancipation*. (World Council of Churches, Switzerland, 1982), 128.

[38] Ibid.,128-133.

we are to remember that addressing God as a father does not necessarily mean that God is male. Instead, this is a metaphor for God. The fatherhood of God should be "open to correction, enrichment, and completion from other symbol forms such as mother, brother, sister and friend. The Bible itself gives us, as we have seen, sufficient indication of this openness to allow us to speak of maternal traits in God."[39] Belleville points out that our human sexuality should not be suppressed because this would be to deny our humanness.[40]

Conclusion

We cannot dismiss the issue of power when talking about leadership. Power is inherent in leadership and without it there will be no action. Jesus himself was filled with the "power" of the Holy Spirit and he used this power to empower others.

The church should reflect deeply on its understanding of power and authority. In so doing, we will learn to be stewards who use power to organize, manage, mobilize, and teach.[41] In this chapter I suggest that young people in the church are also to be stewards of this power, and can use it to nurture confidence and competence in individuals.[42]

It is clear that youth leadership is an issue, which touches both church and society. This is because the church is a microcosm of society (society being the macrocosm). The issue of gender equality is a challenge for the church to reflect on, as the church is called to transform culture not to conform to it. Moreover, the church has to look at how it does theology. It is clear that both women and men are created in the image of God. In stories of the ministry of Jesus, we see that he dismissed attitudes of superiority and inferiority. My argument in this paper is that the church is challenged to be the agent of transformation. Its task is to envisage an egalitarian community. Research findings show that even though women and youth have leadership roles in the church, they are underrepresented. Women and youth, who form the majority in congregations, are represented by one or two people in the executive committee council. The reason is that most women and youth in the church are not familiar with feminist views and, as a result, they have become their own worst enemies.

---

[39] Visser't Hooft, 133.

[40] Linda L. Belleville, *Women Leadership and the Church: 3 Crucial Questions*, (Baker Books, 2000), 98.

[41] Lee, 82.

[42] Ibid., 83.

Recommendations

I recommend that the church accept that women and youth are made in the image of God and should be allowed to participate in all functions of the church. In Matthew 28, we read that women were the first eyewitness of the resurrection.[43] At that time, a woman's testimony was not of value but, in this text, we see a paradigm shift in the role of women.

I further recommend workshops for women where they can learn to have confidence in themselves and others. A workshop is needed where women and children will be emancipated from patriarchal ideologies. This will be a space where women will be allowed to speak their minds without fear. In addition, educational training in theology is essential so that women can realize their potential and the gifts bestowed on them by God. Such platforms should liberate women from oppressive practices and ideologies. This training will unleash the spiritual gifts, which youth received during their baptism. As the Youth League is a moral agent, it is critical that young girls be empowered from a young age.

The church should adopt policies and programs, which ensure that women and youth are part of decision-making structures through capacity building and ensuring that such structures enable the participation of women and youth. The LWF has a quota system of 40 percent each for men and women and 20 percent for youth: ELCSA should ensure that this gender and generational representation is implemented.

Inclusive language in church is not only about changing words or phrases: it is an action, which requires a shift of mind in God-talk.

[43] Tokunboh Adeyemo, *Africa Bible Commentary*, (Zondervan Corporation, 2005), 195.

A Lutheran Perspective of the Nexus Between Justification and Sanctification in the Contexts of Holistic Mission with Reference to the Application of Spiritual Gifts

Wilfred J. Samuel

Introduction: Identity and Practice

We are dealing with a vital question on Lutheran identity and practice in reference to spiritual gifts. Identity plays a significant role in determining how we understand and experience the world (our Christian experience), as well as shaping the types of opportunities and challenges we face. World Lutheran identity has evolved over the centuries in that it has embraced a flexi model in its journey of becoming a communion of churches. In the global context, the reinterpretation process has ideologically and theologically given birth to various identity forms validated as Lutheran. These forms carry within them a conservative outlook, a moderate outlook, and a more liberal outlook. While these may be less theologically complex than the doctrine of justification, there are inevitable differences and complexities in these diverse theological outlooks. It is clear that Lutheran confessions and texts offer a sound theological basis for reflection on pneumatology. However, difficulty may arise when it comes to balancing theology with practice and knowledge with experience. Here, I want to reaffirm that we have been freed and formed with a purpose; we have been entrusted with a responsibility and call to holistic mission—fulfilling the Great Commission and the Great Commandment. Therefore, the practice of our Lutheran faith ought to take into consideration this purpose and consider the application of spiritual gifts as gifts of grace, endowed by Christ through the Spirit to the church.

As a basis and foundation to the Lutheran perspective in the application of spiritual gifts within the missional context, we may need to consider briefly the theological location of Lutheran pneumatology as a holistic approach in the offering and application of the treasure of salvation.

Beyond Justification and Leading to Formation: Offering and Applying the Treasure of Salvation

Lutheran theology generally understands the work of the Spirit in terms of "offering" and of "applying" the treasure of salvation. The "offering" is to be placed in the context of justification the "applying" is related to the post-justification state or sanctification process. Hence, justification is an unrepeatable event, but sanctification is a process involving daily experiences and walking in faith through the power of the Spirit, starting with baptism and regeneration.

The question of baptism and regeneration has always been a thorny issue in baptismal theological debates. Does baptism offer regeneration? Reformation theology with its understanding of "justification by faith alone and grace alone" supported the notion that baptism does hold regenerative capabilities. Hence, infant baptism seemed less of an issue within such context. However, theologies that reject the notion of baptismal regeneration would opt for believer's baptism.

The Work of the Holy Spirit: Location in Lutheranism

In Lutheran theology, the work of the Holy Spirit is generally considered along with a person's reconciliation with God and application of redemptive benefits. It would incorporate themes such as election, union with Christ, regeneration, conversion, justification and sanctification.

Luther could not have been more precise in stating the work of the Holy Spirit, as may be found in his concluding remarks of his interpretation of Psalm 117 (revised edition). He concluded this 1530 document (addressed to Hans von Sternberg) by stating:

> But God, our dear Father, who through His dear Son and our Lord and Savior, Jesus Christ, has so richly enlightened us – may he strengthen us with perfect

> faith through His Holy Spirit and give us power to follow His light faithfully and diligently, and praise and extol Him, both in teaching and in life."[1]

Noticeably, central theological themes related to the work of the Spirit are intricately woven into a single statement, pregnant with meaning. The same is expressly mentioned in article XI of the Epitome in the context of "election": "In addition, he promises the power and operation of the Holy Spirit and divine assistance for steadfastness and eternal life."[2]

In summary, Luther and the confessions corporately understand the work of the Spirit in terms of "offering" and "applying" the treasure of salvation. In justification, the offering

> ... takes place through the preaching of the Word.... God reveals his will in this way, and that in those who He thus calls He will be efficaciously active through the Word so that they may be illuminated, converted, and saved. For the Word through which we are called is a ministry of the Spirit."[3]

Similarly, in the post-justification context, it is the Spirit who "testifies to the elect that they are 'children of God' (Rom 8:16)."[4] The Spirit also ensures that those who are decreed "pray and give thanks, are sanctified in love, have hope, patience, and comfort in afflictions (Eph 1:11–13, Rom 8:25)."[5] For deeper appreciation of the subject (the work of the Spirit) and its location in Lutheran theology, it is helpful to view it under the following headings: Witness, Comforter, and Enabler.

The Work of the Spirit: Formation of a Witness to the Gospel

In Lutheran theology, the "offering and application" of the gift of salvation is first considered on a communicative level. Here the Spirit of God plays the crucial role in communicating the will of God (Jn 16:5–16). The mission of the Spirit of truth is to guide people into truth, which is knowledge of

---

[1] Martin Luther, *Selected Psalms III,* in *Luther's Works.,* vol. 14, ed. Jaroslav Pelikan and Daniel E. Poellot (St.Louis: Concordia Publishing House, 1958), 39.
[2] Theodore G. Tappert, Formula of Concord: Epitome XI:8, *The Book of Concord: The Confessions of the Evangelical Lutheran Church* (Philadelphia: Fortress Press, 1959), 495.
[3] BC, Formula of Concord: Solid Declaration, Article XI: 29, 621.
[4] Ibid., 73, 628.
[5] Ibid., 30, 621.

sin, righteousness, and judgment (Jn 16:9). Luther in his preface to Psalm 2 (March 1532) offers a brief observation (which he would, of course, clarify later in the main text) concerning the operative mode of the Spirit. Here Luther focuses on the Word and worship as chief communicative elements.[6] We may even want to understand that Luther, at this point, is saying Word is indeed worship, since the Spirit is present. Luther cross-references Acts 4:25 in his study of Psalm 2 to assert this notion and indicates that it is the key function of the Holy Spirit to witness to God and God's will. This thought receives a heightened emphasis in Luther's interpretation of Psalms 3, 8, and 51. In these sections too, the concept of the Holy Spirit as the communicator, or revealer, of God is gradually developed into a Christocentric framework. While nature revealed God in a general way (*revelatio generalis*), the Spirit reveals God in Christ in a special way (*revelatio specialis*).

To Luther, these "are divine and heavenly doctrines. Unless they are taught by the Great Spirit, they cannot enter the heart of man."[7] Such testimony, as borne by the Spirit, is an important work of the Spirit in Lutheran theology since human beings are eternally lost in its absence. Truth "cannot be understood without the Holy Spirit for they are abysses of divine wisdom in which the reason is completely submerged and lost."[8] The gatekeeping imagery used by Luther in his interpretation of Psalm 68 is yet another expression of the role of the Spirit: "For if God does not open and explain the Holy Writ, no one can understand it, it will remain a closed book enveloped in darkness."[9]

Work of the Spirit: Comforter in the Context of Spiritual Warfare

Our second point concerns the work of the Spirit as the Comforter. Both the Lutheran confessions and Luther agree that this function of the Spirit should not be understood solely in utilitarian terms—consolation in the midst of emotional sadness or worry. It encompasses a much wider theological perspective with regenerative implications and would then include such themes as "law and Gospel" and "sin and grace". To comfort is to preach about grace and the gracious disposition of God. As elucidated in the Formula of Concord, comfort is spoken into the context of depravity and its tormenting effects. "For the Gospel and Christ are not ordained and

[6] LW 12, *Selected Psalms* I, 4.
[7] Ibid., 303.
[8] Ibid., 266.
[9] LW 13, *Selected Psalms* II, 17.

given us to terrify or to condemn us, but to comfort and lift upright those who are terrified and disconsolate."[10] Similarly, the Augsburg Confession emphasizes that "faith is no idle knowledge, nor can it exist with mortal sin, but it is a work of the Spirit that frees us from death, comforting and quickening terrified minds."[11]

Luther also refers to this comforting role of the Spirit in his interpretation of Psalm 118:6. The context here is spiritual and eternal joy as characteristic features of the Spirit. Luther notes, comfort "does not come to us without the Word, which the Holy Spirit effectively calls to mind and enkindles in our hearts, even though it has been heard ten years."[12] Luther, in synonymy with the confessions, views comforting in the context of sin management. Recognizing the vital connective element of spiritual jubilation between the comforting of the Spirit and the Word (the operative means of the Spirit) is an important location in Lutheran theology. True jubilation, or celebration, is when sin, death, and devil are collectively, and effectively, dealt with.

Since the struggle (spiritual warfare) between the "Old Adam" and the "New Adam" is a biblical reality, the Spirit's aid cannot be ignored. "Thus, the weakness of our own flesh and Old Adam are also in the picture, so that on every hand it becomes difficult and labors to remain steadfast and to await the end. That is why the Holy Spirit has much work to do and comfort his own."[13] It is a process whereby believers are constantly aided in remaining faithful witnesses and performers of good deeds. As the church is a community nurtured by the Spirit, it is endowed with the designation "holy community" or sanctified people. "Until the last day the Holy Spirit remains with the holy community or Christian people. By it he creates and increases sanctification, causing it daily to grow and become strong in faith and in the fruit of the Spirit."[14] Further, the Spirit empowers them with spiritual gifts to be credible witnesses.

The Work of the Spirit: Enabler of Holistic Missiological Formation

Our third consideration concerns the enabling function of the Spirit. It is here that we may find a crucial meeting point in the exercise of the fruit

[10] BC, Formula of Concord: Solid Declaration, Article V: 12, 560.

[11] BC, Apology Article IV: 115, 123.

[12] LW 14, *Selected Psalms* III, 62.

[13] LW 13, *Selected Psalms* II, 179.

[14] BC, *Large Catechism*, Second Part: 52, 417.

of the Spirit and the gifts of the Spirit. In Lutheran theology, as we tread on from the justification scene and cross into the territory of good works, the enabling character of the Spirit is clearly illuminated.

Therefore, we can say, without creating any theological doubt, that Luther and the confessions regarded holy and responsible Christian living with great concern. Holy living is addressed in the context of good works and answers the question "What makes a person holy in the sight of God and induces godliness?" The confessional statement "God is not to be taken lightly"[15] is loaded with meaning in terms of Christian responsibility and virtue. Holiness and godliness are tied with obedience to God, which is mandatory, not optional. It is, in fact, a sign of faith:

> We do not overthrow the law, Paul says (Rom 3:31), but uphold it; for when we have received the Holy Spirit by faith, the keeping of the law necessarily follows, by which love, patience, chastity, and other fruit of the Spirit gradually increase.[16]

The enabling activity of the Holy Spirit induces positive obedience, thus continuing the process of sanctification by ensuring production of good works, virtuous living, and the empowering of credible witnesses.

Here we see the vital role of spiritual gifts in helping to fulfill the missiological task (Lk 6:20–23). To summarize the confessional thought, it may be useful to quote from Luther's preface to Romans.

> Faith is a divine work in us that transforms us and begets us anew from God, kills the Old Adam, makes us entirely different people in heart, spirit, mind and all our powers, and brings the Holy Spirit with it. Therefore, faith is living, busy, active and mighty, so that it is impossible for it not to be constantly doing what is good. Likewise, faith does not ask if good works are to be done, but before one can ask, faith has already done them and is constantly active...It is therefore as impossible to separate works from faith as it is to separate heat from light and light from fire.[17]

Thus far, we have noted that in Lutheran pneumatology, sin management, spiritual warfare, empowerment, holiness, and good works are only possible through the work of the Holy Spirit. The exercise of the fruit and gifts of the Spirit in a constructive and progressive manner results in victorious Christian life. Hence, as we continue to live and serve, it is important that Lutherans who explain the work of the Spirit in this way, also hold in proper balance the centrality of the Word, Trinity, and Christocentrism. I

---

[15] BC, *Large Catechism*, First Part: 149, 385.

[16] BC, *Apology* XX: 14, 229.

[17] BC, *Formula of Concord: Solid Declaration*, Article IV: 12, 553.

believe these standpoints are key to our reflection on the use of spiritual gifts as we endeavor to enhance our Lutheran identity.

Need to Affirm the Essentiality of Spiritual Gifts in Mission

The scriptures lend ample support to confirm that Spiritual gifts are divine tools provided for mission. This includes the gifts mentioned in Romans 12, 1 Corinthians 12–14, and Ephesians 4. From these biblical texts (not to be taken as an exhaustive list) we see how the endowment of gifts is placed within the framework of God's grace and divine will. Although some may doubt the necessity of such manifestations for the modern church, nevertheless, as witnessed by the scriptures, it must be agreed that the early church experienced enormous blessings through the exercise of spiritual gifts. It needs to be reiterated that, contrary to narrow orthodox notions, any theological suggestions which presuppose the withdrawal of spiritual gifts from the church or which limit its function to the early church, need to be reconsidered. The following verses attest to the legitimacy of this thesis.

"For just as the body is one and has many members, and all the members of the body, though many, are one body, so it is with Christ" (1 Cor 12:12).

Here, Paul uses the vivid body metaphor[18] to explain the nature and function of spiritual gifts. He finds it useful to understand the coordinated functioning of the body, with its diverse[19] nature, as the best possible model for the exercise of spiritual gifts in the church. This coordinated functioning is made possible only because every part in the body is functioning as one entity. Paul's frequent usage of "many" and "one" in 1 Corinthians 12, sets forth the idea that his interest rests in affirming unity within diversity. As Pfitzner, the eminent New Testament scholar from Luther Seminary in Adelaide, suggests: "The Corinthians knew this diversity well enough, so the real point is not the variety of gifts and members, but the oneness of

---

[18] "Paul is here using the human body to illustrate the one true Church and its function" (Oliver B. Greene, *The First Epistle of Paul the Apostle to the Corinthians* [Greenville, S.C.: The Gospel Hour, Inc., 1965], 400).

[19] "The congregation of believers and the human body are each an entity in-diversity". Barnett, *The First Epistle,* 231.

the Church."[20] If the body metaphor of Paul is understood well, and applied, the exercise of spiritual gifts will no longer be a thorny issue.

"But as it is, God arranged the members in the body, each one of them, as he chose"' (1 Cor 12:18)

In this verse, Paul not only states the importance of spiritual gifts, but also the need to discern the source and origin of such gifts. Such an emphatic notion, that spiritual gifts are apportioned according to divine wisdom, grace, and choice, is characteristically Pauline. The Corinthian church is, therefore, exhorted to understand this principle. As Greene notes:

> Paul here states the flawless, perfect plan of Almighty God – omnipotent, omniscient, omnipresent – He who knows the end from the beginning. God knows each individual. He knows our ability, our limitation...."[21]

Hence, Paul's body metaphor needs to be interpreted as implying there can be neither envy nor arrogance in the exercise of gifts, since these gifts are gifts of grace. For Paul, each member is unique, with his or her own gift, and no one goes without endowment or empty. This thought, while liberating us of worry or envy, also assures that none[22] have too much or too little.

"But each one of us was give grace according to the measure of Christ's gift ... to equip the saints for the work of ministry, for building up the body of Christ" (Eph 4:7, 12)

Paul finds it necessary to reiterate that the endowment of spiritual gifts is a matter of divine grace. To him, the "ultimate end for which Christ gave his gifts is the building up of the body of Christ; to this end, the equipment of the saints for the work of ministry is the divinely appointed means."[23] The Spirit's sovereignty over the gifts attests that spiritual gifts are gifts of grace—unearned and unmerited. This points us to the necessity and

[20] V. C. Pfitzner, First Corinthians, *The First Epistle,* 195.
[21] Greene, *The First Epistle*, 404.
[22] "Each divine person – God the Lord and the Holy Spirit has gifted each member and 'appointed' each 'member' for a distinctive ministry to the whole, just as He has decided" (Paul Barnett, *The First Epistle,* 233).
[23] John G. Strelan, Ephesians, *The First Epistle,* 55.

validity of spiritual gifts within the church. In Paul's understanding, the church is certainly "charismatic," if "charismatic" refers to presence of the Spirit and spiritual gifts. Understanding, and applying, gifts correctly is a practical question, which then requires spiritual prudence and personal care.

Possible Challenges

- **Fear factor**: There are varied experiences in the Spirit. Spiritual practices and rites must be validated by some biblical or theological standards. But, if properly discerned, the Lutheran church could be open to the work of miracles, supra-rational signs, and wonders, etc.

- **Preoccupation**: The Lutheran church cannot remain inward looking and preoccupied with promoting its brand of spirituality and worship culture alone.

- **Maintaining the perception of balance**: The balance between preaching the law and gospel, grace and good works, Great Commission, and Great Commandment is vital.

- **Failure to reform**: Traditional approaches and theologies are not wrong but could become outdated. Therefore, they need to be constantly evaluated, reformed, and re-expressed.

Lutheran Theological Education and Formation: A Risky Business in Changing African Landscapes

Johannes Habib Zeiler

Introduction

> Now there was an Ethiopian eunuch, a court official of the Candace, queen of the Ethiopians, in charge of her entire treasury. He had come to Jerusalem to worship and was returning home; seated in his chariot, he was reading the prophet Isaiah. Then the Spirit said to Philip, "Go over to this chariot and join it." So Philip ran up to it and heard him reading the prophet Isaiah. He asked, "Do you understand what you are reading?" He replied, "How can I, unless someone guides me?" And he invited Philip to get in and sit beside him. (Acts 8:27–31)

The narrative about the Ethiopian eunuch reminds us about the fact that the interpretation of the scriptures, how we understand tradition and outline the context we live in, or how we read the signs of our time, always need to be undertaken in fellowship with others. In other words, to reflect upon what the gospel means and to be able to adequately respond to what it requires, is not something that we primarily do on our own but in constructive and critical dialogue with one another.

Such a fundamental hermeneutical departure point could easily be applied to the dynamic and growing field of Lutheran theological education and formation worldwide. Among Lutherans generally, the quest for relevant and qualitative models of higher theological education is highly valued and considered necessary to keep the church leadership vital and adequately equipped in the preaching of the Word and the administration of the sacraments. Also, from a broader perspective, to promote and provide Christian education of all sorts to the whole people of God is essential for every church that claims to serve in society and to contribute to its transformation. The biblical narrative from Acts 8 underlines that the communal aspects of the educational enterprise, i.e., reading, praying, and sharing of the gospel, including the fellowship we enjoy while eating and living together, are crucial factors when one explores the contours of the educational task in Lutheran tradition in past and present times.

Educational Initiatives in Context

It is an honor and delight to have presented this paper in Addis Ababa, not only with regard to the guiding principle and spiritual advice delivered by the Ethiopian court official in Acts 8, but also with regard to the fact that it was here that Lutherans across the globe met for the Third All-Africa Lutheran Conference in 1965 which impacted and formed so many of the dreams, visions and initiatives related to the broad field of theological education. Josiah Kibira (1925–1988), by then bishop in the Evangelical Lutheran Church in Tanzania and later president of the Lutheran World Federation, delivered the keynote address and claimed that the African churches were marginalized and hindered from speaking their mind:

> Are we allowed to criticize and think independently without the threat (and consequent fear) of losing our traditional and universal connection, our financial aid, and in some cases, our theological dialogue with other churches; especially those from which we have emerged?[1]

His lecture was titled "A Living Church in a Changing Society" and focused specifically on freedom and unity.[2] For Kibira, these two themes did not merely reflect the socio-political developments over the last decade, but also captured the flavors of the visions and challenges among Lutherans in sub-Saharan Africa at a time of decolonization and societal change.

Already at the end of the fifties, the processes of decolonization had given further impetus for the churches to structurally organize themselves

---

[1] Josiah Kibira, "A Living Church in a Living Society," in *Addis Ababa: A Record of the Third All-Africa Lutheran Conference. Addis Ababa, Ethiopia, October 12–21, 1965*, ed. Department of World Mission, Lutheran World Federation (Geneva: Lutheran World Federation, 1966), 20.

[2] Kibira, 18–27.

in new ways within the education sector, not least in relation to churches and missionary agencies abroad. Lutheran churches across the continent joined newly established networks and organizations through which they started to relate and cooperate with other churches. These radical changes in the life of the African churches have, in current missiological theory, been described as "the fourth self" or as "self-theologizing," indicating the emergence of a new era.[3] The increasing degree of structural independence in the local churches created a seedbed for a new self-understanding on the African continent. The churches started to seek forms of a contextual approach to theology and to carve out a pastoral practice adapted to the diverse contexts at hand. In contrast to the situation during the colonial period, they wanted to better address and respond to the emerging challenges. Broadly speaking, the field of education became a crucial means of decolonization, nation building, and pan-Africanism. Institutions for higher education thus became crucial forces and instruments determining how the churches would evolve and expand in the future.

The decision to privatize the education sector across the African continent challenged the churches and other private actors to join and engage in new ways. From the mid-nineties onwards, many of the theological colleges were transformed into multi-faculty universities. As recently noted by church historian Joel Carpenter and others, today the most comprehensive directory lists nearly 1,500 African institutions for theological

[3] See Dickson N. Kagema, "Leadership Training for Mission in the Anglican Church of Kenya" (PhD diss., University of South Africa, 2008); Jurgens Hendriks, "Reliable Leadership, Sustainable Seminaries: The NetACT Story 2000–2012," in *Handbook of Theological Education in Africa*, eds. Isabel A. Phiri and Dietrich Werner (Oxford: Regnum Books International, 2013), 1001–1017; Paul G. Hiebert, *Anthropological Insights for Missionaries* (Grand Rapids: Baker Academic, 1985); Brian Stanley, "The Church of the Three Selves: A Perspective from the World Missionary Conference, Edinburgh, 1910," *The Journal of Imperial and Commonwealth History* 36, no. 3 (September 2008): 448; Brian Stanley, *The World Missionary Conference, Edinburgh 1910* (Grand Rapids: Wm. B. Eerdmans, 2009), 165–166.

See also Richard E. Trull, Jr., *The Fourth Self: Theological Education to Facilitate Self-Theologizing for Local Church Leaders in Kenya* (New York: Peter Lang Publishing, 2013). The idea of the "fourth self" is linked to the widely discussed theory of the three selves—namely self-government, self-support, and self-propagating—originating from the works of the western missionaries Rufus Anderson (1796–1880) and Henry Venn (1796–1873) in the first half of the 19th century. See, for example: Stanley, "The Church"; Stanley, *The World Missionary Conference*, 132–166, 167–201; World Missionary Conference 1910, *Report of Commission II: The Church in the Mission Field* (Edinburgh: Oliphant, Anderson & Ferrier, n.d. [1910]); World Missionary Conference 1910, *Report of Commission III: Education in Relation to the Christianisation of National Life* (Edinburgh: Oliphant, Anderson & Ferrier), n.d. [1910]).

education.[4] In sub-Saharan Africa, the largest growth of private higher education has been identified among institutions with religious affiliations. Evangelicals, Roman Catholics, Anglicans, Lutherans, and others are all highly involved in the establishment of institutions for higher education. Their various types of academic institutions form global or regional networks with an ongoing exchange of knowledge, ideas, technology, money, students, and staff. Drawn into this expanding, expensive and competitive educational market, the churches, regardless of denominational affiliation, have questioned, problematized, and challenged many of the old concepts and practices. Hence, the growing demand for higher education in Africa has called for reforms of both the African providers of education as well as those international actors that financially support these institutions.

Several African Lutheran churches have taken significant steps within this rapidly growing field. The number of institutions for theological training has both multiplied and become more diverse; so has the number of ministerial students, even though still the overwhelming majority of the students is studying at a lower academic level. Recent data from Tanzania and Ethiopia show that the number of female students in theology continues to increase, partly due to strategic decisions taken by the respective churches. However, the role and status of ordained women in congregational milieus are still of grave concern. The asymmetrical power relations between men and women in church leadership positions need further critical examination.

Additionally, courses and programs for already ordained pastors have been introduced in the intersection of different academic disciplines. For example, two master's programs at Tumaini University Makumira in Tanzania–particularly focusing on gender and health, and on biblical and contextual theologies– have enabled a broad range of Lutheran pastors across the country to engage with new areas of research.

Hence, theological education serves diverse purposes and agendas. It is a crucial factor when promoting theological reflection and research, it is described as a catalyst for theological and ecumenical formation of individuals as well as communities, and it is a strong force in the structural and ecclesial formation processes of a church. Moreover, the discourse of theological education reflects how, and by what means, Lutheran churches claim and become agents of societal change.

[4] Joel A. Carpenter, "To be Agents of a Life-giving Transformation: Christian Higher Education in Africa" *Yale Divinity School Library: Occasional Publication* No. 26 (New Haven, Conn.: Yale Divinity School, 2019).

Theological Education and Formation in the Evangelical Lutheran Church in Tanzania

Let me now turn to my own doctoral dissertation from last year on theological education and formation in the Evangelical Lutheran Church in Tanzania (ELCT), a qualitative study that explores some of the most burning issues related to ministerial formation.[5] The study draws heavily upon interviews and conversations with Lutheran bishops and theological educators in Tanzania. The ELCT is proud of its rich historical and theological Lutheran legacy and, at the same time, is immensely concerned about how to embody and to communicate the Christian faith in its own context in an adequate way. Perceptions of higher Lutheran theological education not only reflect the ideals, structures, values, and ambitions of certain institutions, but also some of the most pivotal challenges related to the diverse contexts in which the church serves its members.

Let's start with two quotations:

> Well, you have the growing number of the charismatic churches, churches without a proper theology, churches without a proper tradition, you know, and you see that our [Lutheran] churches in the urban areas, they are jumping into that bandwagon. They would like to continue to claim to be Lutheran but the way they do their things are completely different from how we are used to, we as Lutherans.[6]

> They [the Pentecostals and charismatics] are voices with a message. So we need to see what are we doing, what are we giving people, how are we approaching people's issues. And what are others doing? Why are they doing what we are not doing?[7]

As noted, Lutherans in Tanzania are drawn into ambivalent processes of confrontation and exchange, dialogue, and strife. On the one hand, the informants considered this diverse influx an external threat to Lutheran identity with a negative impact on the teaching and pastoral practice in the life of the congregations. On the other hand, the fact that there was a growing pressure from below (i.e., highly charismatic Lutheran congregations across Tanzania) obliged the interviewees to revisit and modify their positions and standpoints. The religious landscape is like a kaleidoscope; constantly shifting in color and form, dependent on context and time.

[5] Johannes Habib Zeiler, "Crafting Lutheran Pastors in Tanzania: Perceptions of Theological Education and Formation in the Evangelical Lutheran Church in Tanzania" (PhD diss., Uppsala University, 2018), http://uu.diva-portal.org].

[6] Habib Zeiler, 142.

[7] Ibid., 148.

Denominational Consciousness in the Making

The Roman Catholic theologian Robert Schreiter, who is widely known in ecumenical and missiological circles, underlines the following aspects when commenting upon how religious identity is shaped.[8] According to Schreiter, there are three types of formation of religious identity: formation through resistance, through hybridity, and through hierarchy. I would argue that all of these aspects are of significant importance in the current debate on the nature, character, and role of theological education in the ELCT today, not least the latter one on hierarchical formation, because with education comes also expectations and claims that those who undergo studies will be transformed in a certain direction, and in turn, guide and direct others.

One key issue, as I see it, is to what extent formal theological studies actually provide the students with adequate tools when they are sent to serve in the local congregations.

The ELCT is currently navigating in the midst of a diverse multi-religious landscape, characterized by an increasingly complex mixture of contesting claims and practices. In particular, the informants identified the Lutheran encounters with Pentecostal and charismatic Christianity as one of the most important challenges for them to tackle, particularly as it impacted the denominational identity of the ELCT. These encounters were often depicted in binary opposition, clarifying both commonalities and differences between self and other. However, what was articulated and emphasized on a theoretical and rhetorical level did not always correspond with the pastoral practice in the localities. The informants took overlapping, even contradictory, standpoints and positions. While some tended to describe Lutheran identity in sharp contrast to Pentecostal and charismatic Christianity, others pointed to the fact that the ELCT, throughout its history, had been, and still is, informed and shaped by different revival impulses and movements. The situation generated new questions on if, how, and to what extent, such theologies and practices could, or should, be accommodated within the ELCT.

The informants depicted the denominational identity of the ELCT as multifaceted and complex in character. It is neither monolithic nor static, but defined in relation to historical, socio-political, or theological factors. The local context in which the church conveys its message is crucial in this regard. My study showed that the ELCT could be described in at least three different ways: as historical and mainline, mainline and charismatic, as well as Lutheran and Pentecostal. Importantly, these descriptions do

[8] Robert J. Schreiter, *The New Catholicity: Theology between the Global and the Local* (Maryknoll, N.Y.: Orbis Books, 1997), 73–79.

not necessarily exclude each other. In fact, several of the interviewees sympathized with two or three of the approaches at the same time. Rather, from the informants' point of view, they might be seen as overlapping and complementary perspectives when elaborating upon the self-understanding of the ELCT.

First, the ELCT is one of the historical mainline churches in the country with strong ties and well-established relationships to other mainline churches. It is ecumenically minded and shaped, and through its global networks highly involved in development work. The informants argued that it is important for the ELCT not to be "deluded" or "invaded" by rapidly growing churches that employ teachings, practices, and methods "totally different" from those the ELCT claims to uphold. However, to what extent the ELCT would be able to keep pace with its own members, their needs, preferences, and expectations of the church and what it could offer is an open question. With Schreiter, one could argue that Lutheran identity is carved out through resistance; "We are Lutherans and not like the Pentecostals who are totally other."[9]

Second, the ELCT could be described as both mainline and charismatic. The emergence and development of revival movements within the ELCT is neither new nor alien in relation to the history of the church. The level of "charismatization" in the ELCT may recently have increased or intensified and yet be something that signifies aspects of Lutheran spirituality that have been present and visible in the life of the church since the early twentieth century. The fact the ELCT, when it was established in 1963, was formed out of seven independent Lutheran churches, all shaped by different Lutheran traditions and practices across the country, show that there has always been, and still is, a mixture of traditions—a hybrid if we like—within the Lutheran tradition in Tanzania.

Third, another way of describing the ELCT as charismatic is to explicitly refer to some of the practices traditionally associated with Pentecostalism. The term "Lutheran Pentecostalism" indicates that the ELCT is open to new practices after having critically examined their theological basis. Doing so is one way for the ELCT to respond theologically and pragmatically to many of the current challenges at hand. While some of the practices have to be rejected, others seem easier for the informants to embrace and to incorporate into already existing structures and thought forms.

[9] Habib Zeiler, Chapter 7, 'Encountering Charismatic Christianity', "Crafting," 138-158.

A Risky, Costly, and Contested Business

The fact that the number of institutions of higher education in general has grown substantially reflects demographic changes in society more broadly. As the African population has continued to grow, so the number of students in need of further studies has increased over the years. Modernity is constantly challenging the churches. So is globalization, with its rapid rise of new technology and intensified urbanization. That has changed the general level of knowledge among many of the members of the local Christian congregations. The expectations of the church leadership and its ability to adequately respond to the broad range of needs are, therefore, vast, which in turn raises questions about the nature and purpose of theological education and ministerial formation today and in the future.

However, one has to bear in mind that theological education is far from an innocent or value-neutral enterprise. Rather the opposite, which makes it a risky business for all actors involved. Agreements of cooperation and support, or involvement in diverse exchange programs reveal an asymmetrical and often an unpredictable distribution of financial resources, values, and claims between the so-called donor communities on the one hand—in this case churches and missionary agencies in the global North—and their partners in the global South on the other. In the name of "mission and evangelism" or "development work," new forms of domination and control impact the global links in, and between, churches, missionary agencies, and faith-based organizations in ways that challenge, sometimes even contradict, the sustainability, accountability and unity in the life of the churches. Students, faculty, and the conditions under which the institutions are run have become pawns in a complex theological, financial, and political game.

In other words, an analysis of models and methods of theological training—such as curriculum development, student internships in local congregations, or issues related to content and scope of particular courses—should never be discussed in isolation from these structural and financial aspects of the educational enterprise. In fact, the field of theological education is highly contested and, sadly to say, often embedded in romanticizing and simplistic views on what could be achieved. Therefore, if we are serious about the idea of promoting and strengthening the field of Lutheran theological education, a self-critical and constructive conversation needs to take place between all partners involved. This is very much a question of having a robust and joint conversation within, and between, Lutheran churches and missionary agencies across the globe. For instance, the way financial resources are channeled or how partnership agreements are set up and implemented in practice must be constructively and critically examined anew. Current forms of bilateral support must give way to new forms of multilateral cooperation that are both professionally monitored and well-coordinated. Some of the funds for the Lutheran World Federation Scholarships for Theology and Diakonia program are built around these principles. Such structures could be further developed and strengthened in the future with regard to the field of theological education.

As already indicted, theological education is generally high on the agenda among Lutherans, considered key when strategizing for the future, and often described as "the backbone of the church." While ecumenical cooperation is vital to many Lutheran churches, the discourse of theological education is mainly structured, and talked about, along the lines of denominational affiliation. The logic of privatization and marketisation of the educational field more broadly causes the churches to organize themselves along denominational lines, often at the expense of further institutional ecumenical collaboration. Lutherans do engage in ecumenical theological formation, but only to a certain extent, for instance when running specialized courses for university, hospital, and prison chaplaincies or in the area of inter-religious studies, which are open to students from different churches, sometimes even from other religions.

Moreover, with shrinking democratic space—which is a socio-political reality in several African countries today—come new restrictions that make the education sector vulnerable and fairly complicated for the churches to handle. The requirements for academic recognition, standards, and accreditation—not least when it comes to the formal competence of faculty, the quality of libraries and archives, and how to best use the human resources available in the church—are under constant scrutiny and debate. Furthermore, church synods or dioceses are facing difficulties in finding students who are qualified to embark on higher theological studies. The fact that differing models of theological training exist side by side has, in most cases, served the churches well in terms of equipping the congregations with evangelists, catechists, teachers, and ordained clergy. At the same time, the different institutions are all competitors in a decentralized and liberalized educational market, even within one and the same church. The idea of having one major national institution that provides courses and programs in theology at undergraduate, postgraduate, and research levels is constantly challenged by the rapidly growing trend to set up local or regional institutions. The constant fight for money and students tends, therefore, to ruin the churches financially and to structurally draw them a part.

Concluding Remarks

There is no doubt that Lutheran churches across the African continent have invested tremendous efforts and resources in theological education and benefitted vastly from the establishment of Bible schools, mobile training institutes, colleges and universities. However, many questions need to be further discussed. To what extent are these institutions able to keep pace with the current needs, challenges, and demands? How do we understand the underlying assumptions and ambitions related to theological education when it comes to the formation of solid Lutheran identities of our time? And lastly, are we willing to find joint structures through which we share and allocate human and financial resources in order to achieve the goals?

The issues discussed in this paper on theological education and formation in sub-Saharan Africa could, on a more general level, easily be applied to other Lutheran contexts elsewhere in the world. As noted, the definition of this dynamic field is fluid in character and loaded with diverse aspirations, highly dependent on the context and time.

The questions posed by the Ethiopian court official in Acts 8 and in Kibira's profound keynote address from 1965 are still relevant to discuss and reflect upon, to use as a corrective, and as a source of joy and inspiration. Encountering "the other" along the way means to re-learn much of what we so far have taken for granted. It is a learning process for all actors involved, regardless of our geographical location or theological departure points, to find ourselves on both the sending and receiving end.

Annex

Findings, Learnings, and Steps for Future Reflection

The fruits of theological consultations go well beyond the documentation of essays and papers. *We Believe in the Holy Spirit: Global Perspectives on Lutheran Identities* is the beginning of a communion wide conversation. Participants in the global consultation revealed new perspectives, inspired new directions for future research, and created trans-contextual cohorts for theological reflection that transform our understanding of what it means to be Lutheran today. The major themes that emerged from plenary gatherings, and feedback from small paper presentations and small group conversations were compiled in the report, *Lutheran Identity Process Phase 1: Full Report and Lessons Learned,*[1] which is the annex to this LWF documentation.

As implied by the reference to *Phase 1*, the findings are meant to inform subsequent phases of the study process. On the closing day of the consultation, participants met in regional groups to design survey and discussion guide questions that will be used in Phase 2 of this process. For the churches and local parishes that participate in the study process, the current volume is intended to be a resource, linking the consultation to their ongoing theological reflection. For that purpose, we include the "Major Themes and Findings" here as an appendix.

It begins with an opening statement on the concept of identity in the context of our Lutheran confession. Next, the report summarizes themes that were affirmed, themes that need further elaboration, and themes that we cannot support as Lutherans. Finally, the major findings are summarized.

Major Themes and Findings on Lutheran Identity

On the topic of Lutheran identities, the plenary began under the notion that while our identity is informed by a common theological, normative heritage, our identities are formed in the context of diverse cultures, languages, worldviews and political realities. However, the plenary conversation came around to the possibility that we could still speak of a shared Lutheran

[1] lutheranworld.org/content/resource-lutheran-identity-study-process-phase-1-addis-consultation

identity that is normative, though not prescriptive, and whose unity is expressed in diversity. Participants acknowledged that sometimes one can speak of a shared identity, and at other times identities.

The need to speak of a normative (though not prescriptive) identity was considered significant to churches that are a religious or cultural minority. This requires further exploration in light of questions around particularity and universality, as a communion of churches in the context of ecumenical and interfaith dialogue.

The following summary points were gathered from plenary feedback. They are organized into categories according to what was consistently affirmed, themes that will require further elaboration, and areas that cannot be supported.

Themes that we consistently affirmed

- A common confessional foundation: Lutheran identity is rooted in the *solae* including the Word, the Trinitarian ecumenical creeds, Lutheran confessional documents (recognizing that some churches also recognize the Formula of Concord, Barmen Declaration, etc.) including the Catechisms with special emphasis here on the third article.

- Common marks and spirituality, including prayer, music and worship, the cross, Word and sacraments, service, etc.

- Liturgical spirituality, including Word and Sacrament as a means of grace, is related to the holiness of the church.

- No one cultural expression is prescriptive of Lutheran identity.

- Lutherans have a strong pneumatological foundation but it is not always well expressed.

- The one economy of the Holy Trinity necessarily links Christology, ecclesiology and pneumatology; justification and sanctification; creation, salvation, renewal; *charis* and *charismata*; etc.

- Word and sacraments are constitutive of the church, and means of grace through which the Holy Spirit works.

- Baptism and the priesthood of all the baptized are fundamental to understanding the source of the fruit and gifts of the Spirit, and that the baptized are called and equipped to participate.

- All members of the community are charismatic, if charismata are properly understood in light of the concept of baptismal vocation.

- Theology of the cross and pneumatology are integral to our understanding of the gospel and God's gracious work in the world, and should not be interpreted in isolation from one another.

- There is a need to discern spirits and the spirits of the age (social, political, economic, scientific, theological philosophies that form and inform contemporary discourse).

- We can return to our theological and confessional tradition to ask new questions in order to find new creative expressions of our living faith that speak to contemporary narratives that we face, particularly in relationship to anthropology, care for creation and the social, political and economic spirits of the age.

- *Confessio Augustana V* and *VII* are an affirmation of a way to discern spirits, linking Word/Sacrament and the Holy Spirit.

- We are engaged in this study in the midst of ecumenical, interfaith and interdisciplinary dialogue particularly in situations of Lutherans as a religious, cultural, philosophical or political minority.

Themes to elaborate

- The relationship between pneumatology and Christology (whether that be a Christological pneumatology or a pneumatalogical Christology).

- The Spirit works through the Word and sacraments, but we need to develop our theological understanding of how God's spirit works in the world at large, in light of the sovereignty of the Holy Spirit. The Freedom of God should be a major theme of future theological reflection.

- The relationship of the work of the Spirit in the world at large with earth care.

- A Lutheran-centered process of discerning the Spirit and the spirits of the age (including economic, materialist, political, social, structural, patriarchal, power, etc.).
- Teaching spiritual gifts in a way that is rooted in 1 Corinthians 12 and the theological concept of the priesthood of all the baptized.
- The centrality (or foundational nature) of the priesthood of all the baptized for understanding the work of the Spirit in the world at large, and in the church (through the charisms found throughout the priesthood of all the baptized and in the ecclesial ministries).
- The relationship between mysticism and charisms.
- The need to develop a pneumatology of charisms.
- The relationship between the concept and discourse on mission and the Holy Spirit.
- A more complex notion of colonialism and neo-colonialism as it relates to religious identity and expressions of power (and patriarchy) between churches and within church structures.
- We need to research Lutheran theologies of charisms that already exist or function de facto.
- In the process ahead, we need to engage indigenous perspectives more deeply. Several participants represented indigenous peoples, and the reality of indigenous and traditional wisdom was raised, but not systematically treated. These perspectives are a necessity going forward.

Emerging themes that we cannot support

- Rooted in our confession that we are justified by grace through faith, Lutherans cannot support any use of spiritual gifts that commodifies the gospel or grace, burdens the human conscience, confuses spirituality with special revelation, creates a special class of charisms or has any aim other than building up the body of Christ.

Major Findings

- Lutheran identity and identities are formed in a matrix of normativity and experience that includes all of the *solae* (Word, grace, Christ, faith), our confessional, theological tradition, liturgical tradition as well as the pluralistic societies in which our cultural tradition is formed, multiple religious belonging, and traditional or indigenous belief systems. In this way, the Lutheran tradition is always living, and the expressions are always being negotiated as well as renewed.

- While Lutheran churches are often constituted with different confessional bases (i.e., some ascribe to the Formula of Concord and some do not, while some recognize the Barmen Declaration and some do not), the Augsburg Confession and Luther's Catechism are recognized by all member churches of the LWF. For this reason, a special emphasis was placed on the Catechism, not only as a confessional document, but a teaching tool, and therefore a vehicle of our tradition that continues to be applied in a dynamic, living way in ecclesial settings, and within homes as a means to nurture all baptismal vocations.

- Within the Lutheran tradition, liturgy has a significant role to play within the transmission of the tradition, and as a means of grace where the faithful experience the Holy Spirit as gift and promise.

- Liturgy as performative theology and dialogical aesthetics: The consultation highlighted the special role that liturgy (including Word and the sacraments) plays in forming identity (confessional, anthropological and cosmological), transmitting faith, and shaping the tradition itself. As performative theology, the means of grace do what they say and communicate what God is, and the community or assembly is itself participating in realized eschatology, as well as equipping and liberating us for our vocations. Additionally, as dialogical aesthetics, indigenous or cultural traditions also shape our worship and the way that God's Spirit is active in worship. The consultation recognized the special part that worship plays as a central, lived spirituality, which contributes to the formation of children and informs their education and faith literacy.

- Lutheran identity is open and liberating. Lutheran identity is always formed by ecumenical realities that balance particularity and universality. Lutheran identity always asks us to interpret ourselves in light of the gospel before God and the world and then re-enter into our tradition and context, equipped with a holy dynamism.

- Forming and informing our identity is related to the call to make disciples. In this light, strong emphasis should be placed on the making–formation.

- Multiple religious belonging deeply affects the way our religious and theological identities are formed today. This encourages constructive and critical dialogue with indigenous and traditional wisdom sources of identity, as well as ecumenical and interfaith dialogue.

- Lutherans put an emphasis on discerning the spirits. *Oratio/meditatio/tentatio* provides a method for discerning spiritual gifts for the building up of the body, as well as the "spirits" of the age, such as exploitative power, patriarchy, ethno-nationalism, commodification, fetishism, consumerism, xenophobia, etc., which co-opt narratives of "spirituality" and "spiritual gifts". What is important is that while Lutherans have a rich and strong pneumatology, spiritual gifts are always given in love in order to build up the body (1 Cor 12-13). In order to address spiritual narratives that commodify gifts or suggest special revelations that glorify a new clerical, shamanistic or spiritual class, Lutherans must develop theological frames and mechanisms of discernment (*tentatio*) in order to equip people to differentiate between what gifts are used to build up the body in love and compassion, and what gifts are being exploited through claims of special revelation as a new theology of glory, as a means of commodifying grace in our age.

- Lutheran identity speaks about a method and mode of being in the world. Lutheran identity is not informed solely by a set of theological or confessional propositions. Lutheran identity is formed by the lived spirituality of our experience of God's Spirit through Word, sacrament and service, recognizing and including mysticism. Part of that lived spirituality involves discerning our experience of daily life. A faithful trust in God's presence in the world shapes our mode of being in the world. The *tentatio* of Luther's theological method implies a critical reflection or engagement with the world that trust's the Holy Spirit will help us discern between law and gospel, what is promise and what is contrary to God's desire for creation. The consultation recognized the value of an inductive, pastoral approach to theological reflection and self-understanding that values experience as theological "data", and sees our living theological and confessional documents as normative but not prescriptive.

- To the goal of discerning concepts of charism and the spirits of our age, the consultation repeatedly lifted up the concept of the priesthood of all the baptized as a critical way to frame spiritual gifts as part and parcel of baptismal vocation. The consultation found consensus in that, while criteria need to be developed for discerning spiritual gifts and adapting for the reality of certain spiritual gifts (speaking in tongues or healing), a theology of charisms should be rooted in the baptismal concept of the priesthood of all the baptized. This doctrinal position underwrites the profession that all the baptized have received the same grace from the Spirit of God through Christ, and therefore all gifts are equal. By democratizing administration, teaching, diaconal service, etc. on the same plane as speaking in tongues and healing, then there can be no claim of special revelation (therefore reducing exploitation) related to any "special gifts." This link strengthens the link between *charis* and *charismata* (grace and gifts), as well as justification and sanctification, which is one mark of future Lutheran theological engagement.

- The consultation remarked that liberty is an organizing principle of Lutheran identity. While justification by grace through faith is the cornerstone of the Lutheran tradition, liberation implies that no theological locus or religious practice should ever bind what has been loosed. For that reason, liberation by God's grace (e.g., Paul's letter to the Galatians) implies that nothing given as a gift and promise should be used to burden the heart or conscience, or as a religious means to an end. Like the priesthood of all the baptized, liberty is an organizing principle that will help in constructing any theology of charisms, or criteria for discerning charismata or spirits of the age.

- The concept of liberty also applies to our understanding of God's work in the world at large. To this end, the freedom of God emerged as a significant area for further theological reflection that must be engaged. In many ways, this goes well beyond questions of Lutheran identity. But, in many ways, our Lutheran theological tradition began with basic questions of God's freedom, which eventually led to questions about God's liberty to act through the church, and therefore in the lives of human beings. Most of our anthropological questions are related to the concept of the freedom of God, as are our continuing questions of public theology, ethics and the church in the public space.

However, perhaps most relevant to the discourse of our day, are the ecological implications of the freedom of God. What is our profession regarding God's presence and work in the world? Church's mission in light of the Spirit's work in creation at large? How does that understanding of mission relate the church to other faiths, indigenous traditions and the public space? How does that inform our vocation to participate in God's work in the world as Christians (and therefore Lutherans) and shape our anthropology per se? These are lingering questions that can be explored in the coming years.

Due to their ecological and anthropological significance, perhaps the freedom of God and the Spirit's work in the world at large will be one of the most fruitful arenas for Lutheran theological reflection at the beginning of the next 500 years of our living tradition.

Follow Up and Future Reflection

Already, participants from across the LWF communion have deepened our theological reflection on several of these themes that emerged from this consultation. While the original methodology called for regional reflections, the COVID-19 pandemic was cause for a radical shift in modality toward online meetings. The series of "Being Lutheran" webinars offered an online creative, dialogical space, which models the kind of theological reflection that we hope is inspired by these findings. Recordings of these conversations are curated on the LWF website for use in local parishes.

Finally, an online survey and standardized, open-ended questionnaire was broadcast to LWF member churches, to be used in local fora. Based on the questions produced by the Addis consultation participants, the questionnaire is descriptive and reflexive. It values diverse deductive and inductive responses. It privileges spirituality and experience as theological data, recognizing that Lutheran identity is rooted in a living tradition that includes dynamic practices, and normative but non-prescriptive confessional foundations.

It is our hope that this documentation of consultation papers, including the findings' report, will be read in the context of the questionnaire and the outcomes of this study process. Ultimately, we hope it inspires you to theological reflection on the Holy Trinity's faithful work of continually forming, reforming and transforming our identity as the baptized,

- called to till God's garden and safeguard the conditions for abundant life,
- gathered in communities to resound the good news in Word, sacrament, prayer and praise,
- and enlightened with gifts for loving service to all creation.

Soli Deo Gloria.

List of Contributors

Auvinen, Rev. Dr Mari-Anna, Docent of Ecumenism and Missiology, University of Eastern Finland

Christopher, Rev. Caroline, pastor in Broadway, Chennai, and manager of Working Women and Student Hostel, Arcot Lutheran Church, India

Clapsis, Rev. Prof. Emmanuel, Archbishop Iakovos Professor of Orthodox Theology at the Holy Cross Greek Orthodox School of Theology, Brookline, Massachusetts, USA/Greece

Friedrich, Rev. Dr Nestor Paulo, The Lutheran World Federation Vice-President for Latin America and the Caribbean, Professor at the Faculty of Theology, São Leopoldo, Brazil

Godebo, Rev. Yacob, Dean of Theological Studies, Mekane Yesus Seminary, Addis Ababa, Ethiopia

Halvarsson, Rev. Sofie, MTS Uppsala University, pastor, Church of Sweden

Hutagalung, Ms Novriana Gloria, Jakarta Theological Seminary, Protestant Christian Batak Church, Indonesia

Junge, Rev. Dr Martin, General Secretary, The Lutheran World Federation, Geneva, Switzerland

Kärkkäinen, Rev. Dr Veli-Matti, Professor of Systematic Theology, Fuller Theological Seminary and Docent of Ecumenics, University of Helsinki, Finland

Kim, Rev. Dr Jun Hyun, Professor of Old Testament and Provost, Luther University, South Korea

Madejski, Sebastian, PhD candidate, Christian Academy of Theology in Warsaw, Poland

McDonald, Christopher Lee, MTS Duke Divinity School, former youth and children minister, Anglican Diocese of British Columbia, Canada.

Morudu, Rev. Kagiso Harry, pastor Evangelical Lutheran Church in Southern Africa, and the ELCSA-Youth League, South Africa

Mtata, Rev. Dr Kenneth, General Secretary, Zimbabwe Council of Churches, Zimbabwe

Mulenga-Kaunda, Dr Mutale, independent researcher and member of the Circle of Concerned African Women Theologians, Seoul, South Korea/Zambia

Oberdorfer, Rev. Dr Bernd, Professor of Systematic Theology and Contemporary Theological Questions, University of Augsburg, Germany

Persaud, Rev. Dr Winston D., Professor of Systematic Theology at Wartburg Theological Seminary (Dubuque, Iowa, U.S.A.), Director of the Center for Global Theologies, and Holder of The Kent S. Knutson & United Evangelical Lutheran Church Chair in Theology and Mission, USA/Guyana

Peterson, Rev. Dr Cheryl M., Associate Dean for Academics and Professor of Systematic Theology, Trinity Lutheran Seminary, Capital University, Columbus, Ohio, USA

Pöder, Rev. Dr Johann-Christian, Junior Professor for Ethics (Technology & Medicine) at the Theological Faculty of the University of Rostock, Germany/Estonia

Rimmer, Rev. Dr Chad Michael, Program Executive for Lutheran Theology and Practice, The Lutheran World Federation, Geneva Switzerland/USA

Samuel, Rev. Dr Wilfred John, Director of Lutheran Study Center, Sabah, Malaysia

Wallace, Rev. Dr Beverly, Associate Professor of Congregational and Community Care, Luther Seminary, St. Paul Minnesota, USA

Wasmuth, Rev. Dr Jennifer, Director of the Institute for Ecumenical Research in Strasbourg, France/Germany

Zeiler, Rev. Dr Johannes Habib, Theological Advisor at the Church of Sweden Central Office, Uppsala, Sweden

Anne Burghardt | Simone Sinn (Eds.)

Global Perspectives on the Reformation

Interactions between Theology, Politics and Economics

LWF Documentation 61

160 pages | paperback | 15,5 x 23 cm
ISBN 978-3-374-04840-3
EUR 20,00 [D]

The sixteenth-century Reformation transformed the church and society at large and its key theological insights had a concrete impact on the socio-political and economic spheres. Luther and his fellow reformers reconfigured Christian theology as they explored the liberating concept of justification by grace through faith as a core axiom of theological reflection. Lutheran and other churches of the Reformation continue to be empowered, informed and inspired by these insights, also with regard to their public role in today's societies.

In light of the 500th anniversary of the Reformation, eminent theologians and scholars from all parts of the world offer their insights into the interaction between theological thinking, economics and politics in the twenty-first century.

EVANGELISCHE VERLAGSANSTALT
Leipzig www.eva-leipzig.de

Tel +49 (0) 341/ 7 11 41 -44 shop@eva-leipzig.de

Simone Sinn | Dina El Omari
Anne Hege Grung (Eds.)

Transformative Readings of Sacred Scriptures

Christians and Muslims in Dialogue

LWF Documentation 62

200 pages | paperback | 15,5 x 23 cm
ISBN 978-3-374-05430-5
EUR 20,00 [D]

The interpretation of sacred scriptures engenders vivid debates in religious communities, both at the scholarly and grass-roots levels. Issues of debate are the hermeneutical assumptions, the methods of interpretation, and the constructive and harmful implications of certain readings. For Christian and Muslim communities, themes related to God's grace, violence, gender relations and ecology, are topical. As scholars from different contexts and faith backgrounds together interpret sacred texts they gain fresh insights into their meaning and their transformative dynamics. Essays by authors with expertise in scriptural interpretation, religious studies, pastoral care, philosophical theology, gender studies and pedagogy explore Christian and Muslim perspectives on scriptural interpretation, and discuss how to understand how God communicates with the world today.

EVANGELISCHE VERLAGSANSTALT
Leipzig www.eva-leipzig.de

Tel +49 (0) 341/ 7 11 41 -44 shop@eva-leipzig.de

Jürgen von Hagen | Michael Welker
John Witte | Stephen Pickard (Eds.)

The Impact of the Market

on Character Formation, Ethical Education, and the Communication of Values in Late Modern Pluralistic Societies

300 pages | paperback | 15,5 x 23 cm
ISBN 978-3-374-06406-9
EUR 30,00 [D]

Pluralism has become the defining characteristic of modern societies. Individuals with differing values clamor for equality. Organizations and groups assert particular interests. Social movements flourish and fade. Some see in this clash of principles and aims the potential for a more just human community, while others fear the erosion of enduring culture. Yet beneath this welter stand powerful and pervasive institutions, whose distinctive norms profoundly shape our moral commitments and character–notably the family, the market, the media, and systems of law, religion, politics, research, education, health care, and defense.

In the theoretical, empirical, and historical contributions to this volume, theologians, economists and market practitioners discuss the many tensions between market economics, ethics and the Christian religion, thus adding to the fruitful and much needed dialogue between economics and theology.

EVANGELISCHE VERLAGSANSTALT
Leipzig www.eva-leipzig.de

Tel +49 (0) 341/ 7 11 41 -44 shop@eva-leipzig.de

Michael Welker | John Witte
Stephen Pickard (Eds.)

The Impact of Religion

on Character Formation, Ethical Education, and the Communication of Values in Late Modern Pluralistic Societies

288 pages | paperback | 15,5 x 23 cm
ISBN 978-3-374-06410-6
EUR 30,00 [D]

Pluralism has become the defining characteristic of modern societies. Individuals with differing values clamor for equality. Organizations and groups assert particular interests. Social movements flourish and fade. Some see in this clash of principles and aims the potential for a more just human community, while others fear the erosion of enduring culture. Yet beneath this welter stand powerful and pervasive institutions, whose distinctive norms profoundly shape our moral commitments and character–notably the family, the market, the media, and systems of law, religion, politics, research, education, health care, and defense.
The overwhelming majority of the contributions in this volume deal with the Christian religion, as pluralistic societies today thrive substantially in Christian environments.

EVANGELISCHE VERLAGSANSTALT
Leipzig www.eva-leipzig.de

Tel +49 (0) 341/ 7 11 41 -44 shop@eva-leipzig.de

John Witte | Michael Welker (Eds.)
The Impact of the Law
on Character Formation, Ethical Education, and the Communication of Values in Late Modern Pluralistic Societies

288 pages | paperback | 15,5 x 23 cm
ISBN 978-3-374-06801-2
EUR 30,00 [D]

This volume addresses whether, how, and where laws (variouslyde defined) teach values and shape moral character in late modern liberal societies. Each author recognizes the essential value of state law in fostering peace, security, health, education, charity, trade, democracy, constitutionalism, justice, and human rights, among many other moral goods. Each author also recognizes, however, the grave betrayals of law in supporting fascism, slavery, apartheid, genocide, persecution, violence, racism, and other forms of immorality and injustice. They thus call for state laws that set a basic civil morality of duty for society and for robust freedoms that protect private individuals and private groups to cultivate a higher morality of aspiration.

EVANGELISCHE VERLAGSANSTALT
Leipzig www.eva-leipzig.de

Tel +49 (0) 341/ 7 11 41 -44 shop@eva-leipzig.de

William Schweiker | Michael Welker
John Witte | Stephen Pickard (Eds.)

The Impact of Academic Research

on Character Formation, Ethical Education, and the Communication of Values in Late Modern Pluralistic Societies

216 pages | paperback | 15,5 x 23 cm
ISBN 978-3-374-06803-6
EUR 30,00 [D]

This volume addresses whether, how, and where academic research has an impact on ethical education, character formation, and the communication of values in late modern pluralistic societies. It reflects the great impacts of a global network of research universities, with the enormous range from the natural sciences to mathematics, historical and theological investigations. It offers praises of the institutionalized impact of the search for truth and the defense of tested truth-claims, but also skeptical voices with respect to the ethical impact of academic research today.

EVANGELISCHE VERLAGSANSTALT
Leipzig www.eva-leipzig.de

Tel +49 (0) 341/ 7 11 41 -44 shop@eva-leipzig.de